IMAGES
of America

BURLINGTON

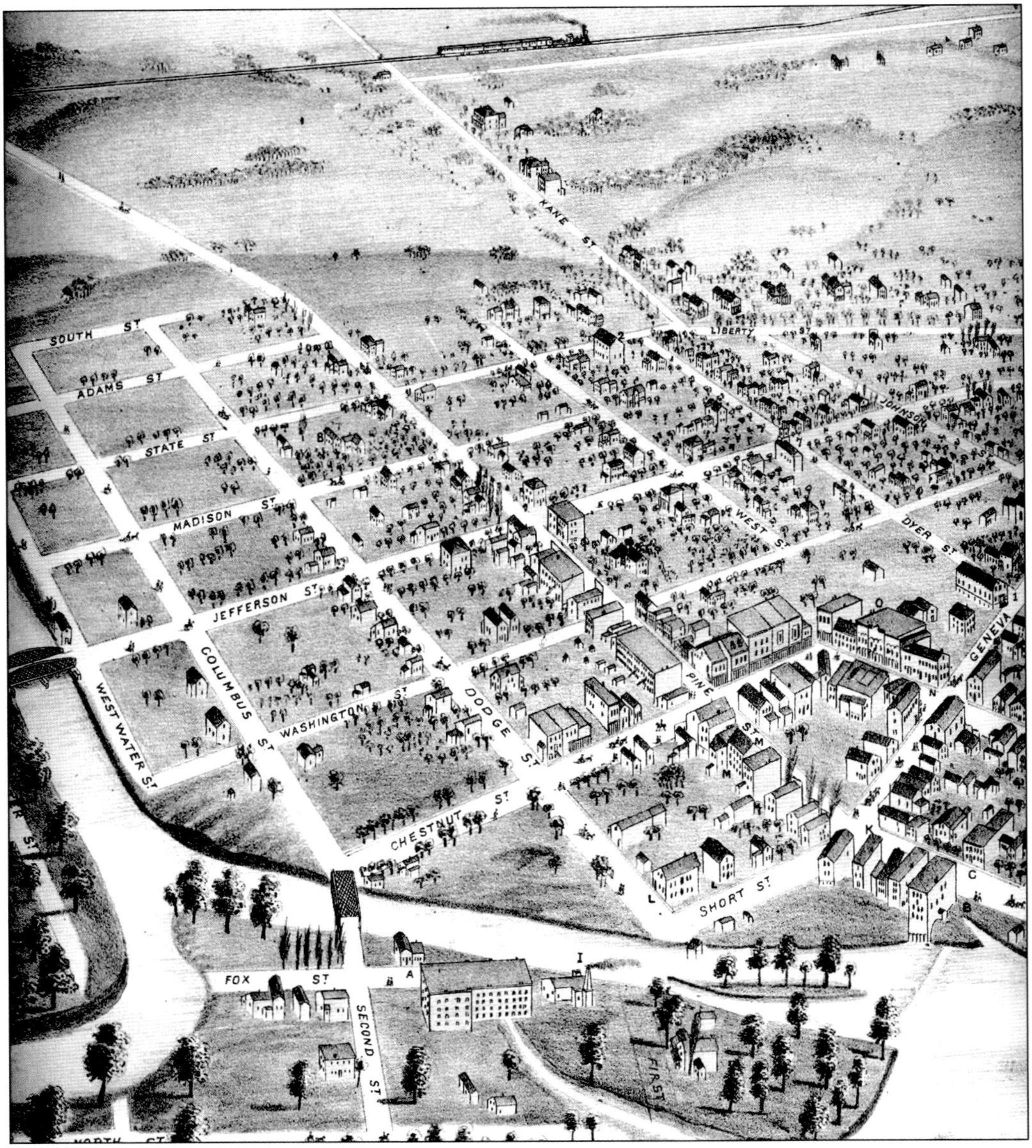

"The Heart of Burlington" is captured in this cut from an 1871 lithograph drawn by H. H. Bailey and published by T. M. Fowler & Company, Madison, Wisconsin. It looks south from what is now the Echo Park area (bottom) toward the former Chicago, Milwaukee & St. Paul Railroad tracks (top). The Fox River Bridge on Jefferson Street is at left and the White River Bridge from Chestnut to Second Street is left of center near the bottom. The mill dam is at bottom right. The referenced buildings include Teutonia Hall (1), School House (2), Baptist Church (7), Perkins Woolen Mill (A), Perkins Flour Mill (B), Wagner Foundry & Machine Shop (C), Burlington Tannery (I), Benson Livery Stable (K), Nims & Voorhees Carpentry (L), Exchange Hotel (M), Jones House (N), and Jones Block (O).

IMAGES
of America

BURLINGTON

Burlington Historical Society

Dennis P. Tully and Donald J. Vande Sand

ARCADIA
PUBLISHING

ISBN 978-0-7385-3427-5

Published by Arcadia Publishing
Charleston, South Carolina

Printed in the United States of America

Library of Congress Catalog Card Number: 2005926573

For all general information contact Arcadia Publishing at:
Telephone 843-853-2070
Fax 843-853-0044
E-mail sales@arcadiapublishing.com
For customer service and orders:
Toll-Free 1-888-313-2665

Visit us on the Internet at www.arcadiapublishing.com

(Cover) This picture was taken at the former Conkey Street (later Cooper) School and is believed to be of the senior class of 1909 with Principal J. S. Miller (standing, third from right). The two class members standing at the right are Barbara Kasner (Mangold) and Rudolph Uhen. Other class members (not specifically identified in the picture) were Della Burritt (Karcher), Gladys Foote (Fraser), Theodora Jacobson, Frances Mealy (Potter), Edith Mittlestadt (Ritterhoff), Irene Sutton (Verick, Henry), Donna Tindall (Linneman), Sarah Wegge (Hoelz), Erma Wilson (Mathews), Jeannette Wilson, Ermina Zimmermann (Treichel), Louis Brehm, Donald Jones, and Joseph Reminger.

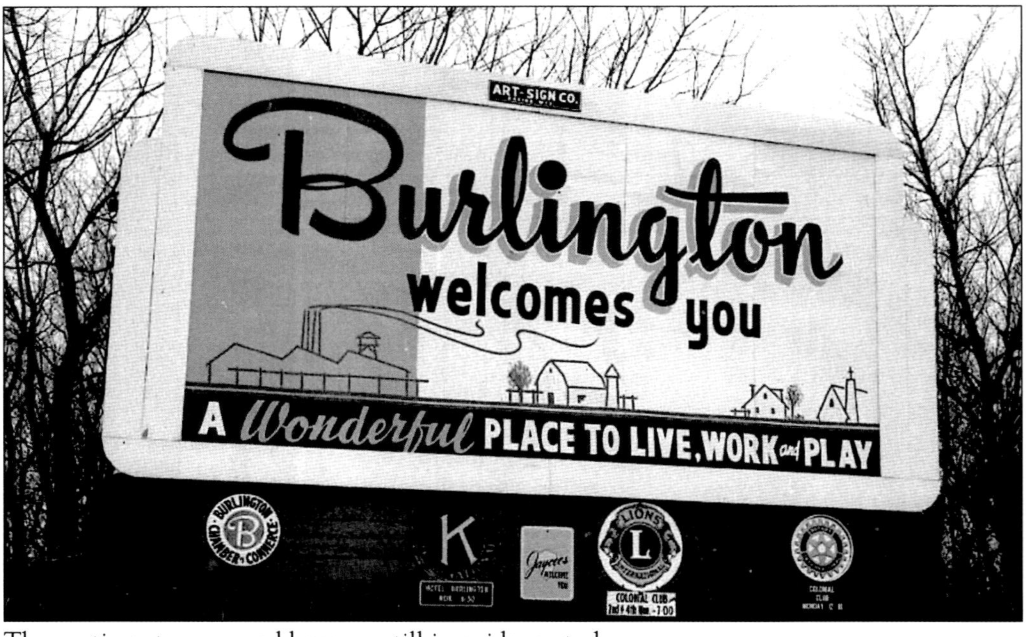

The sentiments expressed here are still in evidence today.

Contents

ACKNOWLEDGMENTS

This book is the product of many people who have contributed their time and given their talents over the years to photograph the scenes they saw in and around Burlington, to record the names and places and events pictured, and to collect and preserve the images for posterity. The 230 or so photographs selected for this book are a very small sample of the thousands and thousands of photographs, negatives, postcards, and slides that have been donated to the Burlington Historical Society over the years.

The photographers who took the pictures as long ago as the 1860s, when photography was in its infancy, up to the present time include R. D. Kesler, George Law, J. W. Johnston, Adolph Moestue, Charles Clench, Joseph Wagner, Alphons E. Hatch, Robert Fitch, Peter Angsten, Leonard J. Smith, Thomas J. Shouldis, Howard Wood, Otto R. Heinemann, John K. Asder, Charles H. Warner, John Zwiebel, R. Glenn Adams, Elmer Ebert, Emmett Raettig, and numerous others.

Those who recorded the names and places and events include not only the photographers themselves and their helpers, but the newspaper reporters, the business and factory owners and employees, family members, and local historians. Special gratitude goes to the present and former members of the Burlington Historical Society who have searched through records and, not infrequently, through their memories to recall and identify what the photographs show. The former members of the society, starting with Antoinette Meinhardt Fulton and the other founders, are also due thanks for collecting and preserving the images on behalf of the present and future residents of Burlington and the surrounding area.

Among those who have donated extensive or unique collections of photographs, negatives, postcards, slides, and other images to the society are Cornelia Pettibone Dudley, Ernest Foltz, Joseph Dyer, Harriet Dyer Adams, James Stammers, Elmer Ebert, Emmett A. Raettig, Mrs. Henry Allen Cooper, Arthur D. Smith, William and Clara Devor, Henry and Joan Mangold, John Zwiebel, Doug Lind, Francis Meurer, Otis Hulett, Margery Adams Ray, Seth Fratt, Don Reed, Marie Angsten Shaw, John Pieh, Susan Nienhaus Kott, Gerald Karwowski, Ken Amon, Roger Bieneman, Michael Schiller, the Glenn Hintz family, the Enoch Squires family, the Helen Hicks and Clarence Gleason estates, and many others.

Because of the nature of this book and the limited space available, we did not include photographs of individuals and family groups nor, except in a few instances, of social, organizational, and business and factory groups. We also left for another time, and for other compilers, photographs of sporting events and teams and of school and church and many community events. Some photographs of those types, as well as additional photographs of scenes and buildings similar to those in this book, are available for viewing on our website, www.burlingtonhistory. org.

We want to express our thanks also for the encouragement and help of our Arcadia editor, Elizabeth Beachy, and the other Arcadia employees who contributed to the publishing of this book.

INTRODUCTION

In March 1885, Enoch D. Putnam, an early Burlington resident, wrote to the *Burlington* (Wisconsin) *Standard* that he had

> *first visited the site where Burlington now stands in July 1836, and was greatly delighted with the natural beauty of the place. I predicted at the time that it would become an important point, which prediction has since been fully verified. The place was then called Lower Forks, and when that season a stage was started by a Mr. Rork, . . . in his advertisement he called the place Foxville, a name which it retained but a short time. . . .*

A couple of weeks later, Putnam wrote again. He said that, in 1836, Enoch D. Woodbridge and others had engaged him to lay out the quarter section at the forks of the Fox and White Rivers into village lots. After the work was done, the proprietors came to see the place and name it. They brought with them Milan G. Tobey and his wife, who kept the hotel at Kenosha, to cater for the company. Putnam wrote:

> *After dinner was over, the subject of naming the town was discussed, and as no one proposed a name, Mr. Woodbridge who acted as chairman, said that inasmuch as I had done all that had been done there, I ought to have the honor of naming the place. Mr. Woodbridge's proposition was adopted by a unanimous vote. I was taken wholly by surprise, as I had not even thought of a name; but after a moment's thought I said that the State of Vermont, from which I came, had one town celebrated above all others for the beauty of its location and scenery, I would propose the name of that town—Burlington— as a name for this new town. The question was then put, 'Shall this town be called Burlington, as proposed?' It was decided in affirmation by a unanimous vote, and three rousing cheers were given for Burlington.*

While Enoch D. Putnam may have given Burlington its name, the first ones to stake out claims on the present site of Burlington were Moses Smith and William Whiting. On December 15, 1835, the two carved their initials on a tree near the present-day Standard Press building, left the area for about two weeks, and then came back with Benjamin Perce and Lemuel Smith. The four built a temporary shelter near the bend in the Fox River and proceeded to explore for mill and farm sites. Moses Smith and Perce were Mormons; Lemuel Smith, a brother of Moses, and Whiting were not.

More settlers arrived starting in 1836, mainly "Yankees" from New England by way of the Great Lakes. A rock and log dam and mill races were built to power a saw mill and a grist mill, with a woolen mill following a few years later. The grist mill was an important source of flour for Milwaukee, Racine, and Kenosha, and was the first in Wisconsin to ship flour to New York. The woolen mill made the first roll of cloth turned out in Wisconsin. The woolen mill's cloth was also used for Union soldiers' uniforms during the Civil War.

The mills served the many farmers and their families who settled in the area. Wheat was the leading farm product through the Civil War days, when livestock and dairying, which had made inroads by 1860, became the major farm industry. Businesses were established to serve the farmers, including plow and agricultural implement makers and dealers, wagon makers, and blacksmith shops.

A brick school house was built in 1840, which was used also by some Protestant groups for services until their churches were built starting in 1852. The Germans, mainly Catholic, began arriving in 1841; put up a small stone church building in 1844; and, if not farmers, built houses in areas near the church. In 1844, James Jesse Strang founded a Mormon settlement called Voree just west of Burlington.

Several people in Burlington and the surrounding area, led by Dr. Edward G. Dyer, were active in the abolition movement and a number of freedom-seekers on the Underground Railroad were sheltered in the Burlington, Rochester, and Spring Prairie area. They included 16-year-old Caroline Quarles, who was hidden for several days before being taken by buggy to Detroit, where she crossed the river into Canada; and Racine resident, Joshua Glover, who, after being freed from the Milwaukee jail with a battering ram, spent several weeks in this area before being taken to Racine and put aboard a boat bound for Canada.

In 1855, the Racine and Mississippi Railroad (later a part of the Chicago, Milwaukee & St. Paul Railroad) built a line through Burlington to Savannah, Illinois. Over 30 years later, another railroad, the Wisconsin Central (later a part of the Soo Line and now a part of Canadian National) built a second line through Burlington. From 1909 to 1938, Burlington was also served by an electric rail line that ran to St. Martins (near Milwaukee).

Burlington supplied many soldiers to the Union cause in the Civil War, usually avoiding having to draft anyone because volunteers filled the quotas. Groups organized in Burlington included the Utley Guards (Company C, 1st Infantry), the Burlington Rifles (Company E, 5th Regiment), and the 9th Battery of the Light Artillery. 23 men were either killed in battle, died of disease, or died at home of wounds.

After a slow-growth period following the Civil War, an electric company was established in 1888 and a city water system was installed in 1890. These were followed by several manufacturing firms making products invented or perfected by Burlington residents. These included the Burlington Blanket Co., which made the Stay-On horse blanket; the Burlington Brass Works, which made industrial steam valves and other plumbing products; the Security Lightning Rod Co.; the Wisconsin Condensed Milk Co.; A. Zwiebel & Sons, which made windmills, folding wooden ironing boards, and other products; and the Multiscope and Film Co., which made Al-Vista panoramic cameras. Other industries included the Burlington Brick & Tile Co.; the Burlington Canning Co.; the Burlington Malting Co.; Finke-Uhen Brewing Co.; F. G. Klein Bottling Co.; Citizens Gas Co.; the Badger Basket and Veneer Co.; John J. Wolf's sauerkraut factory; and in 1925, Murphy Products Co., which made animal feed concentrates.

Today, other manufacturing firms have taken their place, including a Nestle Co. chocolate plant; St. Gobain, glass containers; Air Liquide, industrial products; Lavelle Inc., rubber and plastics molding; Packaging Corporation of America; NEL Frequency Controls; and Circle Inc., paper shipping holders.

The Burlington Liars Club started awarding an annual championship medal in 1929 for the best tall tale, and became world-famous, even broadcasting its picks over national radio in some years. The annual contest is still held, drawing entries from the United States and even some foreign countries.

The Burlington Historical Society was established in 1928, and is the oldest historical society in Racine County. Its buildings include a museum housed in a former church building, Pioneer Log Cabin, and the 1840 school house. Its collections include more than 100,000 images, including photographs, negatives, postcards, and slides. Included are some early tintypes and daguerreotypes; stereoscopes, glass plates, and Al-Vista panoramic pictures taken in the late 19th and early 20th centuries; negatives from local newspapers from 1949 to 1955 and from 1965 to 1967; negatives and photos of various aspects of community and area life taken by local photographer Emmett Raettig from 1948 to 1988; several family photo albums, some with area scenes; and many photographs donated over the years of buildings, houses, street scenes and vistas, individuals, groups, and activities ranging from the 1880s to the present time.

This book presents a small sample of the society's image collection—truly a community treasure.

One

Cityscapes and Street Scenes

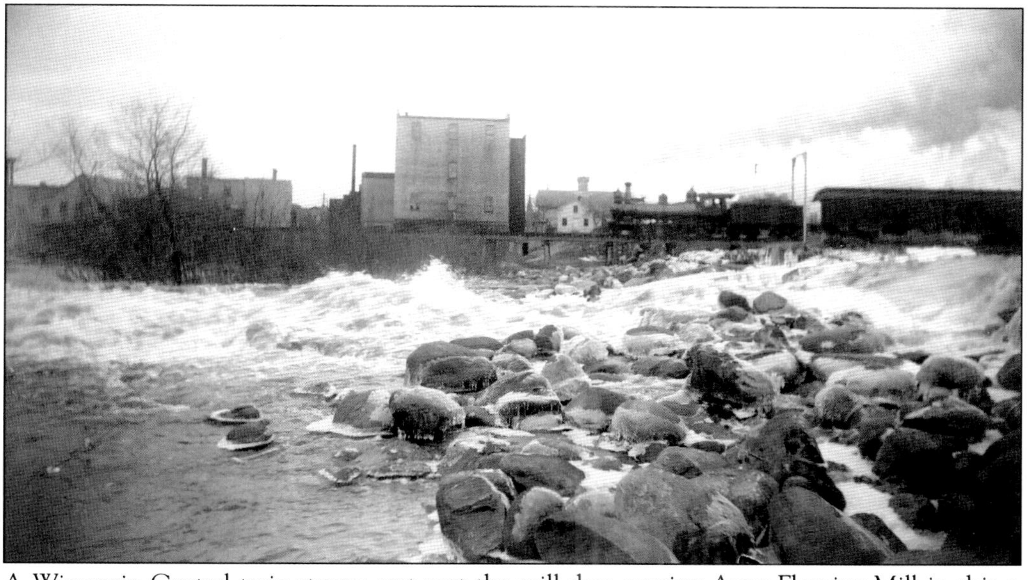

A Wisconsin Central train steams east past the mill dam nearing Ayers Flouring Mill in this *c.* 1890s picture looking southwest from the area that is now Echo Park. When Pliny Perkins and his father, Ephraim, moved to Foxville (as Burlington was then known) in 1837, they bought the unfinished dam and sawmill that Moses Smith and Samuel C. Vaughn had begun on the White River. After completing the dam and sawmill, they also built a small, frame grist mill. Both the dam, after damage from floods, and the grist mill, after damage from fires, had been rebuilt and improved over the years. Between the mill and the engine is the water works building, completed in 1890. The Wisconsin Central, later a part of the Soo Line Railroad and now part of the Canadian National Railroad, laid its tracks through the Burlington area in 1886.

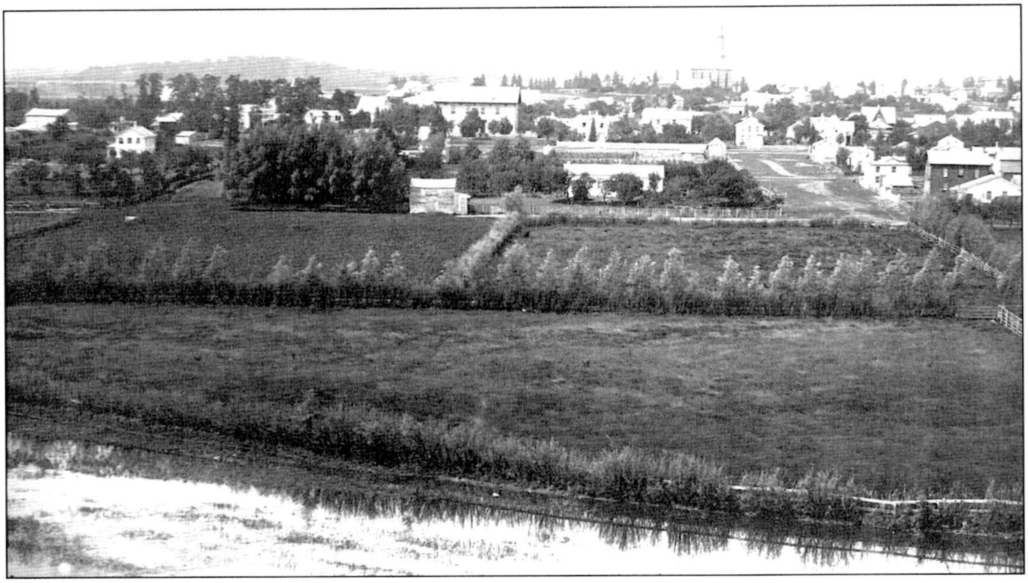

The four pictures on these two pages, taken by George Law from Muth's wooden brewery building on the east side of the Fox River (now site of the Malt House Theatre), show Burlington in July 1868. Landmarks in this first picture, which looks southwesterly, include the Union High School (upper center), called Lincoln School since 1911, and the 1859 Church of the Immaculate Conception, now used as St. Mary's school annex. The broad street to the right is Madison Street.

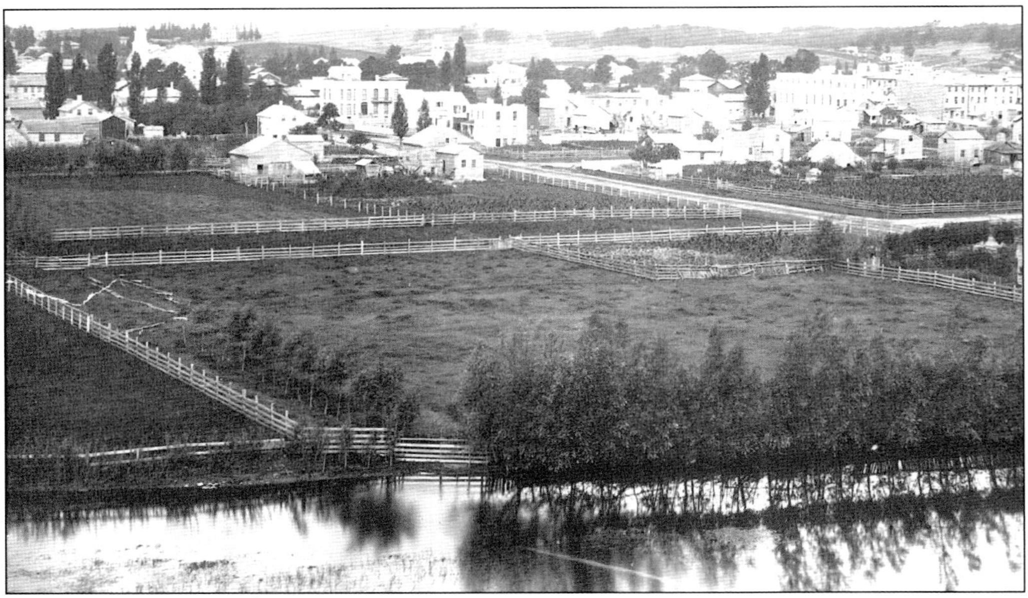

The long building with two windows nearest the camera at left is Burlington's first school building at Dodge and Madison Streets. Now known as Whitman School, it was moved in 1986 to Beloit Street. Dr. Frederick Kords' 22-room multi-windowed house left of center is at Jefferson and Pine Streets, now site of the public library. The row of multi-windowed buildings at the right still stands on the east side of Pine Street between Washington and Chestnut Streets.

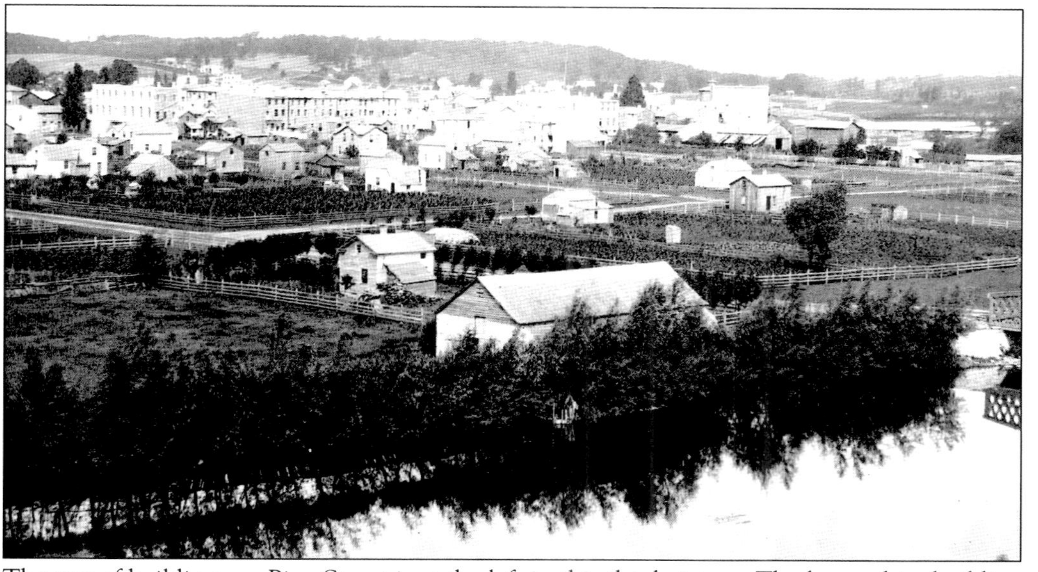

The row of buildings on Pine Street is at the left in this third picture. The large white building near the horizon right of center is the Perkins (later Ayers) Flouring Mill on what is now Commerce Street. Portions of the mill pond are to the right of the mill. The building with the cupola partially hidden by the mill is Floral Hall, a part of the Racine County Fair held in Burlington from 1864 to 1885, after which the Wisconsin Central railroad built its depot in that area.

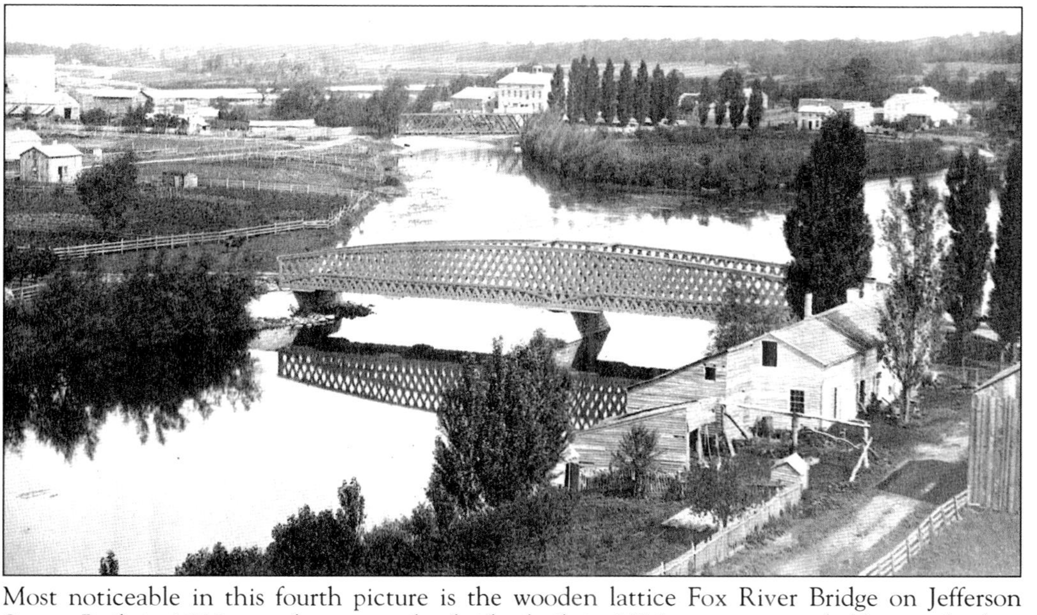

Most noticeable in this fourth picture is the wooden lattice Fox River Bridge on Jefferson Street. Built in 1866 to replace a wooden bridge built in 1836, it was succeeded by iron bridges in 1876 and 1893, and by the current concrete bridge, which dates to 1949. Other landmarks are the Perkins flouring mill (top left), the woolen mill (top center) in the area that is now Echo Park, the iron bridge near the woolen mill on what is now Bridge Street, and the point where the White and Fox Rivers meet.

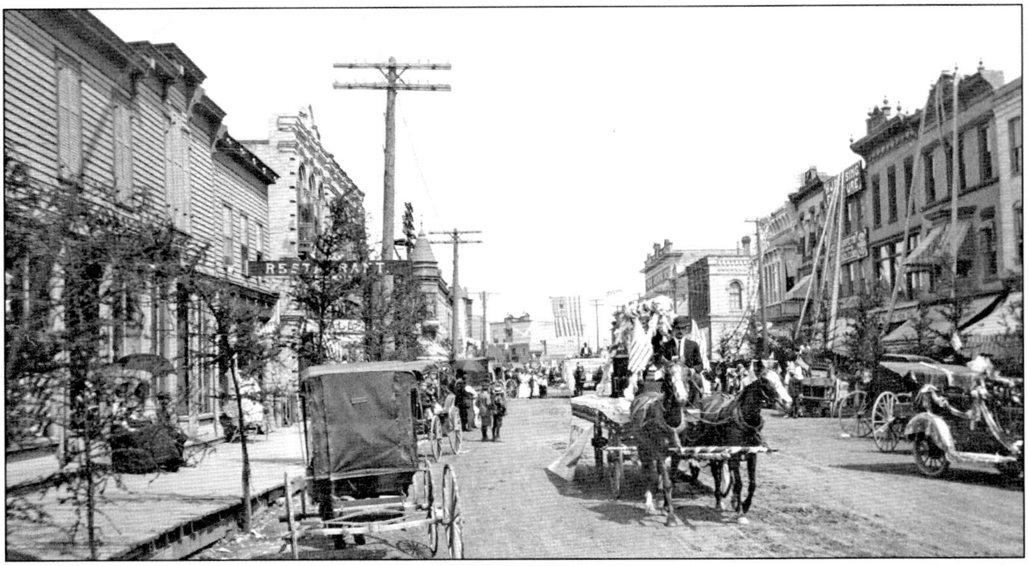

The 1907 Fourth of July parade heads south on Pine Street toward Washington Street. The wooden Keuper building at left housed a variety store, a plumber, a real estate office, and a restaurant. A brick building, which replaced it in 1914, has housed, among others, Rosenberg's dry goods store, Montgomery Ward, and Schuette Daniels furniture store. The buildings on the right have changed little, although they have different occupants. The automobile was one of the few in Burlington in 1907.

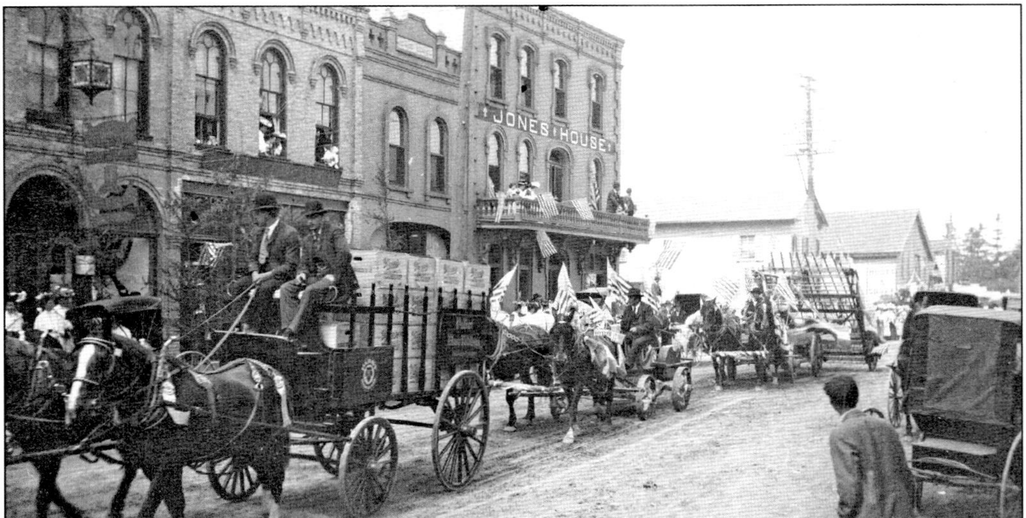

The F. G. Klein & Co. wagon nears the Chestnut Street bend on July 4, 1907. The firm, which made carbonated beverages such as ginger ale, cream soda, and German-style birch beer from "Celebrated Burlington Rock Spring Water," also bottled Pabst's beer. At the left are Matt Cunningham's clothing and dry goods store, the Bank of Burlington, and Mrs. Arlina DeLaplain's millinery store. The upper floors of the Jones House (later the Badger Hotel) were demolished after a 1968 fire.

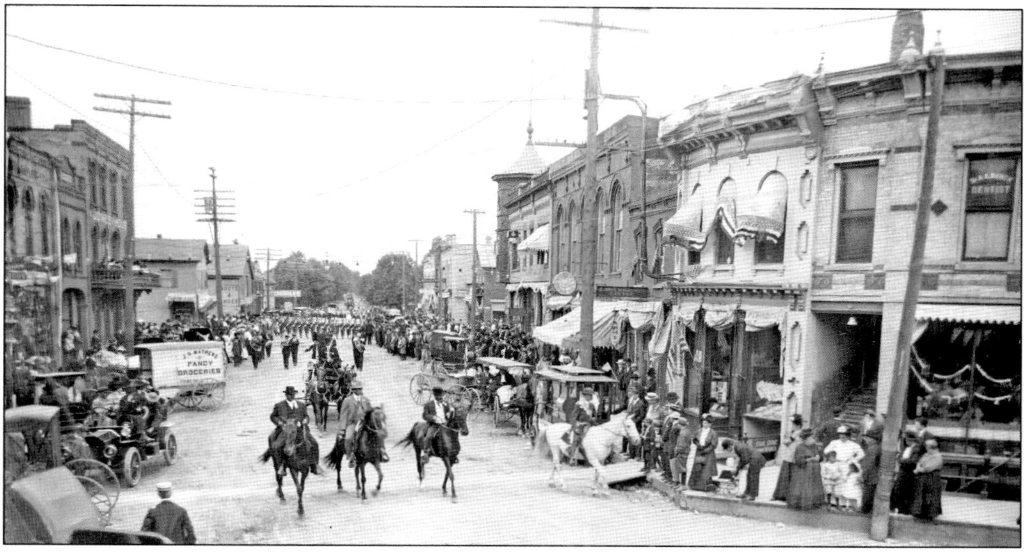

Four horsemen make the bend in Chestnut Street *c.* 1909. Except for the Jones House, now one-story, the buildings still look much the same. Businesses in the near block include Effie Carr's City Book Store, Frank Reuschlein & Son's insurance and real estate, lawyer E. John Wehmhoff, Eugene & Emma Wehmhoff's jewelry and millinery, and John P. Gill's Red Fox Inn. In the far block are Egizo Giannini's Burlington Fruit Store, F. Stoffregan's boots and shoes, Ed Zwiebel & Bros. plumbing and automobiles, and William Rosenberg's dry goods and clothing.

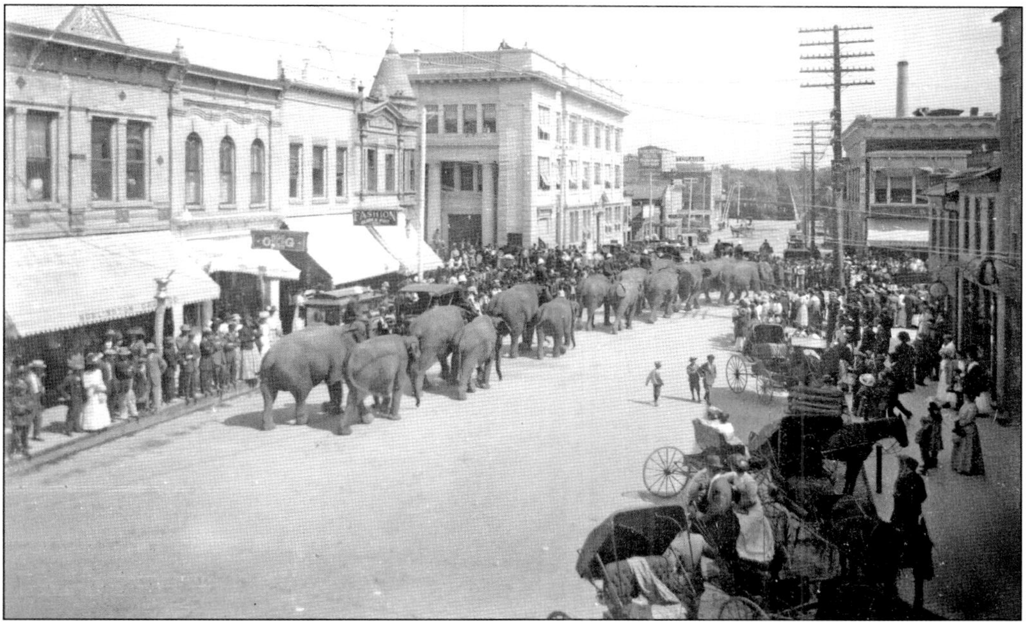

The lead elephants turn on Pine Street as the others follow on Chestnut Street east of the bend *c.* 1912. On the north side of Chestnut Street were Thomas G. Buchan's Burlington Drug Co., marked by the mortar and pestle on the post; Fred Oberg's Palace of Sweets, with his popcorn wagon at the curb; Fashion Cloak & Suit; and Nic Gill's saloon in the building with the tower. Across Pine Street is C. B. McCanna's Bank of Burlington, erected in 1909.

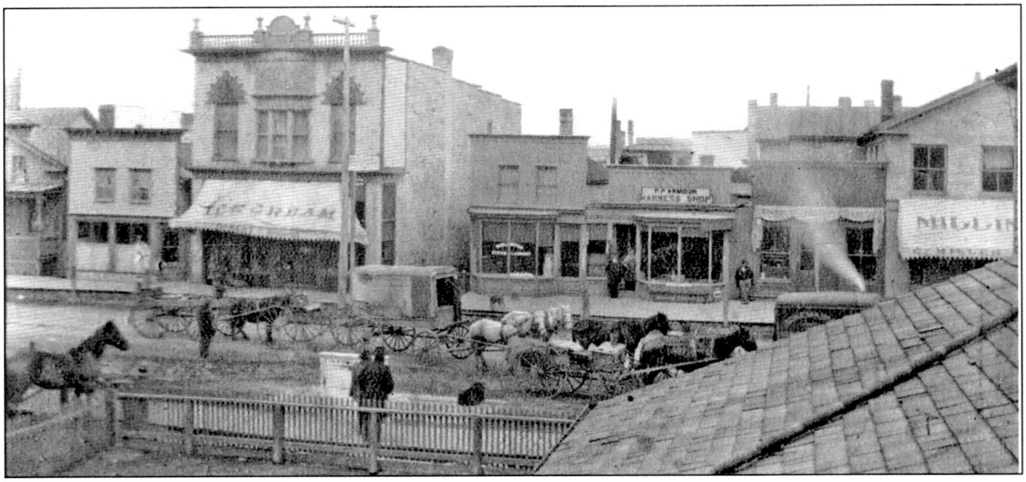

Standing on the north side of Chestnut Street between Mill Street and what is now Milwaukee Avenue (then Geneva Street) in 1899 were, from left to right: the Nic May family residence, May's meat market, John Rose's bakery and restaurant, Burlington Steam Laundry, Perley P. Armour's harness shop, John R. Schneider's jewelry store, and Lottie Miller's millinery store. Except for the Rose and millinery store buildings, the other structures have since been replaced by other store buildings.

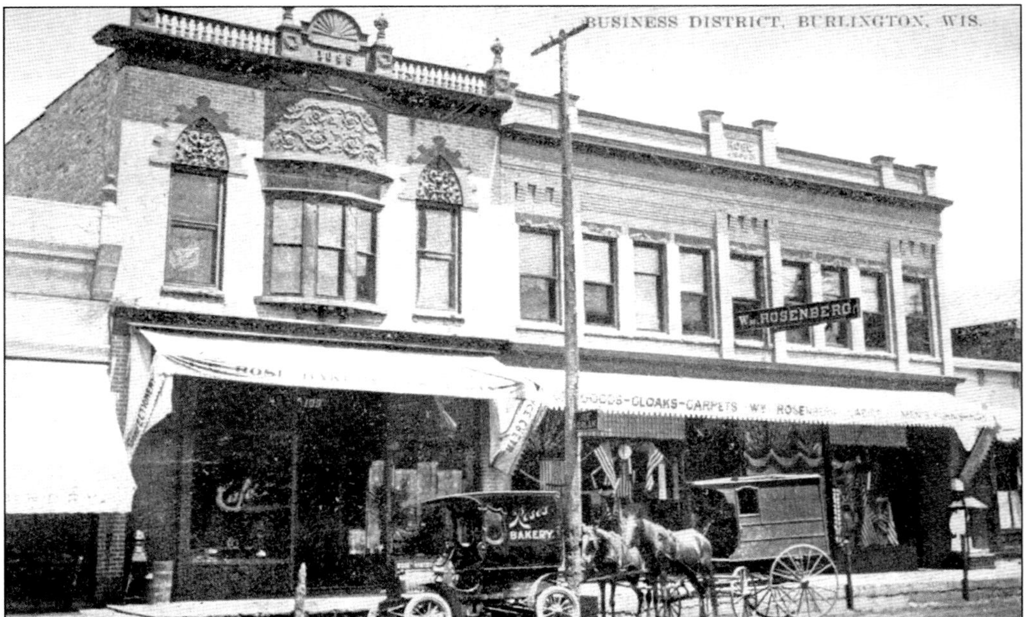

John G. Rose's two buildings on the north side of Chestnut Street west of Geneva Street (now Milwaukee Avenue) have maintained their basic appearance since this c. 1907 picture. The "medallioned" building, erected in 1895, was a Rose's Bakery until 1973. Rose constructed the larger building in 1906 for William Rosenberg's department store. After Rosenberg moved to a new building on Pine Street in 1915, Rose opened a five and ten cents store which operated into the early 1940s.

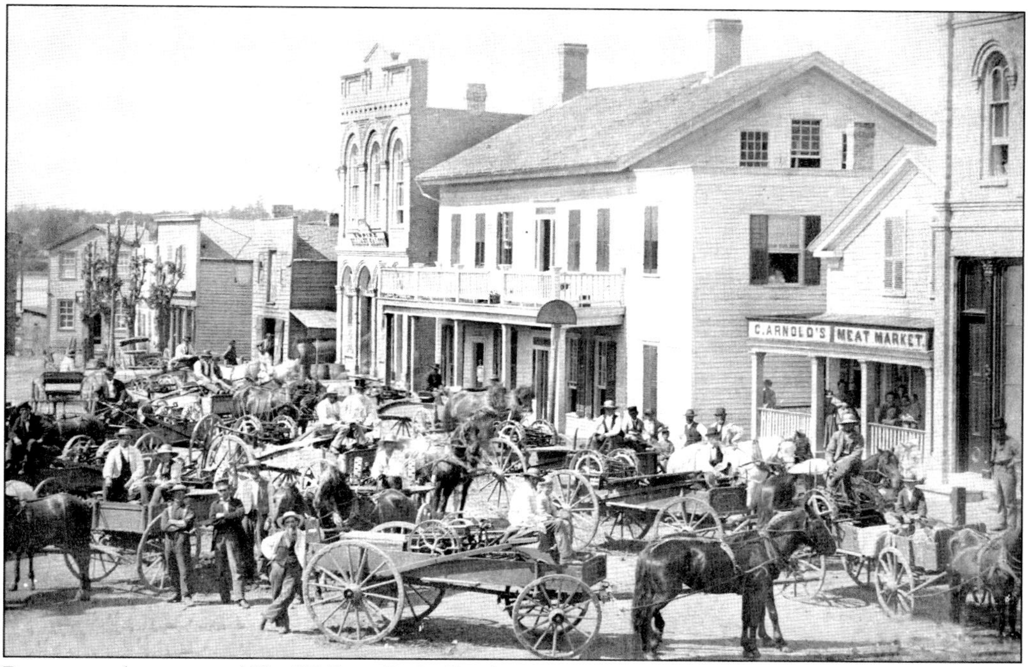

Reapers and mowers sold by William P. Goff gather on Pine Street north of Chestnut Street on May 30, 1874, for a picture by Adolph C. Moestue. The large wooden Exchange Hotel was replaced in 1902 by the brick Hotel Burlington. Charles Arnold's Meat Market, now a residence at Wainwright Avenue and South Pine Street, was replaced in 1897 by the brick Bankes building. Lewis Konst's Empire saloon building (with point at top of cornice) still stands, minus the cornice.

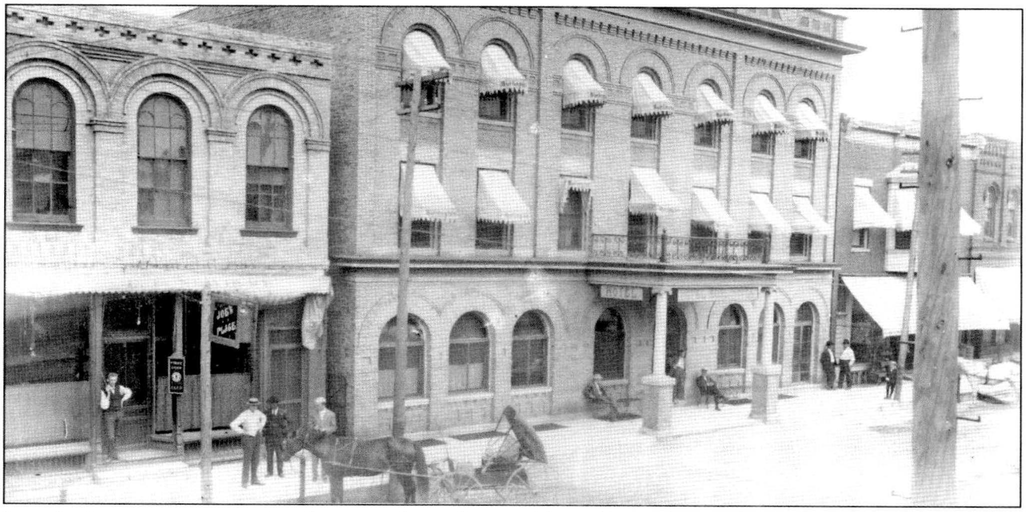

Joseph Rittmann, arms akimbo, stands in front of his saloon, Joe's Place, in the former Empire Saloon building—minus the cornice—on Pine Street north of Chestnut Street c. 1905. Seated under the canopy of John Mutter's Hotel Burlington are Mutter, left, and John Cunningham, right. F. Bankes & Son's agricultural implement store occupies the building with the bay window (partially hidden by the utility post). The Veteran Saloon (right) was moved in 1909 to make way for McCanna's Bank of Burlington building.

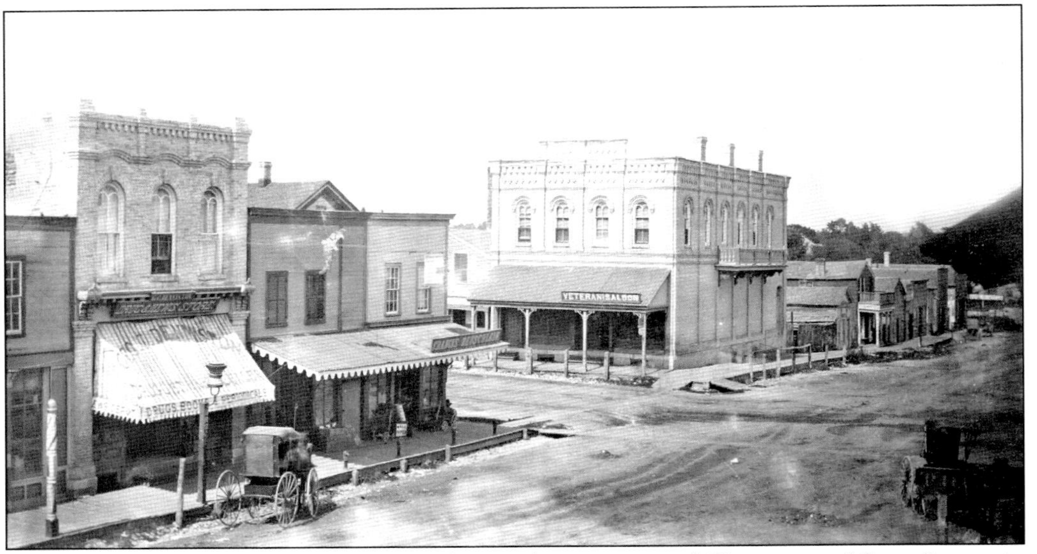

William Laske's Veteran Saloon sat on the northeast corner of Chestnut and Pine Streets in 1889. To the west, left to right, are Kettlehut's barber shop (barber pole), Denniston's drug and news store (mortar and pestle), Stang's boot and shoe store ("Punch in Boot"), and Reuschlein's general store. The drug store building is still a fixture, while the wooden buildings have been replaced. The Veteran Saloon was moved in 1909 to make way for the McCanna-Bank of Burlington building.

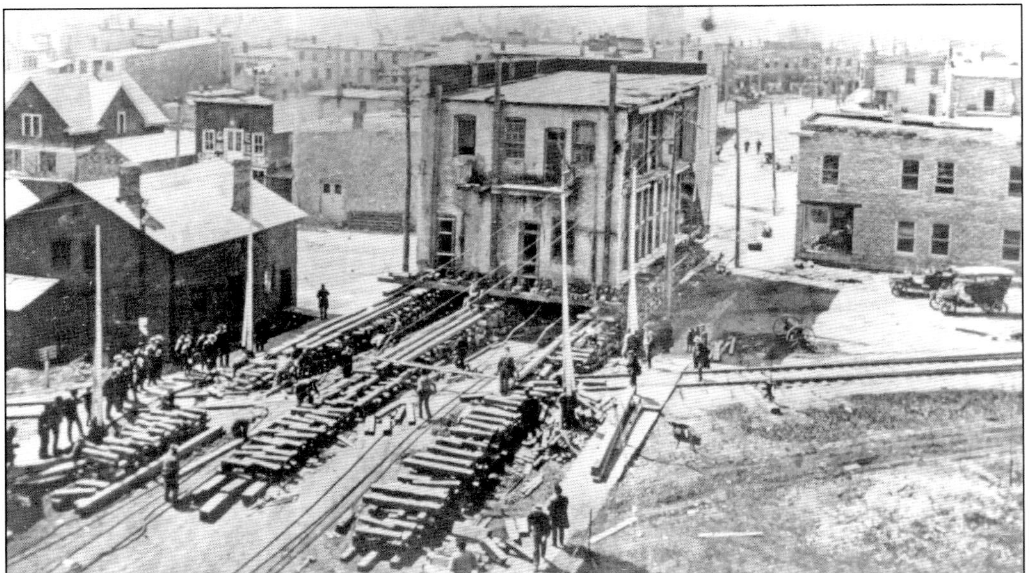

The Veteran Saloon building is at Dodge Street ready to be moved across the Chestnut Street tracks on April 15, 1909. The tracks, closed at noon, reopened at 4:25 p. m. Timbers shore up the right side, which shared a wall when the building stood on the corner of Chestnut and Pine Streets. After its move, the building housed a feed company, can plant, freight warehouse, and Hi-Liter Graphics Co. The building was demolished in 2001 for the City's riverfront development project.

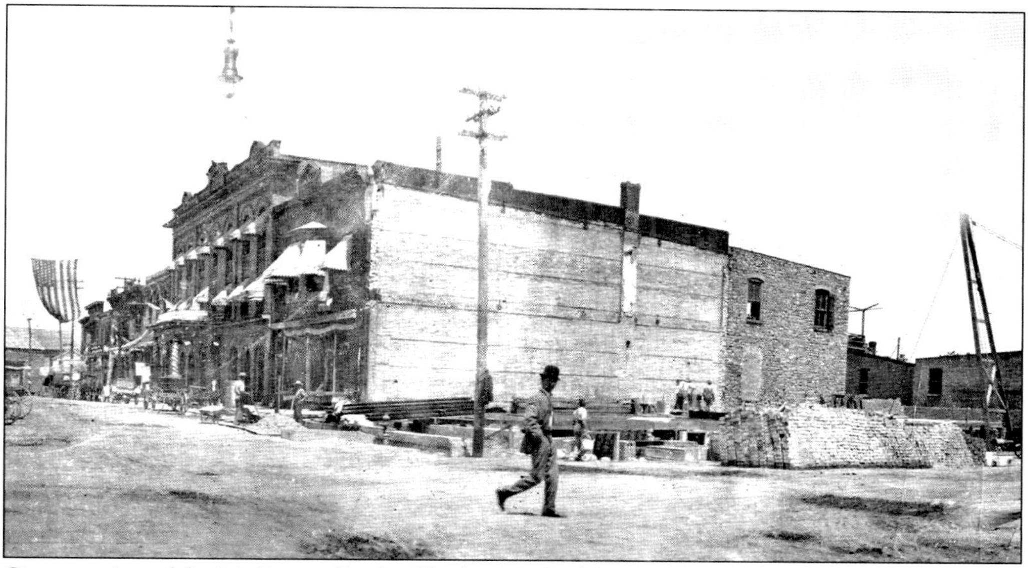

Construction of the McCanna-Bank of Burlington building on the northeast corner of Chestnut and Pine Streets is in its early stages in 1909 after the Veteran Saloon building was moved off the site. The saloon building had shared the wall of the adjoining Bankes building, which at that time was occupied by Reineman Hardware Co. The Hotel Burlington is the tallest building north of the construction site.

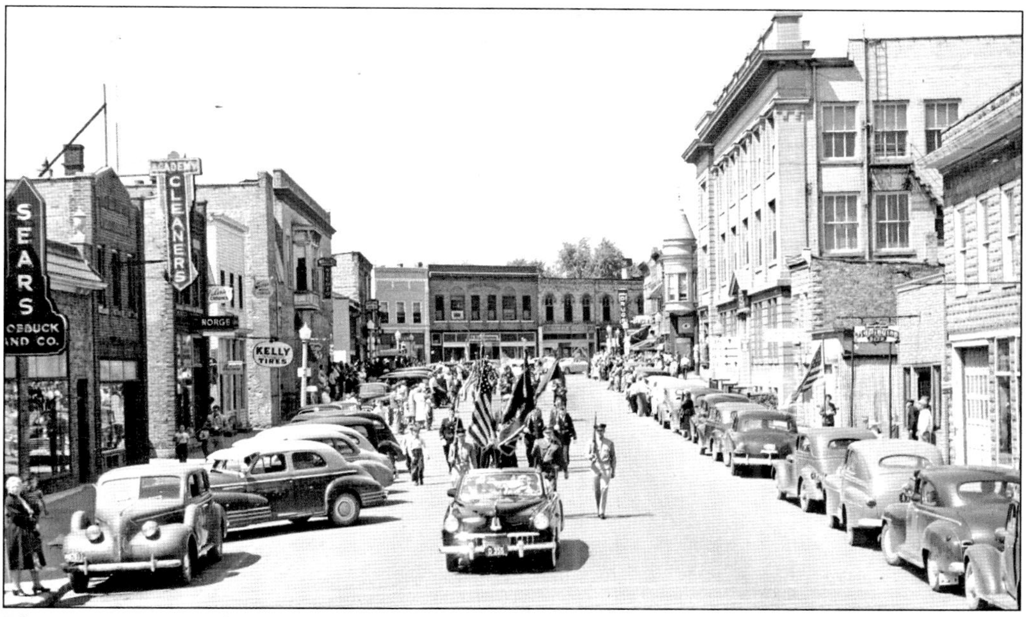

The 1949 Memorial Day parade nears Dodge Street as it heads east on Chestnut Street. Businesses on the south side of Chestnut, from Dodge to Pine Street, include Sears Roebuck & Co., Academy Cleaners, Whitton's appliances, Valerie's Candies, and Lois tire shop, with Al Writer's music studio above. Businesses on the north side, from the Bank of Burlington building east, include Reineman's plumbing, heating, and sheet metal department and Hoffman's tavern. The Lee Koch Implement Co. occupied the building partially visible at the right.

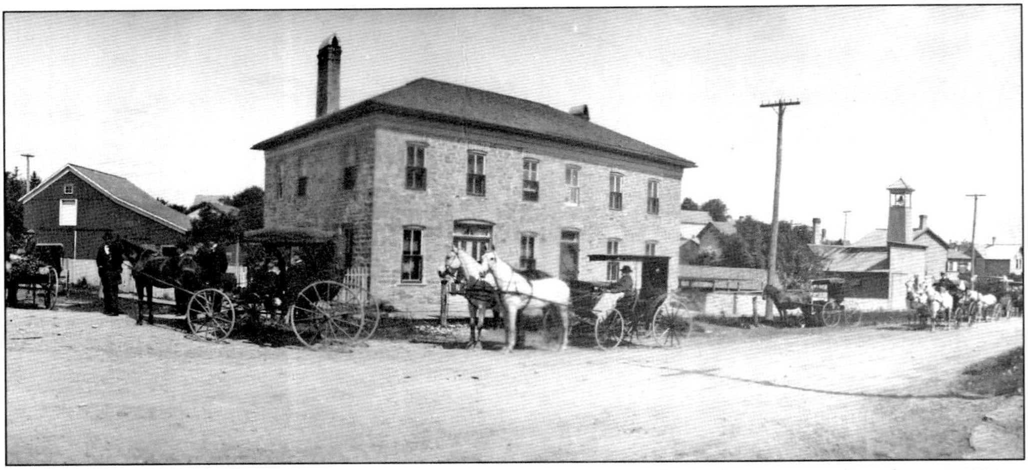

B. J. "Barney" Wentker bought the Triangle area on the Hillside from Peter Smith in 1897, a few years before this *c.* 1900 picture. The stone hotel, with an addition built in 1901, was on the northwest corner of McHenry and Liberty (now State) Streets until 1959, when it was replaced by a gas station and convenience store. The fire bell tower at right was on Wentker's wooden saloon building, which he replaced with a brick building in 1908.

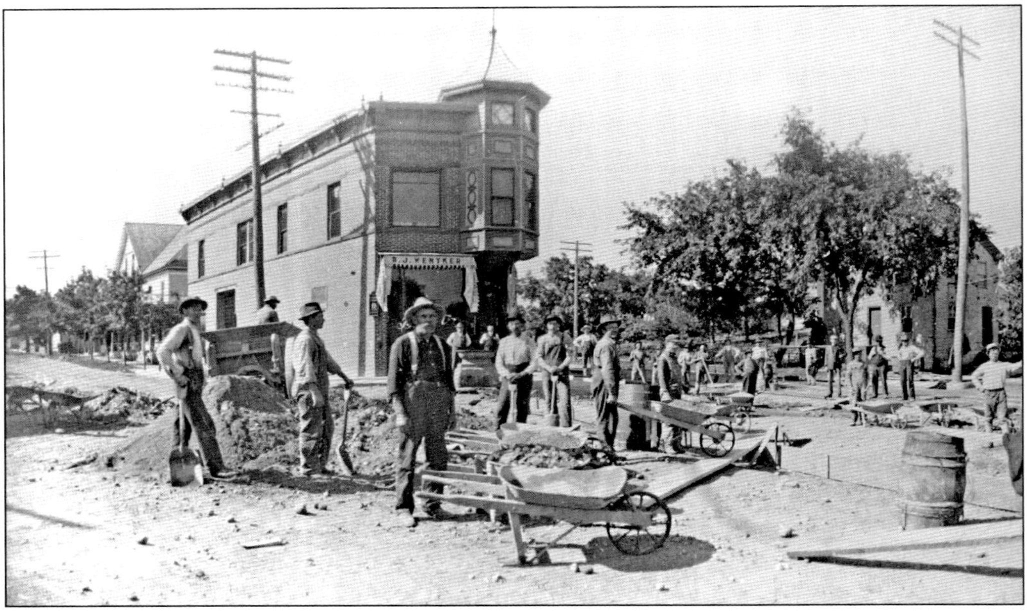

The bricking crew takes a break at the intersection of Geneva (now Milwaukee Avenue) and McHenry Streets in 1909. The interurban electric car rails being laid along Geneva Street (to the right) went west to the area of St. Mary's Cemetery. B. J. Wentker built the brick tavern in 1908 to replace a wooden one. He also owned the hotel building sitting beyond the tavern. The Wentker tavern building and the house at the right, built in 1856, are still fixtures on the street.

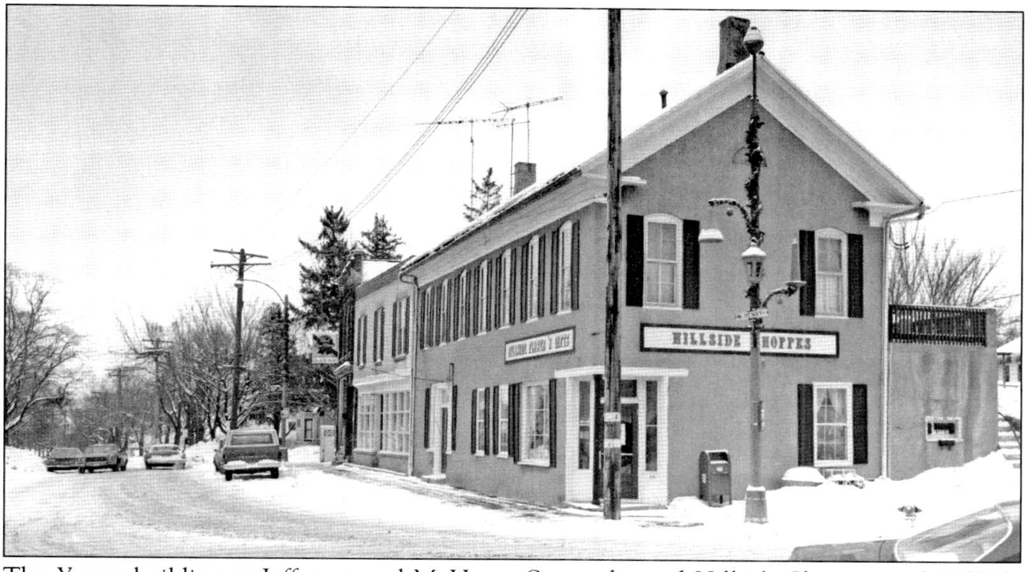

The Yanny building at Jefferson and McHenry Streets housed Hillside Shoppes and Hillside Flower 'N Gifts in February 1979. One of the city's oldest buildings, it originally housed the Catholic school and Sisters residence. Joseph Yanny bought the building in 1895, using the ground floor for a milk depot, followed by a meat market and grocery store. An upstairs hall, used for social activities, later became apartments. Yanny built the adjoining building, next to the Log Cabin tavern, in 1906.

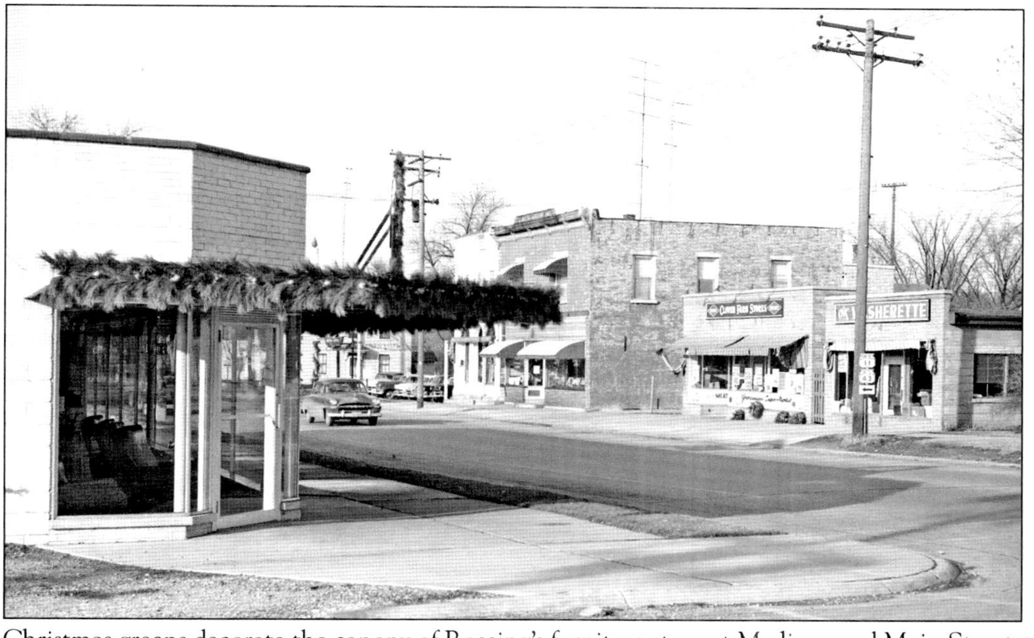

Christmas greens decorate the canopy of Roesing's furniture store at Madison and Main Streets on the east side of the Fox River in 1960. Across Main Street are Union Chevrolet's used car lot on the corner of Jefferson Street, the Canadian Club tavern, Phelps paint store, Grossman's Clover Farm super market, and O'Keefe's O'K Launderette. Burlington's east side, sometimes called "Canada," has had that nickname since at least the 1880s.

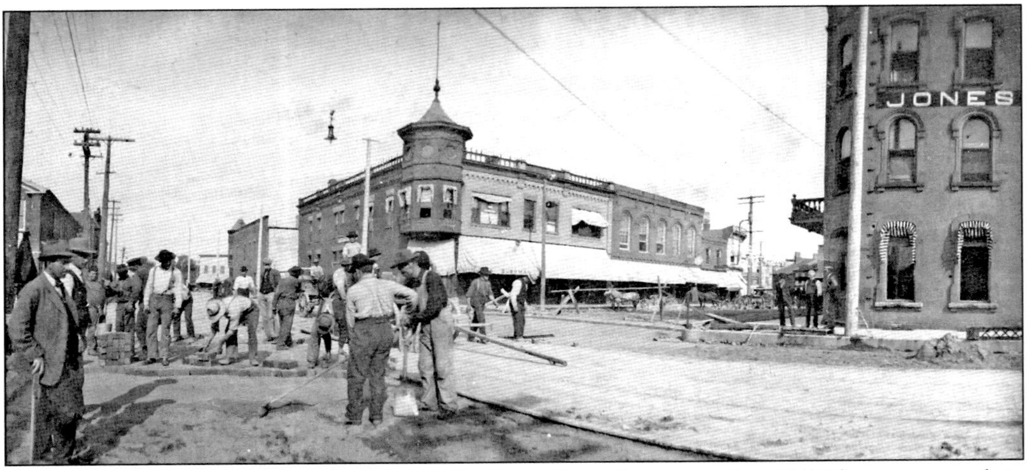

Geneva Street (now Milwaukee Avenue), from Pine Street to the Hillside, was paved in 1909 with vitrified brick laid on a cement base. Rails were also laid for the interurban electric cars, which ran from Burlington to St. Martins (near Milwaukee) from 1909 to 1938. Along Chestnut Street are Bushman & Denig's saloon (with the tower), Gill's Red Fox Inn, Mathews' grocery, Wehmhoff's jewelry and millinery, Wehmhoff's law office, and Effie Carr's City Book Store. The Burlington Business College was above the Mathews and Wehmhoff stores.

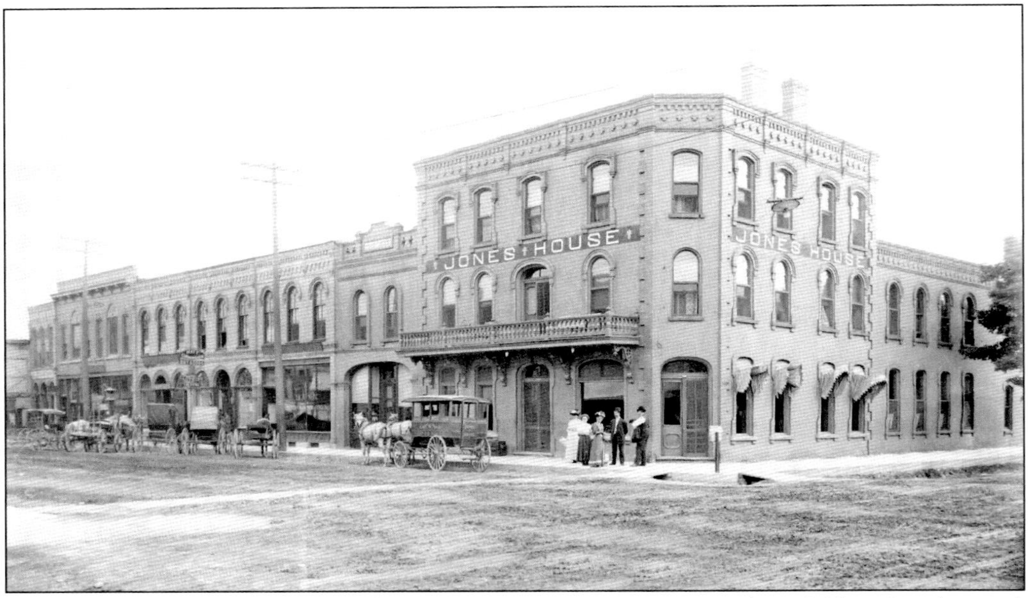

William Gill's omnibus waits on Chestnut Street near Geneva Street (now Milwaukee Avenue) c. 1908. Going left toward the "bend" from the Jones House are Mrs. Arlina DeLaplain's millinery, the Bank of Burlington, Matt Cunningham's dry goods, Prasch Bros. Eagle drug store, C. G. Foltz & Son clothing, and Frank Stang's gents' and ladies' clothing.

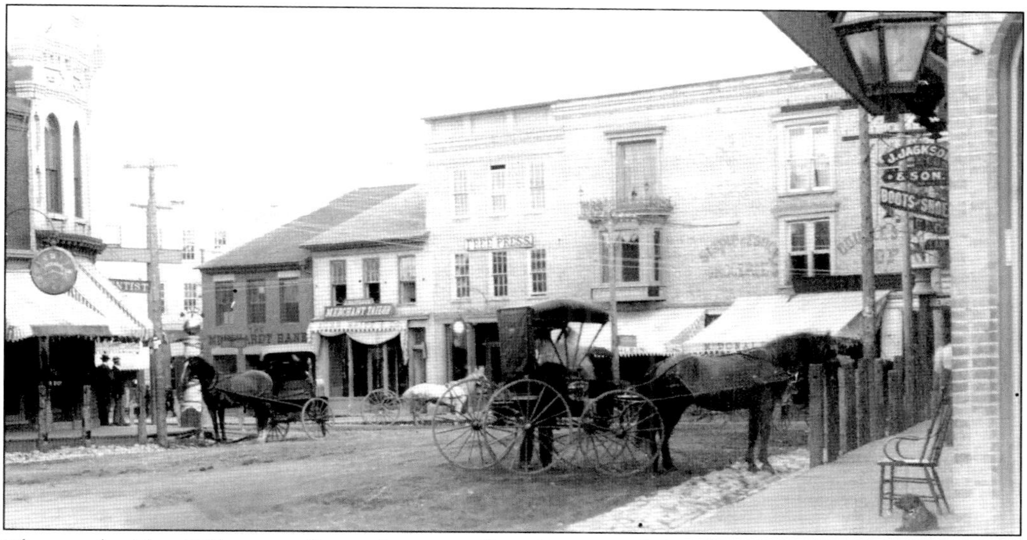

The south side of Chestnut Street between Pine Street and the "bend" is shown *c.* 1892. The Meinhardt Bank opened in the corner building in 1891. John Haitz, merchant tailor, was in the Neuhaus building from 1888 until 1899. Mrs. William Wheeler's three-story building housed Adolph Helfrich's jewelry store, the Free Press newspaper office, and the Masonic lodge rooms. In the large "double" building were John Itzin and Louis Reuschlein's harness shop (below the bay window) and Oliver and John McDonald's grocery store.

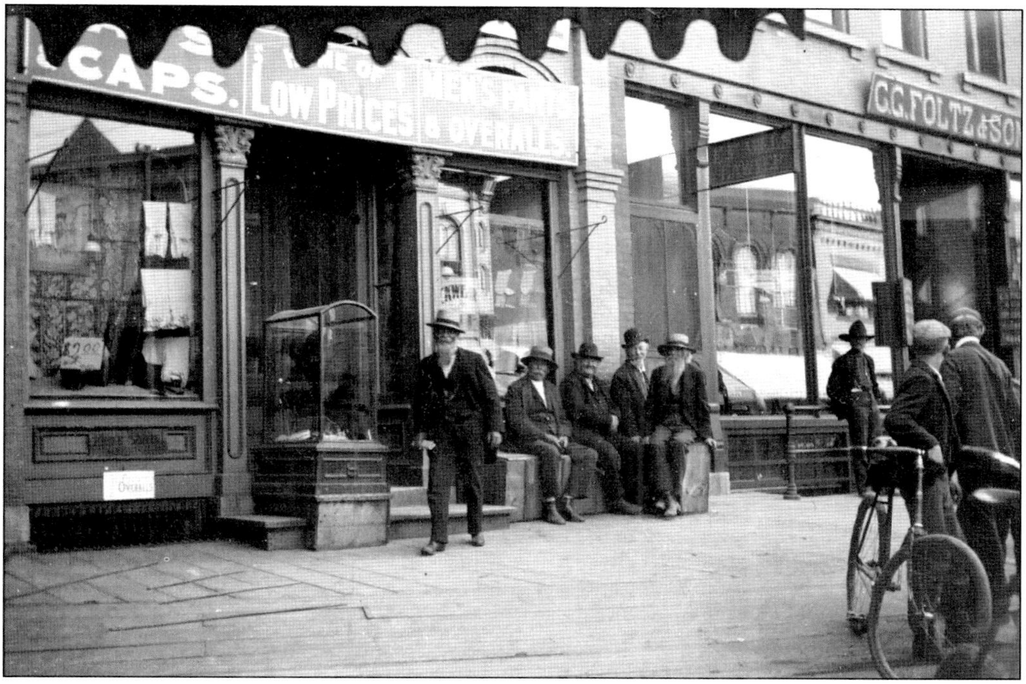

John Mathews, Charles Ball, Richard Baxter, and John O. Montgomery, seated in front of Frank Stang's Enterprise store, watch Loring O. Webber (walking left) and the rest of the world go by at the Chestnut Street "bend," *c.* 1900. Joining in the activity are the boys at right and Mr. Stowell, standing in front of the C. G. Foltz & Son store.

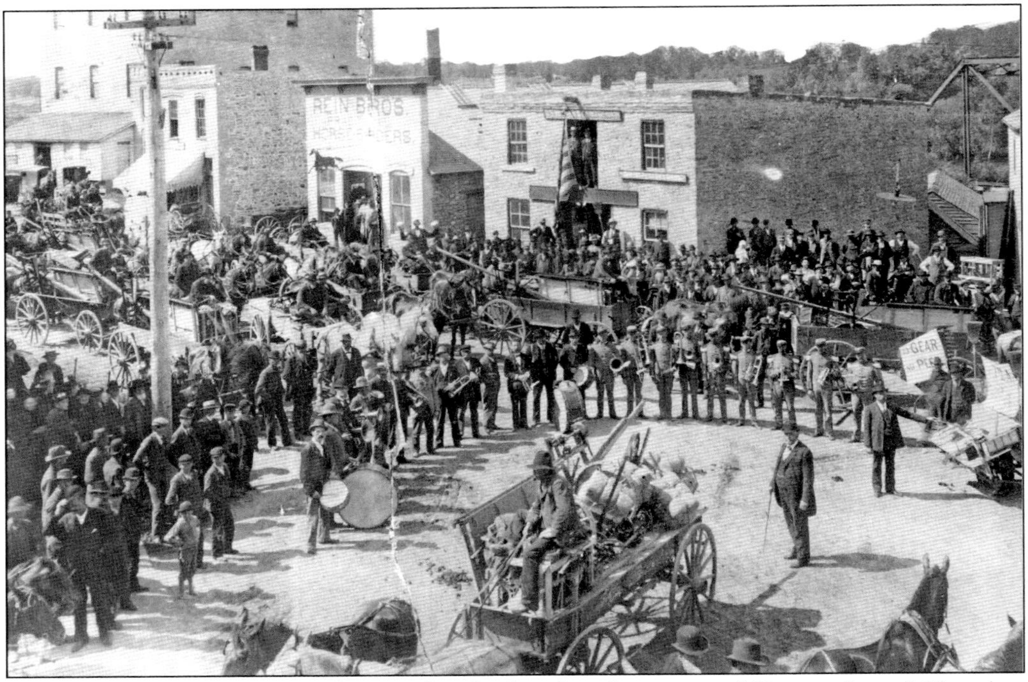

The Burlington and Waterford cornet bands played at the corner of Geneva (now Milwaukee Avenue) and Pine Streets on May 28, 1896, when a large number of Jones binders and reapers, sold by Henry Plucker and Joseph Wackerman, were delivered. Along what is now Commerce Street, from left to right, are Ayers flouring mill, Jerome Mutchler's store, Rein brothers' blacksmith shop, and Plucker and Wackerman's implement depot. The two men standing at the right are thought to be Plucker (with cane) and Wackerman (pointing).

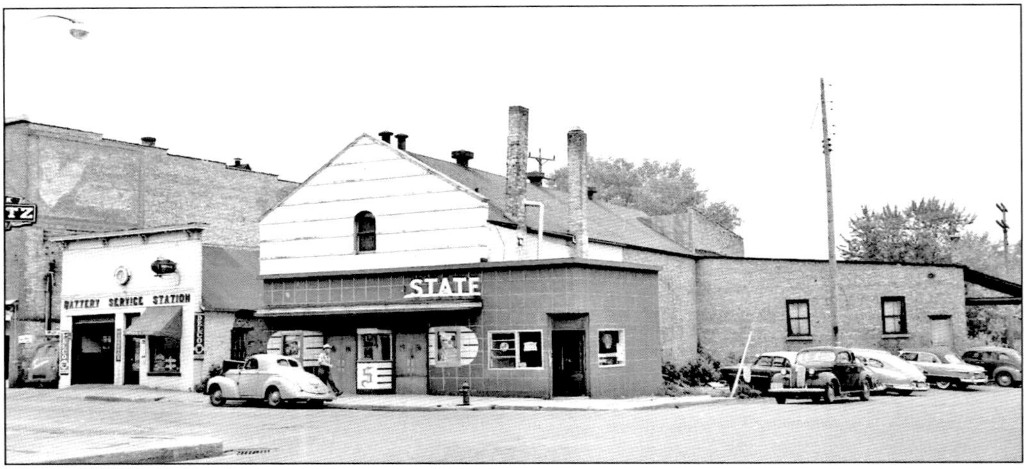

The State Theatre, pictured in 1949 at Pine and Short Streets (now Commerce Street and Milwaukee Avenue), opened in 1935 in this building, which was expressly built for its predecessor, the Crystal Theatre, in 1911. In 1953, the City bought the building and the adjacent Battery Service Station and demolished them to make way for a parking lot. The Battery Service building had previously housed the Rein blacksmith shop, which William Rein had started before 1860.

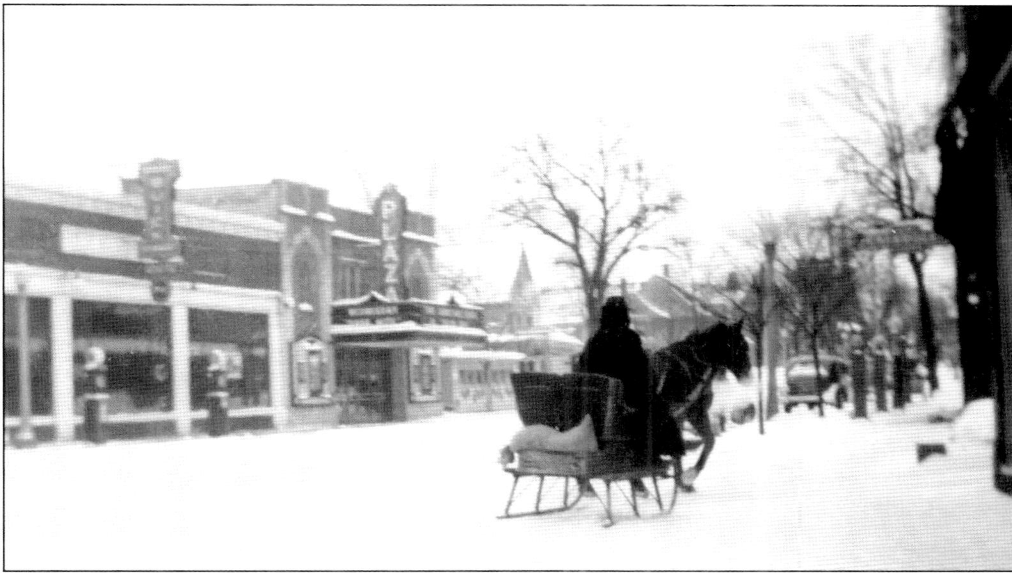

A sleigh heads southwest on Geneva Street (now Milwaukee Avenue) in February 1936. The Agner building at left, then occupied by Cunningham Buick, and the Plaza Theatre are still in use. The Lunch Box, next to the Plaza, was moved to the front of a house on the Hillside in 1945, where it remains, although no longer a diner. The Verhalen house beyond the diner served as a Badger Hotel annex for about 30 years before being demolished in 1949.

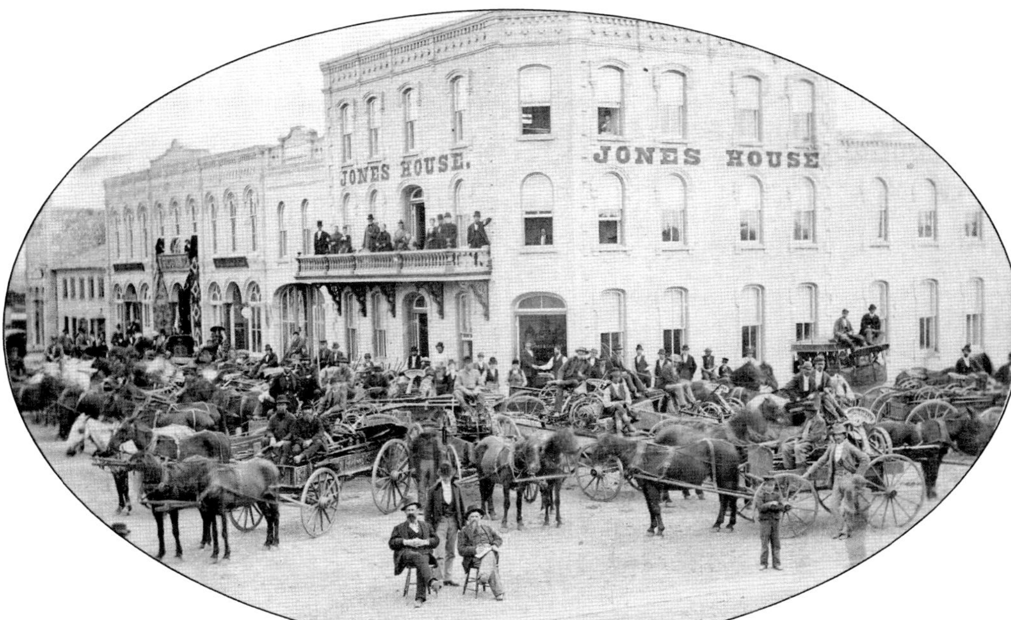

Captain J. W. Johnston photographed the teams and loads of Champion reapers and mowers that assembled in front of the Jones House hotel on Chestnut and Geneva (now Milwaukee Avenue) Streets, on Monday, May 10, 1875, when 24 farmers picked up the implements from William P. Goff. Goff is seated at right nearest the camera. Joseph Wackerman is seated at left.

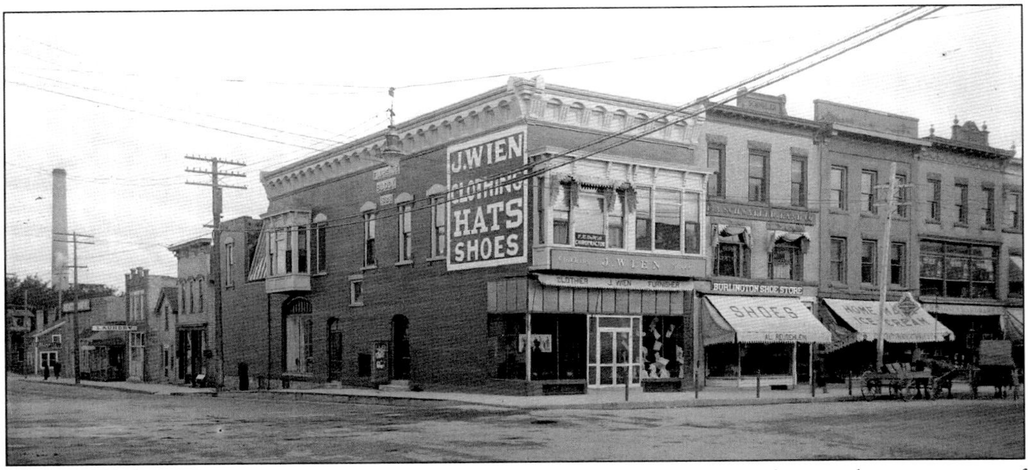

T. W. Buell built the Florence Block, named for his daughter, on the southeast corner of Chestnut and Pine Streets in 1888. Jacob Wien, whose men's wear store occupied the building from 1904 until 1939, bought the building in 1915 and, after renovations, named it the Wien building. Subsequent occupants included Kessler's variety store and Rogan's shoe store. Also along Pine Street *c.* 1915 were Al Reuschlein's shoe store, Egizo Giannini's fruit and confectionery store, and C. B. Wagner's Hardware Store.

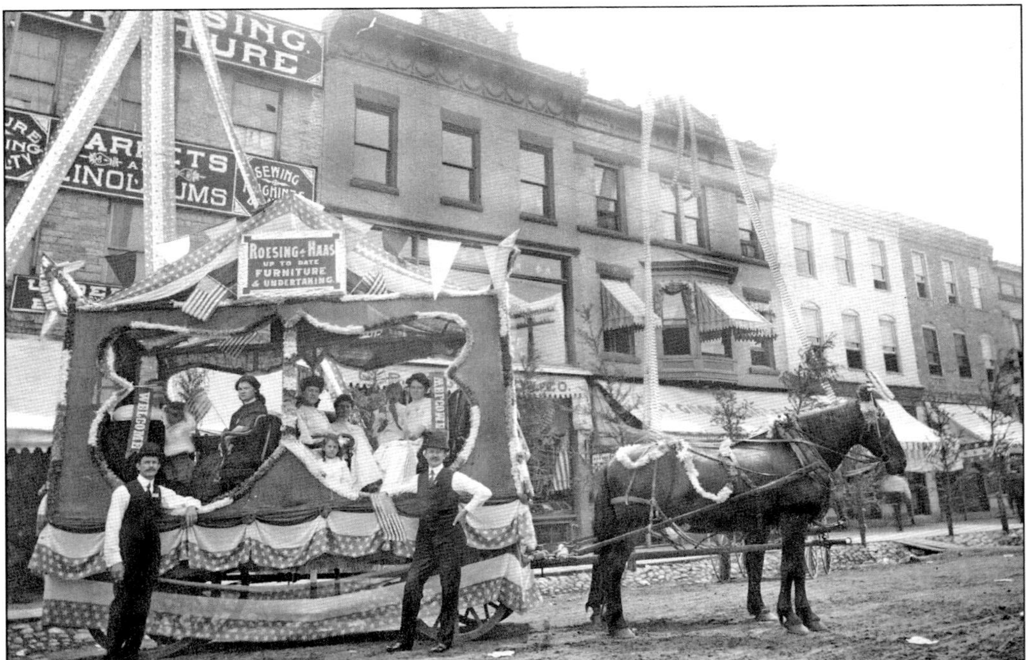

John Haas and Henry J. Roesing and their families pose in front of their furniture and undertaking business on July 4, 1907. Businesses to the south are Charles B. Wagner's hardware store, Frank H. Vos' grocery and dry goods store, John Cunningham and George May's meat market, and Henry Busch's saloon. Before 1906, Wagner's hardware store had been further south on the block. Roesing and Haas moved to the northwest corner of Washington and Pine Streets in 1911.

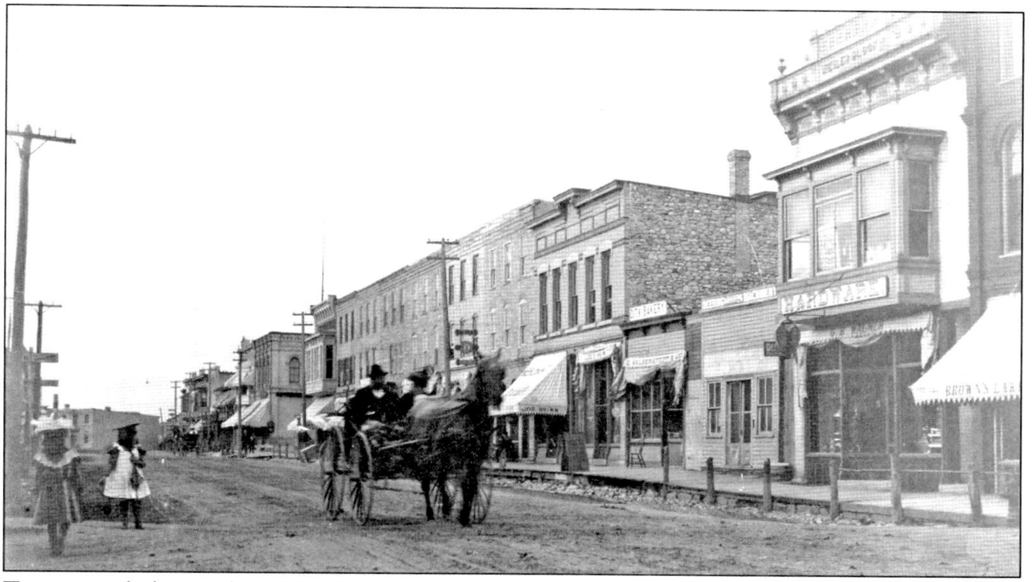

Two young ladies in their "Sunday best" look on as a horse-drawn runabout heads south on Pine Street near Washington Street c. 1898. Businesses, from the white awning near the horse's head to the right, are Joseph Brimm's tailor shop; Louis Rein's meat market; Charles Halberstadt's bakery; the building used by Charles B. Wagner to store Deering farm machinery; Charles B. Wagner's hardware store; and John Hoelz's saloon, called "Brown's Lake Exchange."

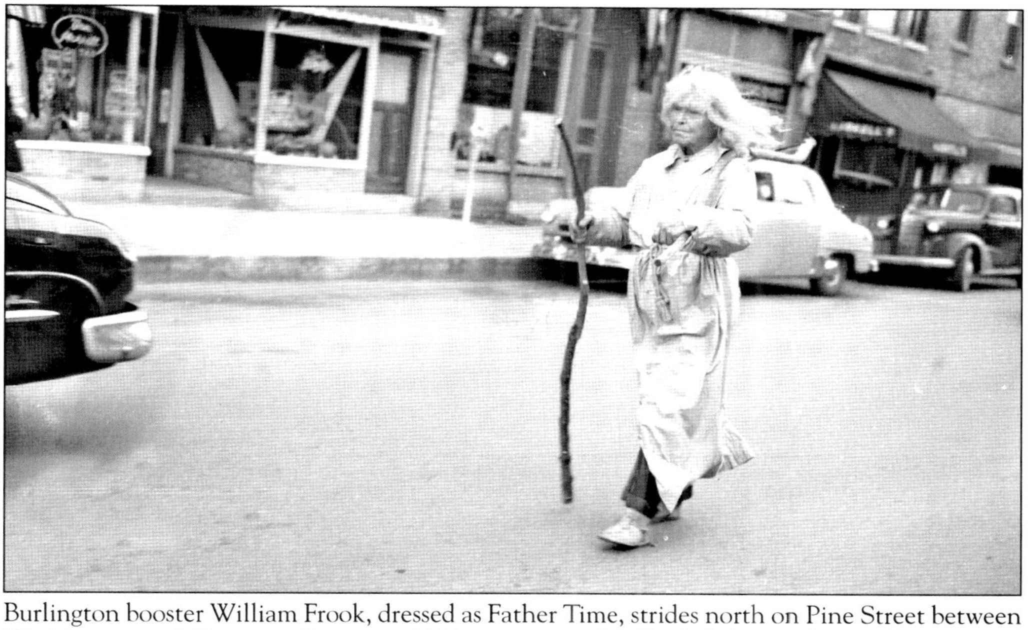

Burlington booster William Frook, dressed as Father Time, strides north on Pine Street between Washington and Chestnut Streets in 1951, protesting the City's failure to have a ceremony to mark completion of the repaving of Pine Street and Wilmot Avenue. Over the years, Frook proposed many ideas for community improvements. One—a bridge across the Fox River at State Street—which he first advocated in 1928, was realized in 2003 when the State and Adams Street Bridge was completed.

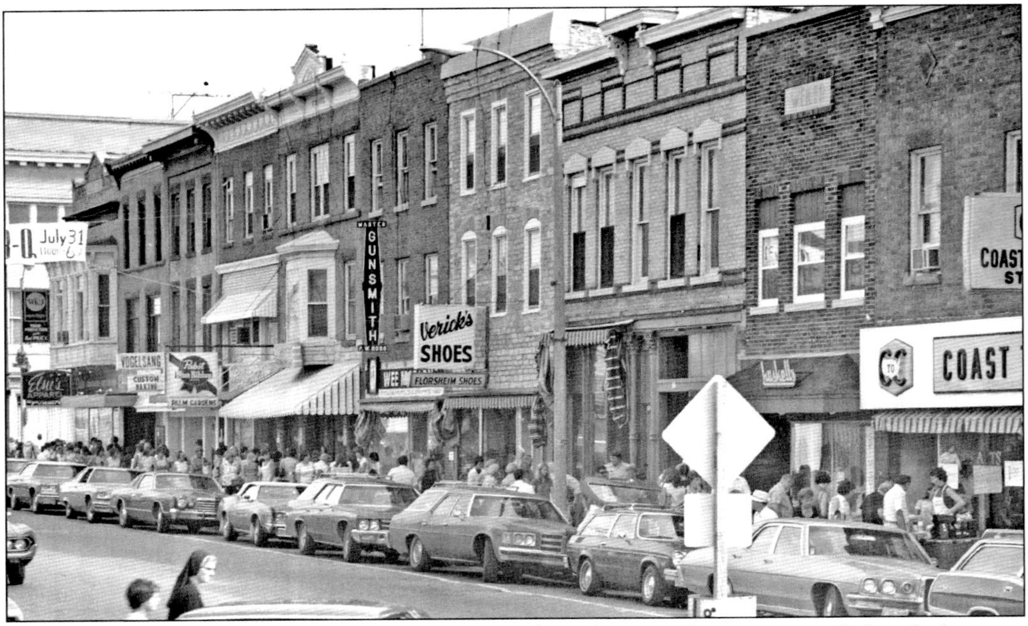

The east side of Pine Street between Chestnut and Washington Streets is crowded with shoppers during Maxwell Street Days in 1976. From left to right are Elsie's women's wear (which, at the time, also occupied the former Kessler store on the corner), Vogelsang's bakery, Palm Gardens tavern, Wee Moderns children's clothing, Verick's shoes, Itzin's shoes, management consultant Benton B. Hale, Haskell's women's wear, and Coast to Coast hardware. Gunsmith P. W. Ross was above Wee Moderns.

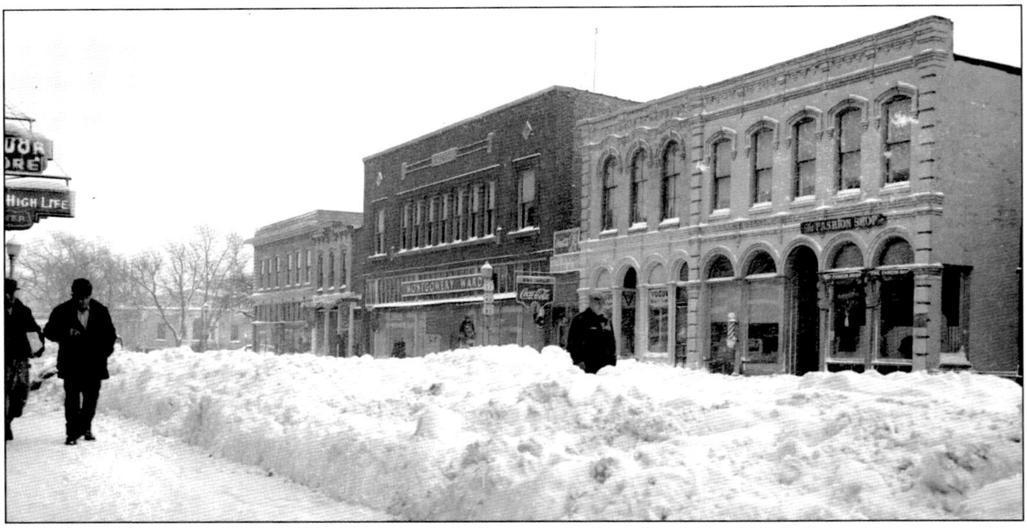

Snow fills Pine Street between Washington and Chestnut Streets *c.* 1947. Businesses on the west side of Pine, from left to right, are A. J. Roesing's furniture store, William and Lenora Graves' Smart Shop clothing store, Montgomery Ward department store, Mary Leadley's Little Skyscraper lunch counter, Vogue Beauty Shop, Allan Vogt's barber shop, and Evelyn Dwyer's Fashion Shop. The first three buildings are still standing, while those on the right were demolished in 1971 to create a bank drive-through.

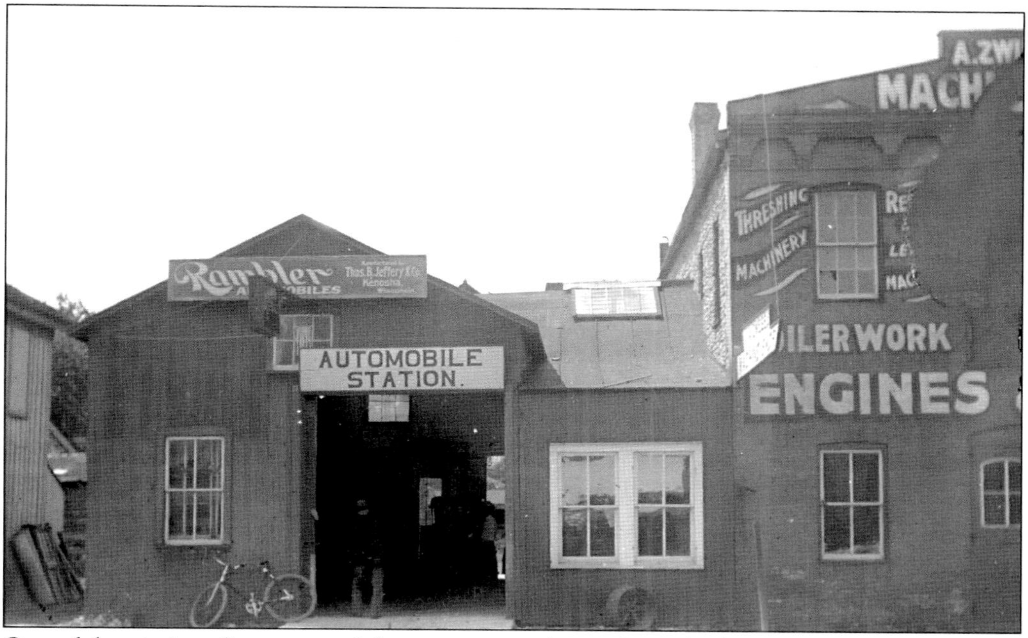

One of the city's earliest automobile services was Anton Jr. and Edward Zwiebel's Automobile Station on the south side of Chestnut Street, west of Geneva Street (now Milwaukee Avenue). The firm opened in 1906 in part of Anton's machine shop. Their father, Anton Sr., one of Burlington's most prolific inventors, had established the machine shop in 1865 in the former Benson livery building (at right). These buildings were replaced in 1908 with a large brick building. (Courtesy of the Henry Mangold Collection.)

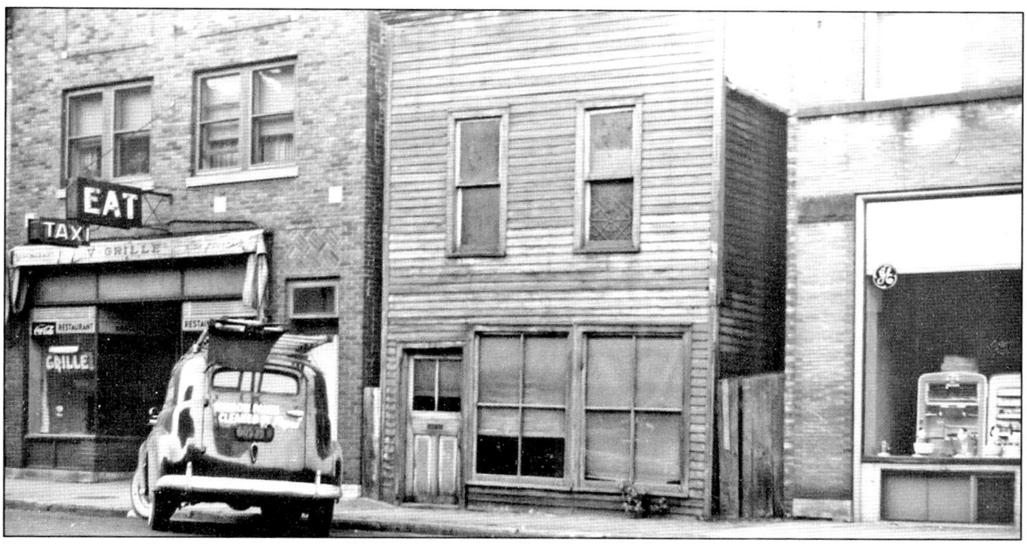

The last wooden downtown building—Charles Mole's barber shop—is shown c. 1949 on Pine Street north of Chestnut Street between the V-Grille, where Harold Boulden had a taxi stand, and the Wisconsin Electric Co. store. Mole, who bought Frank Stang's barber business in 1893 and the property in 1895, barbered until 1949. He also had the last wooden sidewalk in Burlington, replaced in 1928. In 1953, Edwin Boyle built a brick law office, still used by the family's third generation.

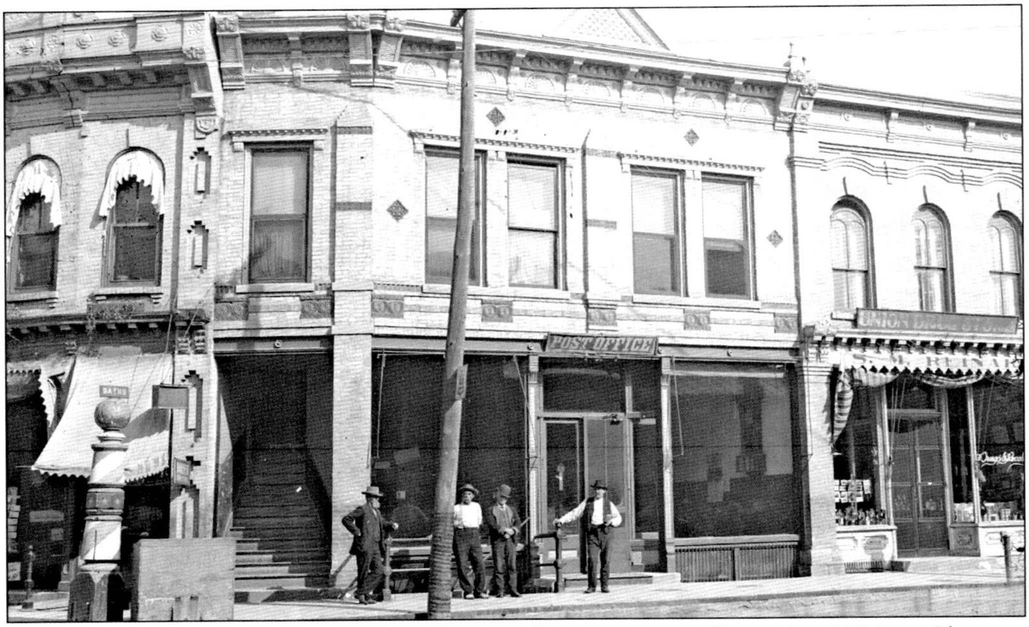

Frank Stang (in derby, third from left) and three others (unidentified) stand, *c.* 1904, on Chestnut Street just east of the bend near the Hoch building, which housed the post office from 1891 to 1908. S. M. Reinardy's Union Drug Store was in the Smith building at the right from 1902 to 1910. The barber pole denotes Charles Teut and Cady Farmer's barber shop, below George Denniston's book and news store in the Miller building at left. (Courtesy of the Henry Mangold Collection.)

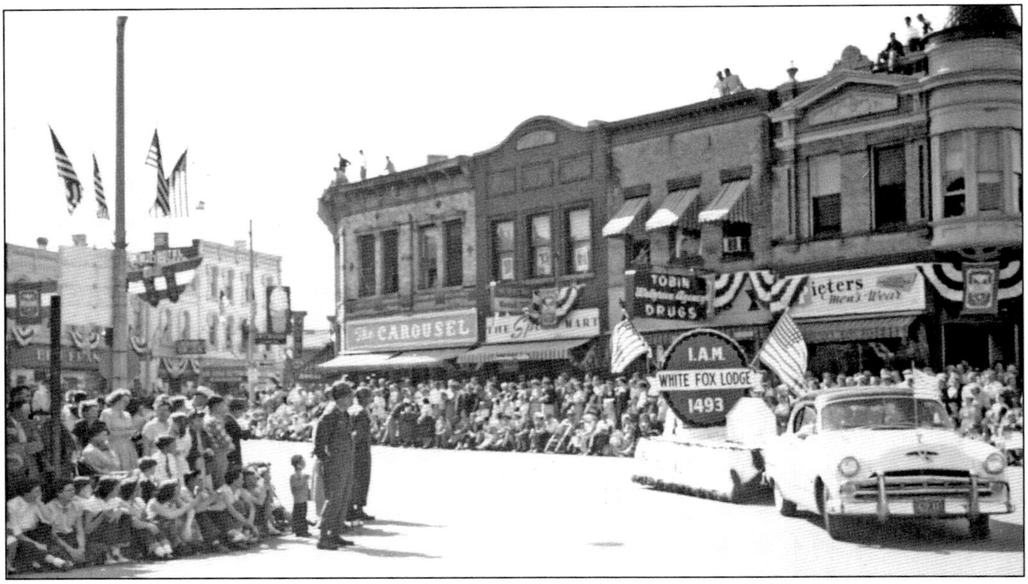

The downtown streets were lined several spectators deep as the May Day, U.S. Way parade went by on May 1, 1955. This was the second year for the event. Burlington had been selected in 1954 by the Wisconsin American Legion as the first community to sponsor a May 1 patriotic celebration of American heritage and traditions which would be the opposite of the communist May Day holiday.

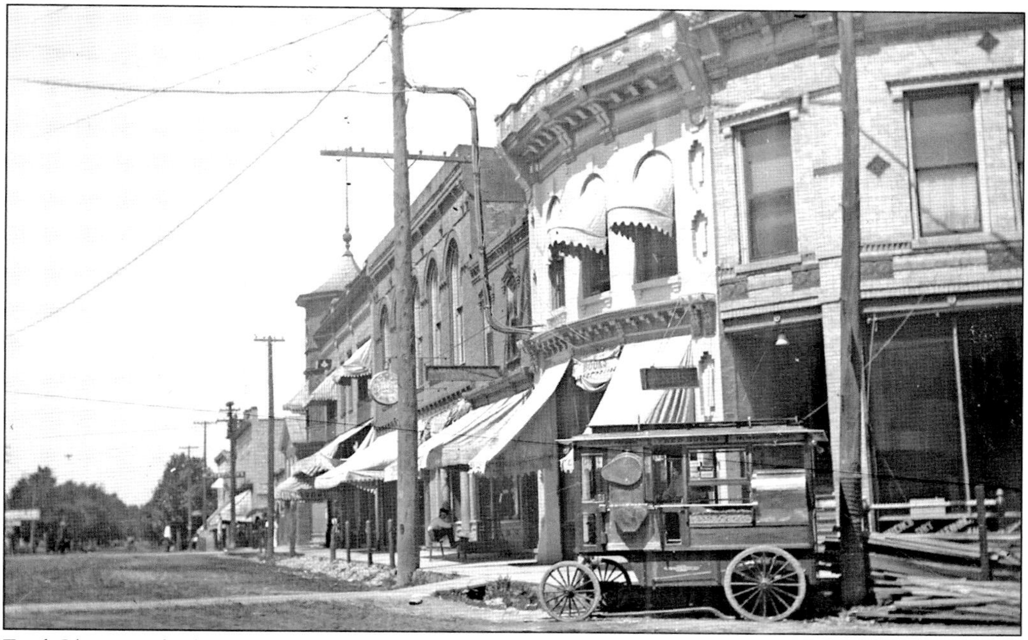

Fred Oberg's refreshment wagon stands on the north side of Chestnut Street at the "bend" in 1908. The Hoch building (at right) is being remodeled for Thomas G. Buchan's Burlington Pharmacy after the post office moved to the Hoelz building at Pine and Washington Streets. To the left of Oberg's refreshment wagon is George C. Denniston's book and news store, which he sold to W. R. Jones a month or so after this picture was taken. (Courtesy of the Henry Mangold Collection.)

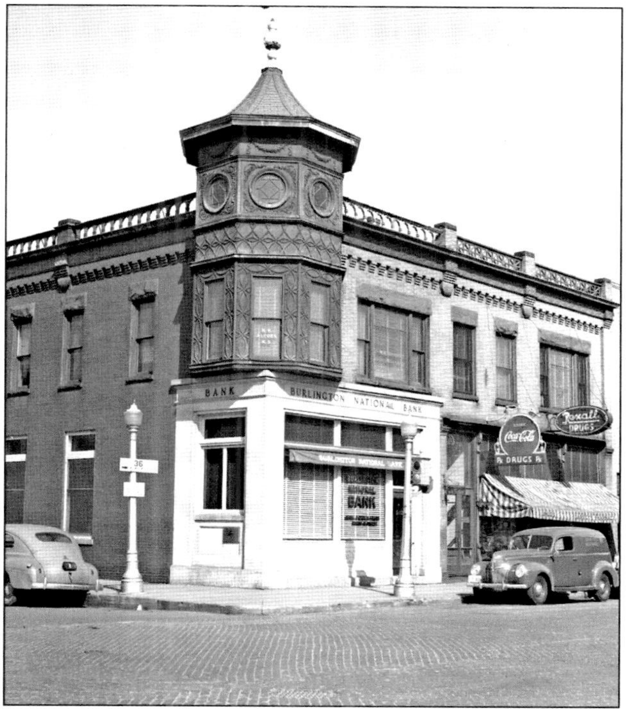

The Burlington National Bank opened on the corner of Chestnut and Geneva (now Milwaukee Avenue) Streets in 1921 and remained there until 1960. This 1949 picture by John Zwiebel also shows Edward Garvey's drug store and the brick-paved street. Both of the buildings are now occupied by Oldenburg Insurance. The corner building, put up by John P. Gill in 1895 and sold to B. J. Bushman in 1900, was used as a saloon until being remodeled for the bank.

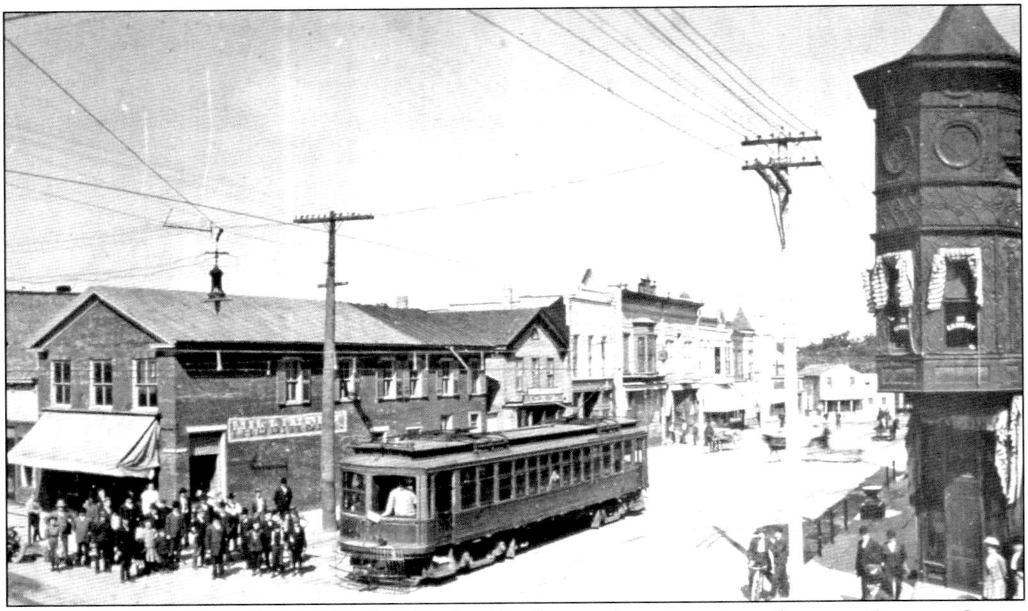

The first Milwaukee Electric Rail & Light Co. Interurban electric railcar on Geneva Street (now Milwaukee Avenue) is shown at the Chestnut Street intersection in this October 1, 1909, picture by Leonard J. Smith. The car then continued to the west city limits near St. Mary's Cemetery. The electric cars had been coming to Burlington since July 1, 1909, but did not cross the White River until the bridge there and the tracks on Geneva Street were completed.

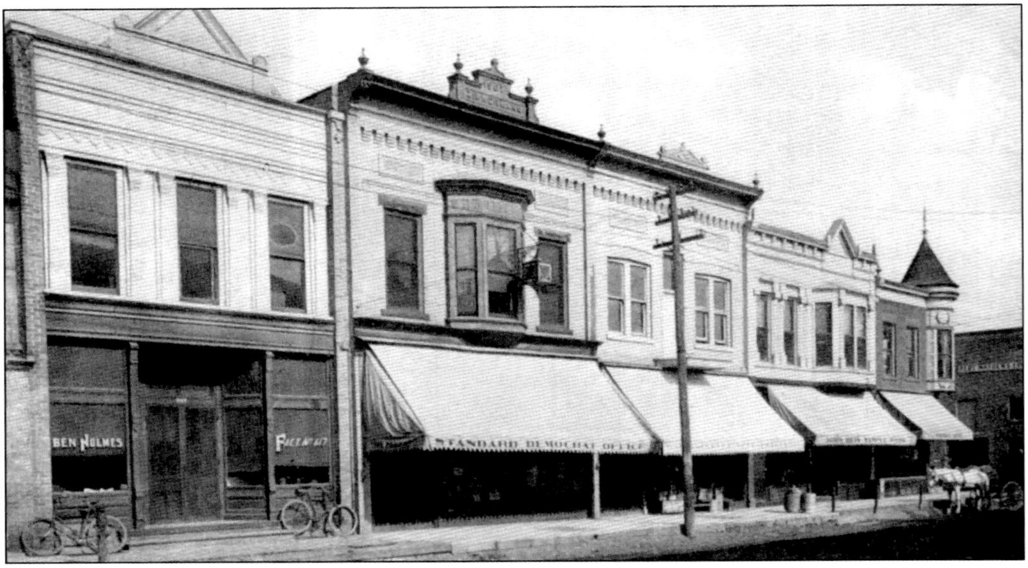

Businesses on the northwest side of Geneva Street (now Milwaukee Avenue) between Chestnut and Pine Streets *c.* 1906 include Ben Holmes cigar factory, the Standard Democrat newspaper and printing office, Peter Strassen's grocery store, John Beix's saloon, and Henry Woeste's saloon (building with tower). Except for the decorative cornice tops and the second story of Beix's saloon, the buildings retain much the same look today. Bert Mathews livery building, far right, was across the street from Woeste's saloon.

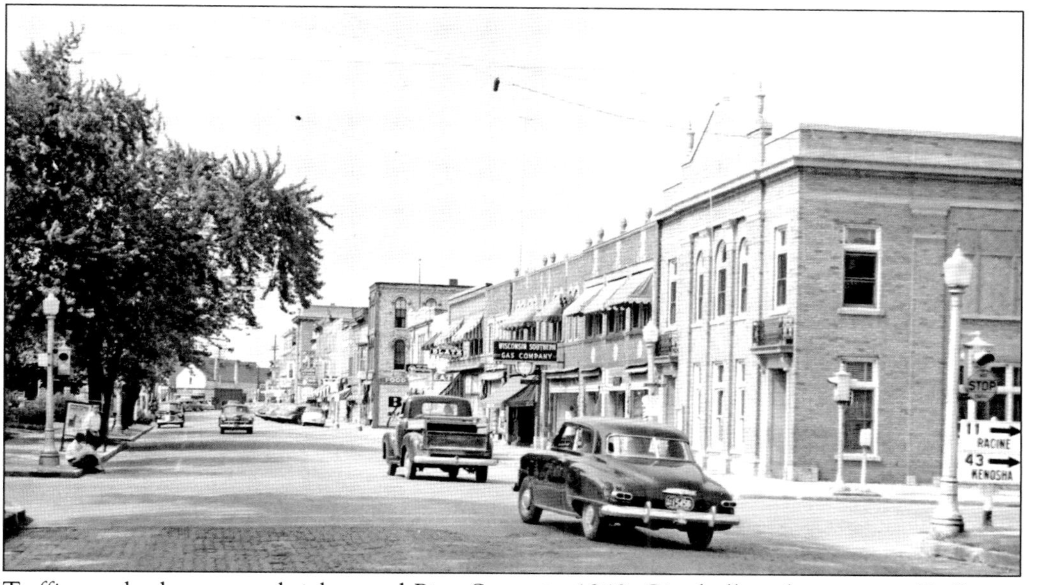

Traffic ran both ways on brick-paved Pine Street in 1949. City hall at the corner of Jefferson Street housed City offices, the public library, and the police department. Next north is Art Jacobs' barber shop, then Gilmore Gulbranson and William Larsen's insurance and real estate office, Elmer Ebert's Free Press newspaper office, Wisconsin Southern Gas Co., Katherine Pieh's Partee Gift Shop, Co-op grocery, Francis Sommers and Alan Castleberg's Palace Recreation Center, Herman Soetenga's appliances, and Joseph Bazal's creamery.

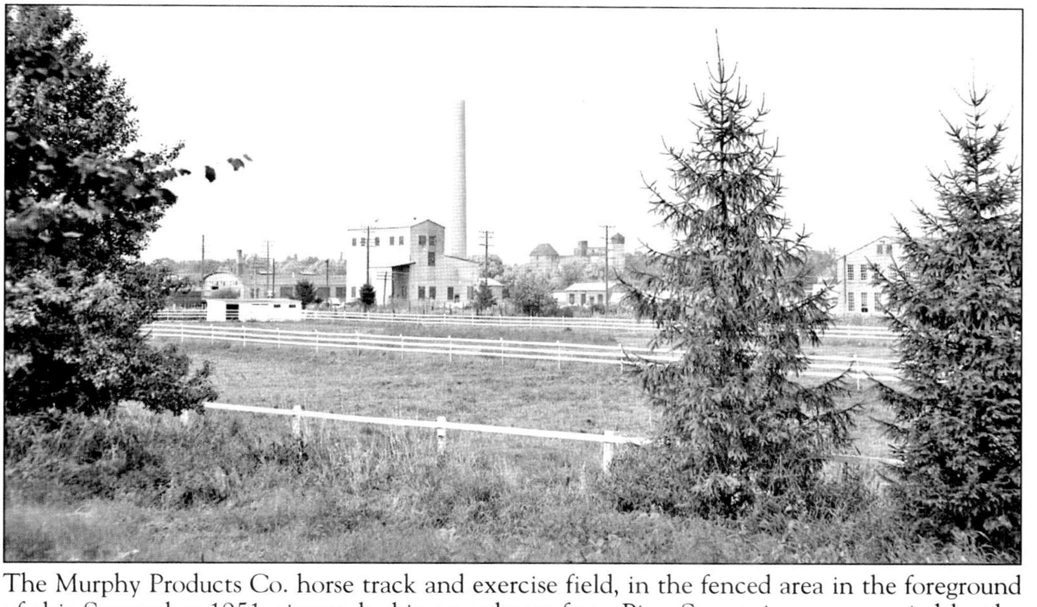

The Murphy Products Co. horse track and exercise field, in the fenced area in the foreground of this September 1951 picture looking northeast from Pine Street, is now occupied by the Pinecrest shopping center. Buildings across Calumet Street include Quality Milk Carriers (left, with the rounded roof line), the gas plant (left center, with the smokestack), the malt house on the east side of the Fox River (right center), and the former Basket factory (right, partially visible between the trees).

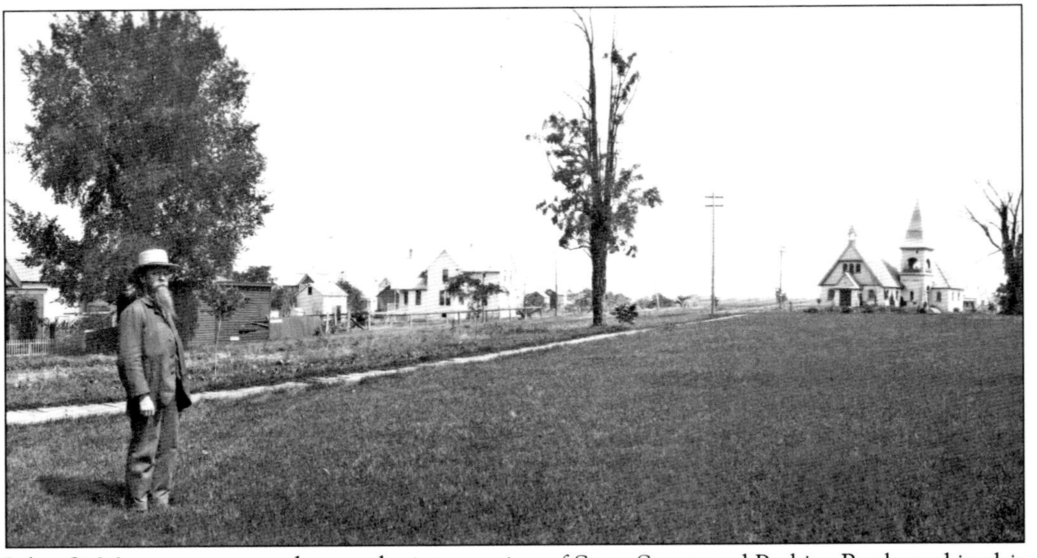

John O. Montgomery stands near the intersection of State Street and Perkins Boulevard in this *c.* 1900 picture. St. John the Divine Episcopal church (at right) had been dedicated in 1894. Until 1893, this area had been part of the Frederick Stanton Perkins farm, which stretched from State Street on the north to what is now Market Street on the south, and from Pine Street on the east to Kane Street on the west. That area has become largely residential.

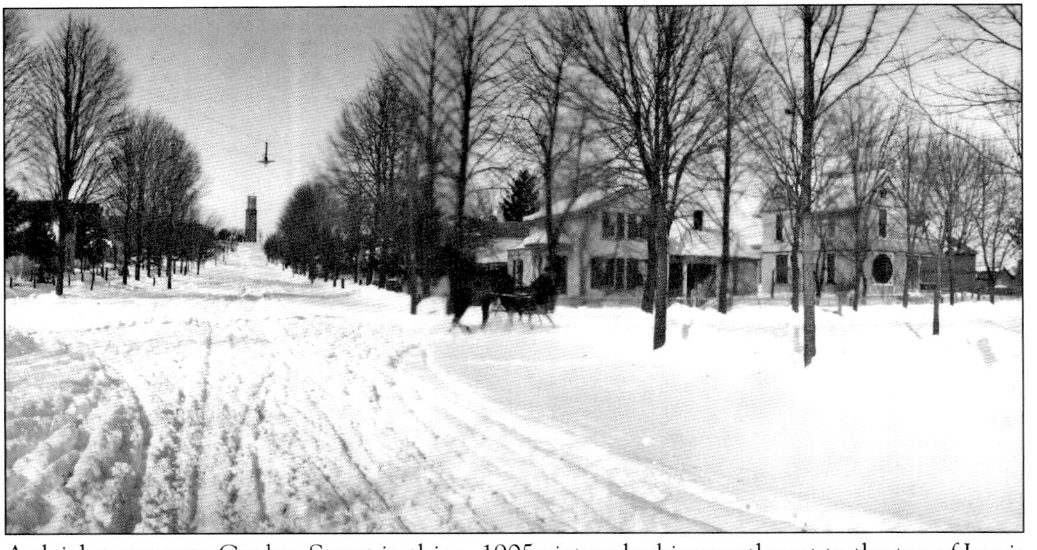

A sleigh turns onto Conkey Street in this *c.* 1905 picture looking northwest to the top of Lewis Street where the 1890 water tower sits. The tower served the Village and then the City of Burlington for over 60 years. The house just right of center still sits on that corner. The house at the right with the round window was moved to Edward Street in 1956 to make way for a schoolyard and parking area for St. Charles Borromeo Catholic Church.

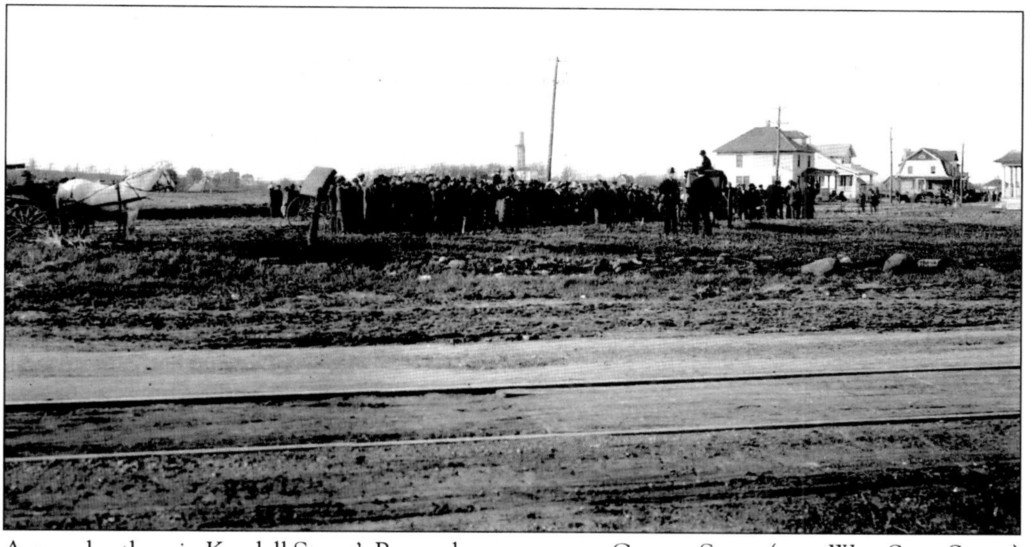

A crowd gathers in Kendall Street's Bensonhurst area near Geneva Street (now West State Street) for a lot sale in November 1912. The Lewis Street water tower is at center. The large hip-roofed house at right center was built by Edward D. Perkins in 1911. The interurban railcar tracks (foreground) ended about this point near St. Mary's Cemetery. For a time, the last incoming car each day stayed here overnight before heading back to St. Martins, near Milwaukee.

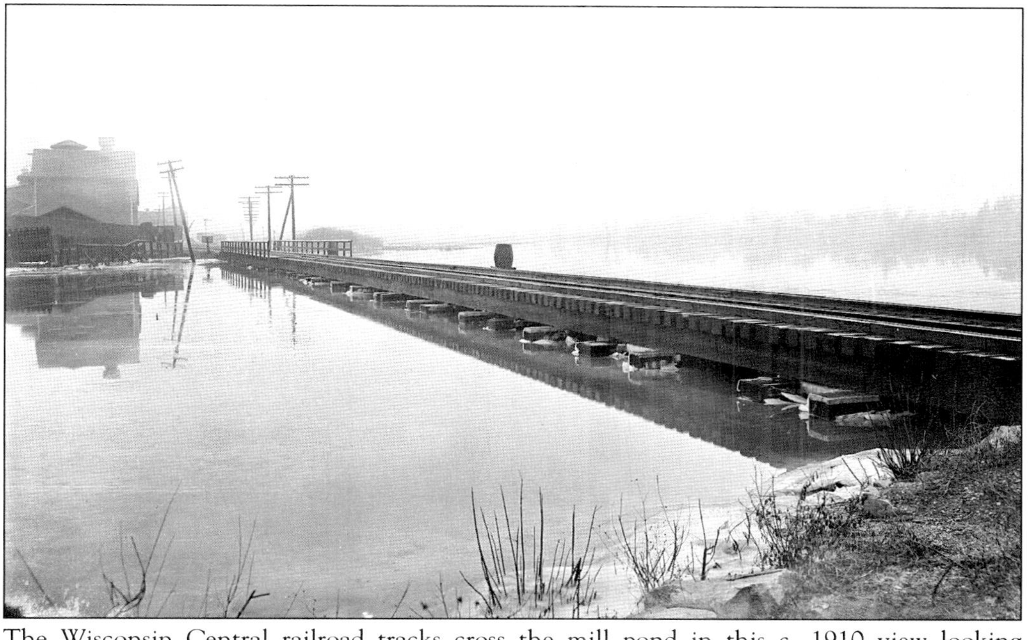

The Wisconsin Central railroad tracks cross the mill pond in this *c.* 1910 view looking northwest from the area of the dam and Ayers Flouring Mill (now site of the Standard Press building) toward the train depot near what is now Commerce Street. The large buildings at the left are grain storage buildings. In 1919, the Soo Line, successor to the Wisconsin Central, filled in this area with gravel to allow trains to run on solid roadbed.

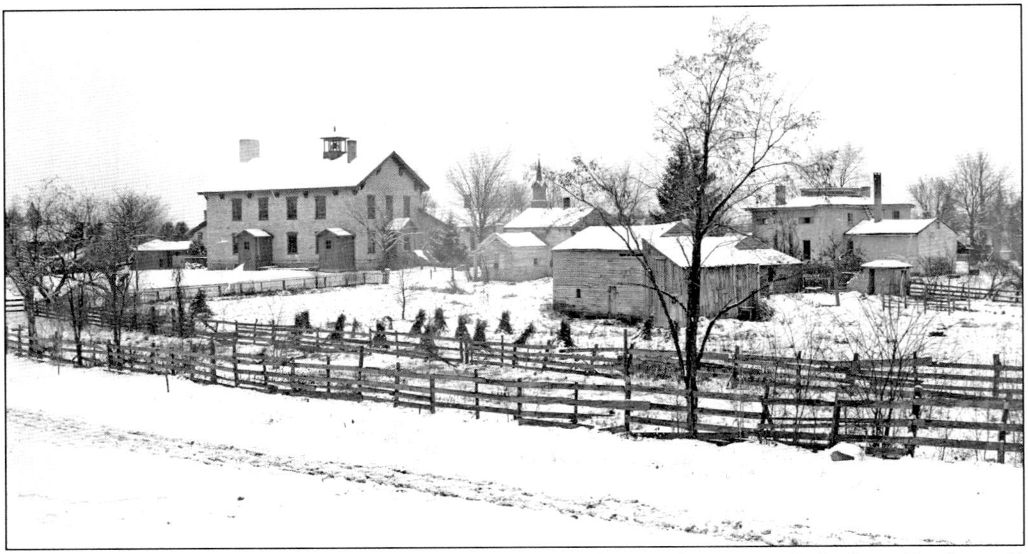

The Union School on State Street between Kane and West (now North Perkins Boulevard) Streets is pictured in the late 1890s looking northeast from Kane Street. The building, erected in 1859, was used as a school until 1896, when the Conkey Street School (later known as Cooper School) was opened and the students were moved there. The one-story addition extending east along State Street to West Street, put up in 1884 to provide additional school space, was moved off the site in 1910.

The school building was used as a manufacturing facility and for other purposes for several years, before being remodeled and reopened in 1911 as Lincoln School. Kindergarten and early primary classes were held at Lincoln School until 1981, when the school district moved its offices there.

The corn shocks and outbuildings are on the corner where C. Roy and Elfrieda Becker McCanna built a residence in 1920. Following Mr. McCanna's death in 1975, the former residence was occupied by a funeral home, a furniture store, and a collection of shops and offices.

The former residence of Dr. Edward G. and Ann Eliza Morse Dyer (center, with the steeple of St. John's Lutheran church in the background) and the former Origen and Julia Dyer Perkins residence (the large square building at the right with the rear attachment) were stations on the Underground Railroad in the years before the Civil War. Dr. Dyer, Burlington's first doctor, was an ardent abolitionist, who gave Liberty Street (now part of State Street) its name. The house, which was bought by John Pennington Mather in 1877 and later lodged foreign laborers, was moved off the property around the end of 1915. The Perkins residence, built in 1846, still stands as one of the city's treasures.

The Dr. Joel Henry and Persis Allen Cooper House, partially seen at the left behind the school building, also is reported to have been a shelter for freedom-seekers on the Underground Railroad. Their son, Henry Allen Cooper, who grew up in the house, represented this district in the United States Congress for 31 years.

Two

STORES, SHOPS, AND BUSINESS VEHICLES

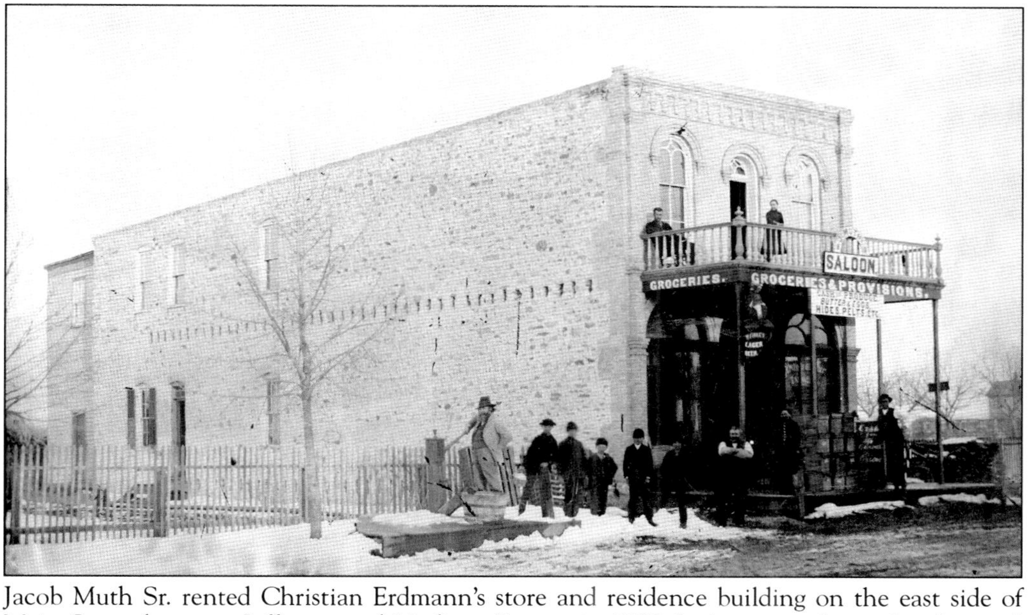

Jacob Muth Sr. rented Christian Erdmann's store and residence building on the east side of Main Street between Jefferson and Madison Streets in 1880 for his general merchandise and saloon businesses. Erdmann earlier had a saloon here. The building, pictured c. 1882 in this tin plate image, still stands, minus the porch and canopy. The well (center) was drilled in 1881. Muth moved his saloon to his residence on the southeast corner of State and Main Streets in 1890. This building has been occupied by a succession of taverns over many years, including the Canadian Club, the Embassy Club, P. J. O'Reilly's, and Rumors Never End.

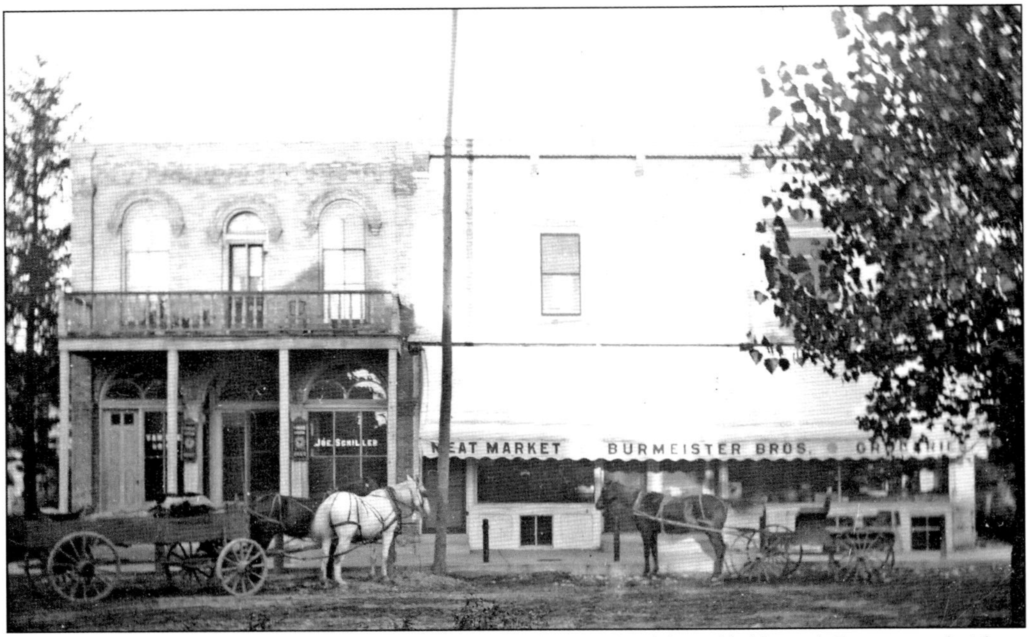

Joseph Schiller's saloon occupies the former Erdmann building (left) and Ernest and Alvin Burmeister's grocery store and meat market occupies their building on the east side of Main Street south of Jefferson Street in this 1911 picture. Schiller, who exchanged a flour mill in Marytown, Wisconsin, for the saloon business in 1907, operated the saloon until the end of 1911. The Burmeister brothers opened the business in their new building in September 1911. The Burmeister brothers' building burned in 1965.

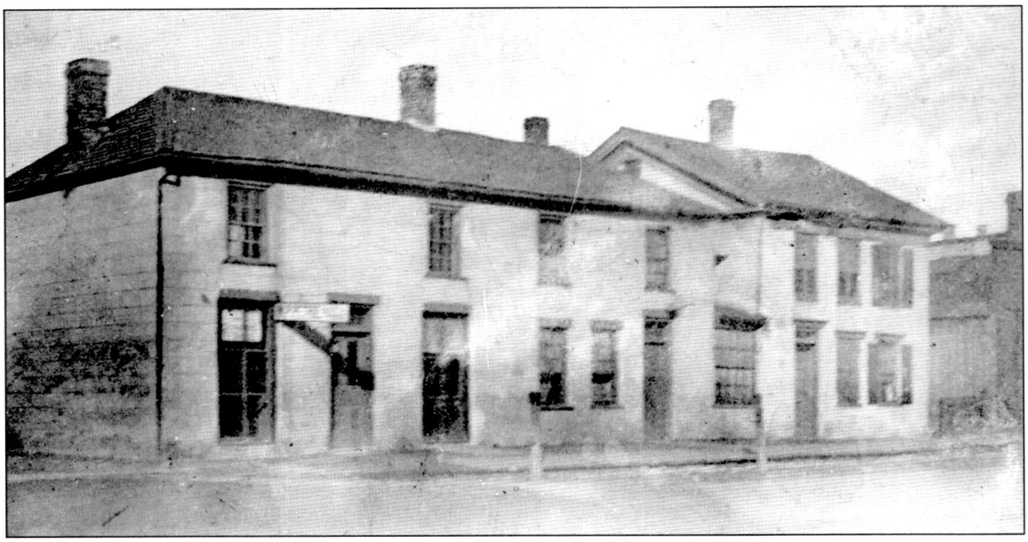

The Meakins store and residence, pictured c. 1880, sat on the northwest corner of Pine and Washington Streets for over 50 years. The three connected grout buildings were owned by Thomas and Mary Meakins until 1885. Meakins was a jeweler, shoemaker, and barber, who also pulled teeth and took in boarders. Cook and Willich's meat market was the last occupant in 1908, when Mathias P. Petrie put up the two-story cement block building that now stands on the corner.

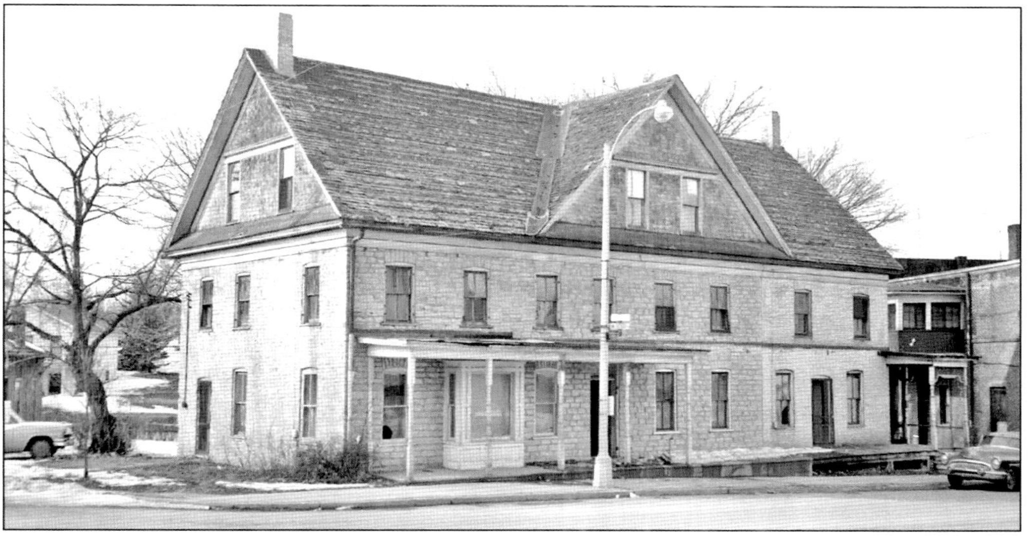

This hotel and boarding house, shown just before it was razed in 1959, was a fixture on the Hillside Triangle bounded by McHenry, Liberty (now State), and Geneva (now Milwaukee Avenue) Streets from the late 1870s. Peter Smith built it after a fire had destroyed his residence and other buildings on the property. Barney Wentker, who bought the Triangle in 1897 and had a saloon next to the hotel, sometimes operated the hotel and other times leased it out.

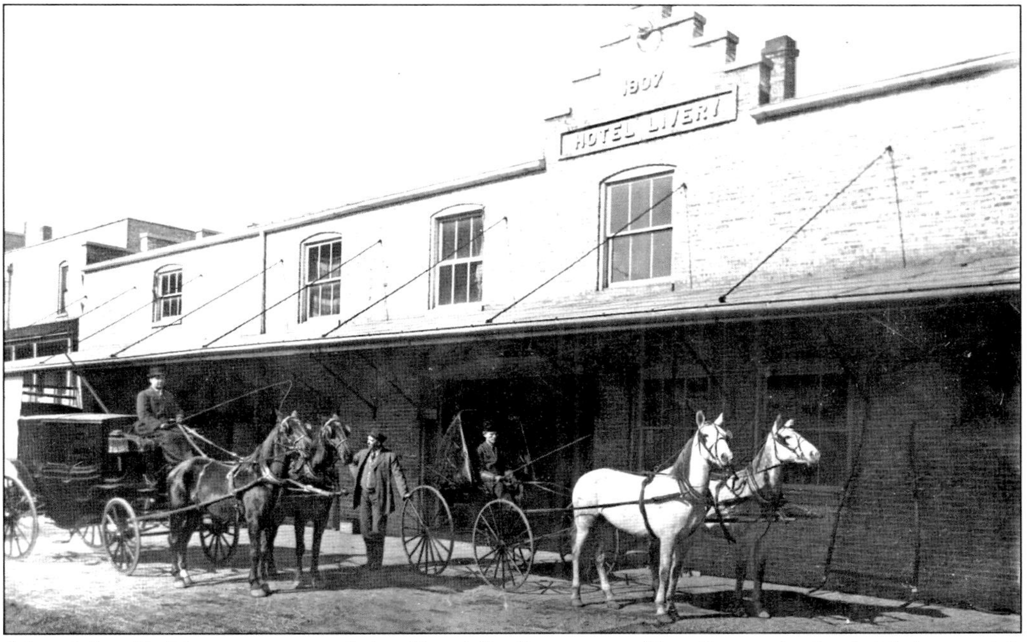

After John G. Mutter, owner of the Hotel Burlington on Pine Street, had a brick barn with cement floors built in the rear of the hotel in 1907, Henry Tichlofen and Frank Rambo moved their livery business there. In 1908, Richard "Dick" Kelly bought Rambo's interest, and Tichlofen and Kelly leased land and laid an entrance road to Chestnut Street. Following Tichlofen's death in 1910, Kelly became sole proprietor. The livery barn, pictured c. 1910, has been demolished.

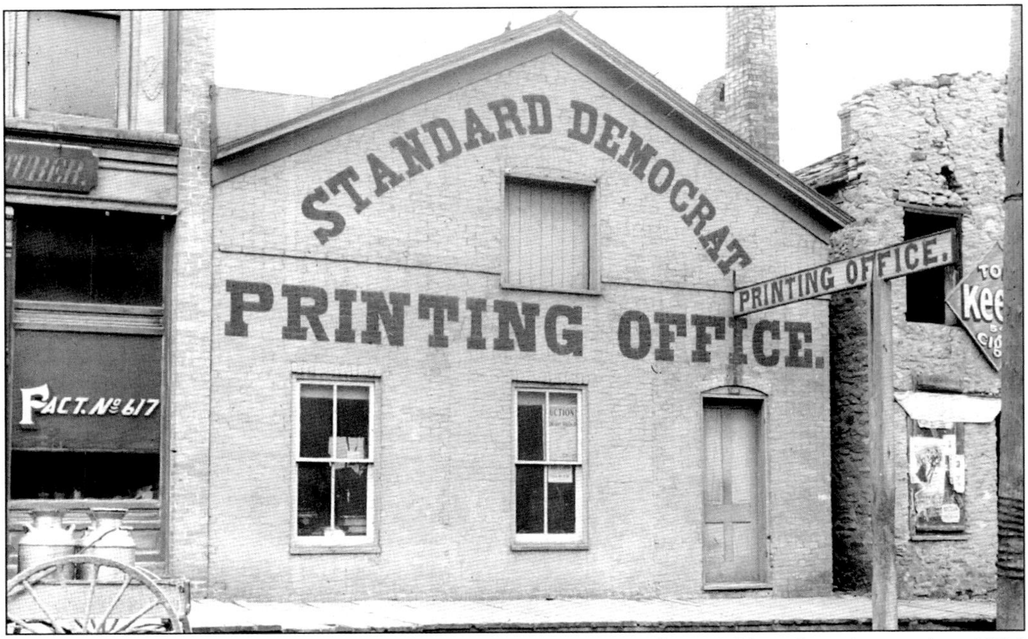

Henry Zimmermann bought this building on Geneva Street (now Milwaukee Avenue) in 1896 and moved his Standard Democrat newspaper office there. The building, pictured *c.* 1905, had been Charles Wagner's blacksmith shop from 1860 (or before) until 1888, and had then served as a horse barn and the Derby Bicycle Club's meeting place. The building was replaced in 1907 by a two-story brick building where the newspaper remained until 1984. The Spinning Top Museum now occupies the 1907 building.

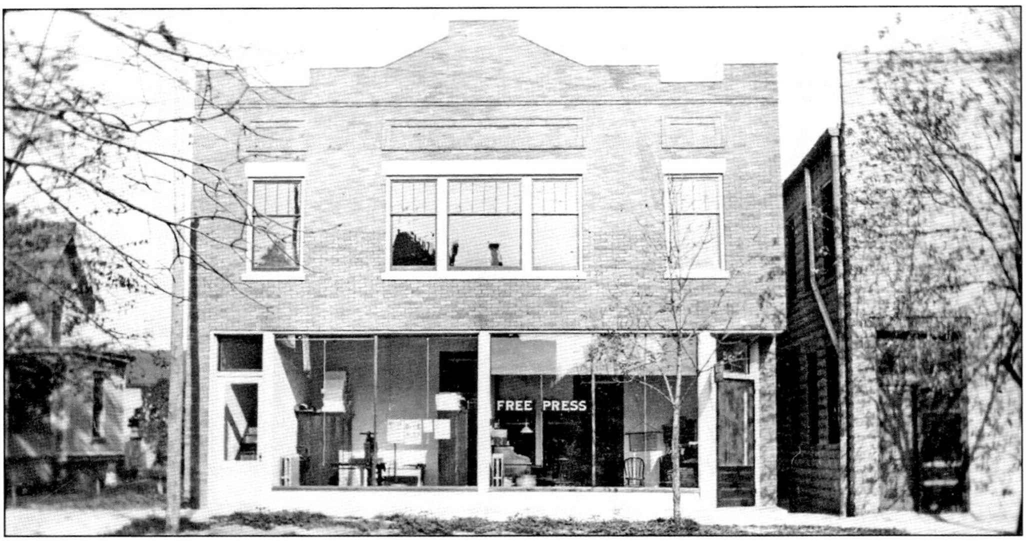

William Devor, owner of the *Burlington Free Press* from 1891 to 1920, erected this building on Washington Street, near Pine Street, in 1914. A. J. Cunningham bought the property in 1922 and leased it to Joseph Bazal, who opened a creamery. In 1926, Bazal moved to the former city hall property less than a block away. A meat market and an electric shop occupied the building before it was sold in 1944 to Stanley Szydlowski, who opened the Music Mart.

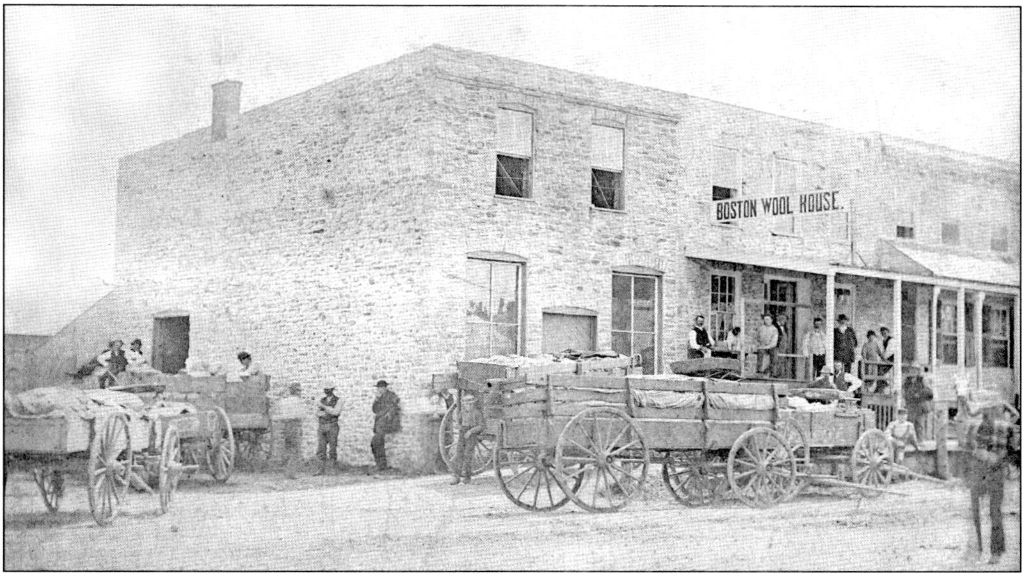

In 1881, Elias Nelson White bought land on the southwest corner of Chestnut and Dodge Streets and built a two-story stone building, shown *c.* 1885. White used the building and the adjoining one, connected by an arched doorway, as a wool depot, called the Boston Wool House. In the ensuing years, Burlington became known as one of the largest and best wool markets in the northwest. In 1907, Matt Rewald bought the building and remodeled it into a planing mill.

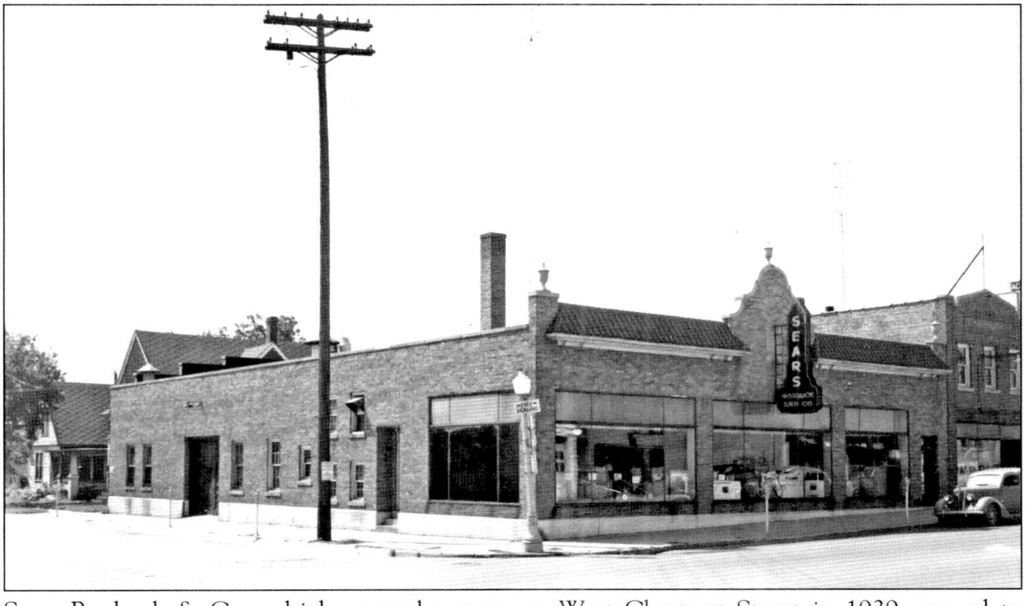

Sears Roebuck & Co., which opened a store on West Chestnut Street in 1939, moved to this building at Chestnut and Dodge Streets in 1940, succeeding the building's first tenant, Champion Motor Co. The building, shown *c.* 1950, was erected in 1929, replacing the former planing mill and wool depot. After Sears moved out in 1961, this building was occupied by the Burlington Discount Center, Clinton Lumber Co., H. W. Theis plumbing supply, and Adelita's Mexican Store. The building burned in April 2005.

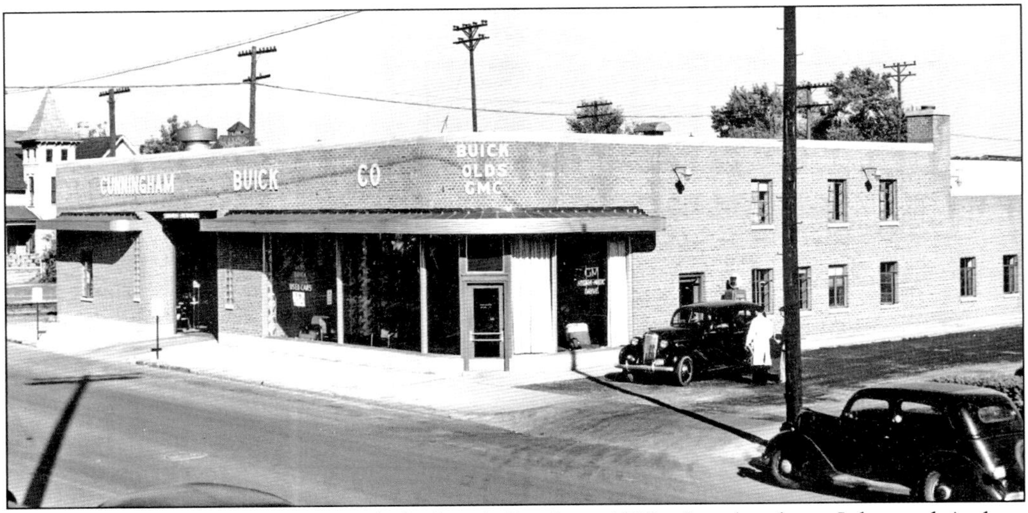

The Cunningham name was first linked with Buick in 1909 when brothers, John and Arthur, bought a Buick touring car from Hugh Agner. In 1914, Arthur took the Buick agency for Burlington and opened a garage on Washington Street. After moving to different buildings in 1917, 1927, and 1933, Cunningham Buick bought this site on Jefferson Street, built a new garage, and moved here in 1947, the year before this picture. The firm added the Oldsmobile agency in 1932.

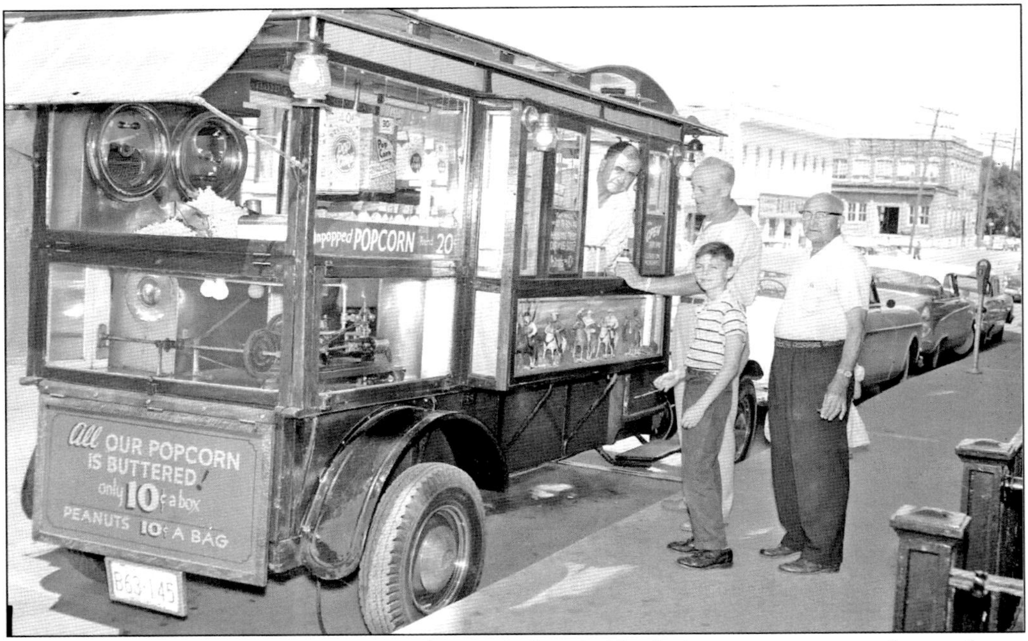

McCormack's popcorn wagon, pictured in 1958 beside Kessler's variety store on the southeast corner of Chestnut and Pine Streets, was a familiar downtown sight for many years, first at the Badger Hotel corner and then here. Floyd "Mac" (in the window) and Florence McCormack bought the 1921 Model T Ford popcorn wagon in 1924 from Fred Oberg, who obtained it in 1922. The wagon, which the McCormacks also took to various community and area activities, was moved to Chicago in 1966.

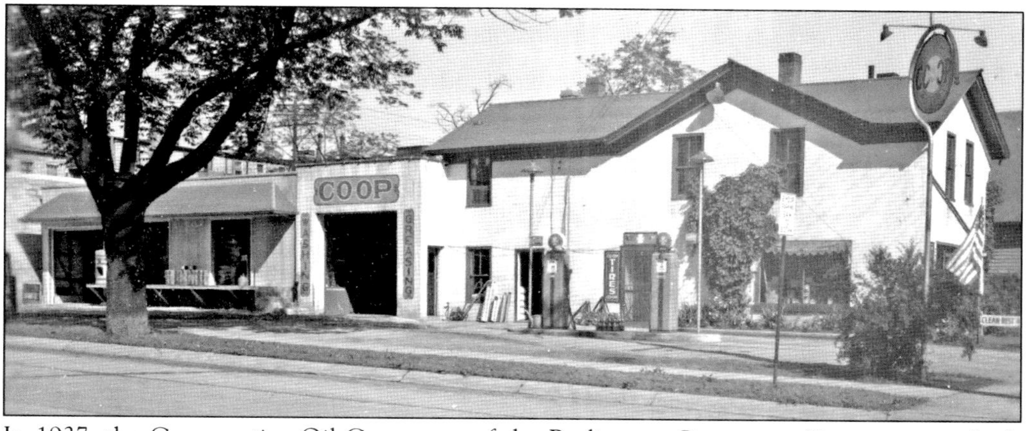

In 1937, the Co-operative Oil Co., a part of the Burlington Consumers Co-operative which was organized that year to handle petroleum products and put up a filling station, bought the Andres house on the northwest corner of Washington and Dodge Streets and installed a filling station, shown here in the 1940s. In 1959, the house, used for office and storage space, was torn down to enlarge the service station.

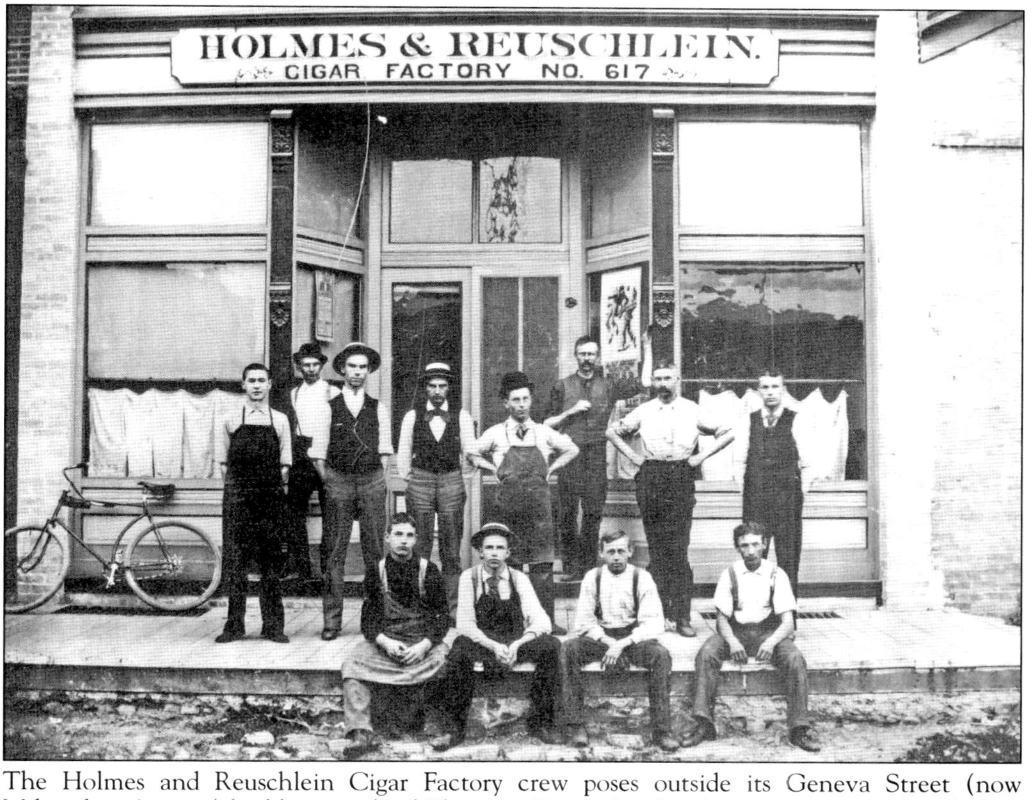

The Holmes and Reuschlein Cigar Factory crew poses outside its Geneva Street (now Milwaukee Avenue) building north of Chestnut Street shortly after moving to the building in May 1894. Owners Louis Reuschlein (in hat and suspenders) and Ben Holmes (with left arm raised) are at the back. Edwin Moe is seated far right; others are unidentified. The partnership dissolved in January 1895, with Holmes continuing the cigar business. Holmes moved his cigar business to a Pine Street building in 1909.

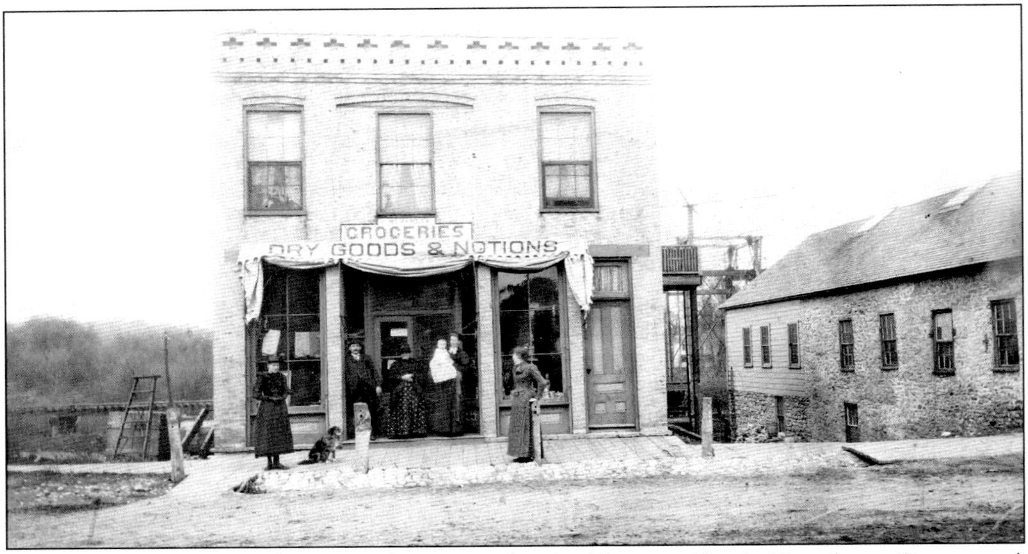

Jerome Mutchler opened a general store in this building on North Pine (now Commerce) Street in 1894 after buying the building from Henry Kline, who had a saloon there. The building had been erected in 1865 by Elliott C. Benson as a livery stable. Later in 1894, Mutchler and two neighboring businesses, including the Rein blacksmith shop (right), put new stone gutters in front of their buildings. The Wisconsin Central Railroad tracks can be seen in the left background.

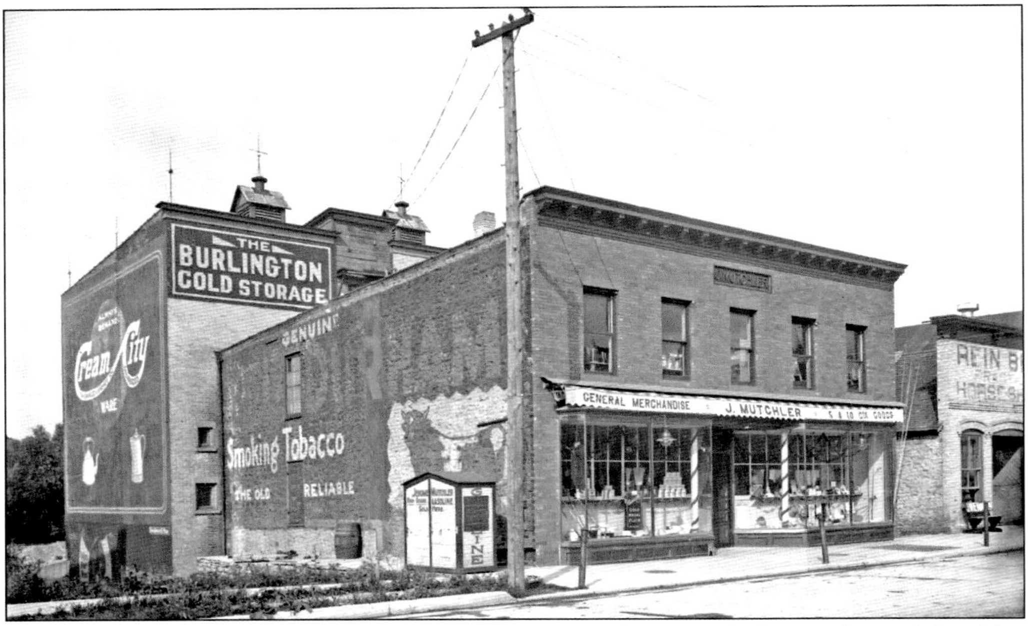

After building a cold storage warehouse and an elevator for use with the warehouse behind his original store on the east side of North Pine (now Commerce) Street in the early 1900s, Jerome Mutchler renovated his store building in 1913, putting on a modern front, as pictured here. Albert T. Spiegelhoff became Mutchler's partner in 1915 and bought Mutchler's interest in the general merchandise business in 1916. Mutchler and his son Leo continued the cold storage business.

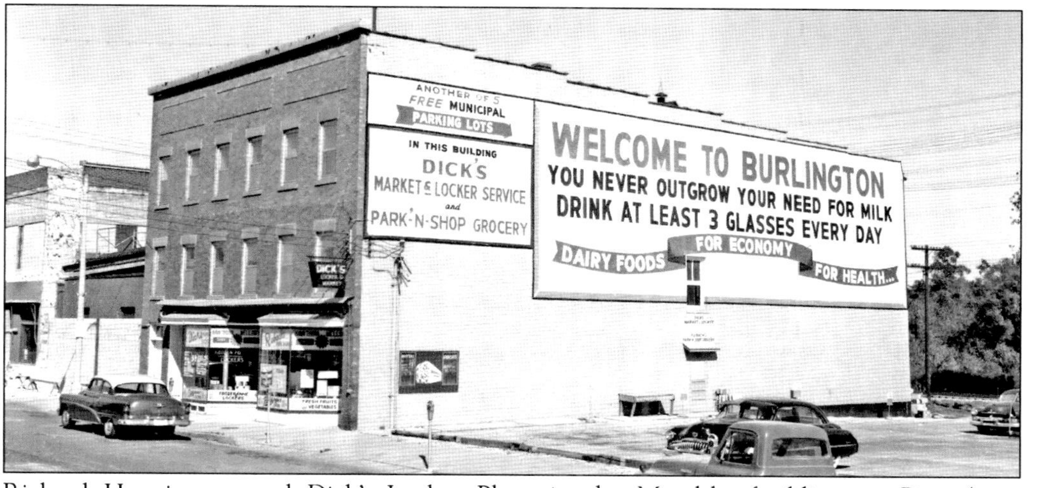

Richard Huening opened Dick's Locker Plant in the Mutchler building on Pine (now Commerce) Street in 1940 after his lease on a quick-freeze locker plant on Wilmot Avenue (now South Pine Street) expired. In 1953, Roger Rubach opened a grocery store with the locker plant as the meat market. Huening sold the locker service and grocery in 1955. The municipal parking lot beside the store was put in after the Battery Service Station and State Theatre buildings were demolished at the end of 1953.

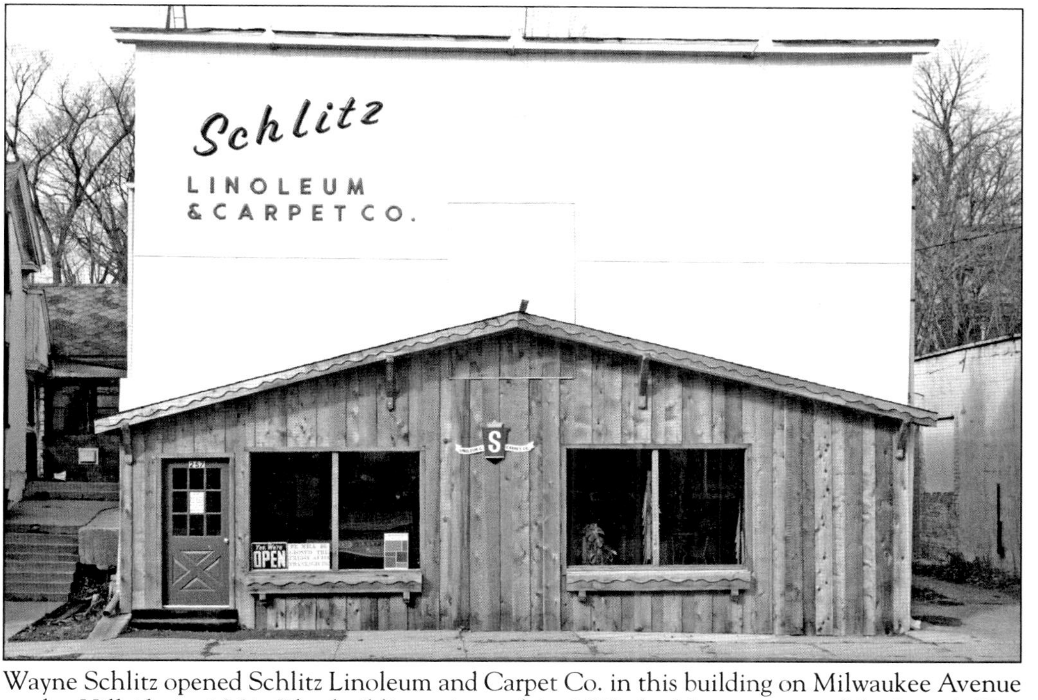

Wayne Schlitz opened Schlitz Linoleum and Carpet Co. in this building on Milwaukee Avenue at the Hillside in 1964. The building, pictured in 1972, had been occupied by Large's Tire Service, which moved there in 1953. Earlier occupants included Alois Grossman's wagon shop, Henry A. Rueter's workshop, George Henry's and Max Daniels' meat markets, a variety of automobile and related businesses, Edwin Subrod and Paul Zerneke's feed business, Eugene "Sam" Martin's Hitching Post restaurant, and Mrs. Emma Norris' Rainbow Snack Shack.

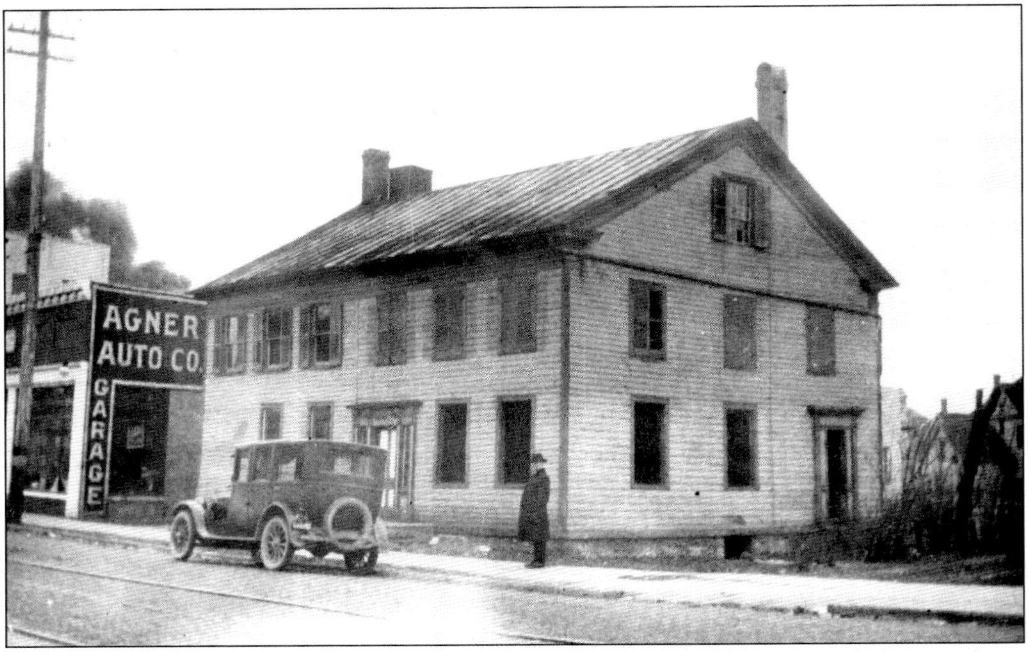

This frame building, which originally stood on the corner of Chestnut and Geneva (now Milwaukee Avenue) Streets, was moved south to this spot on Geneva Street about 1866 to make way for the Jones House hotel. It was built in 1839 by Pliny Perkins and Hugh McLaughlin as a hotel and store building. After the move, it was used as a rooming house. The building, pictured c. 1920, was razed in 1924 to make way for the Plaza Theatre.

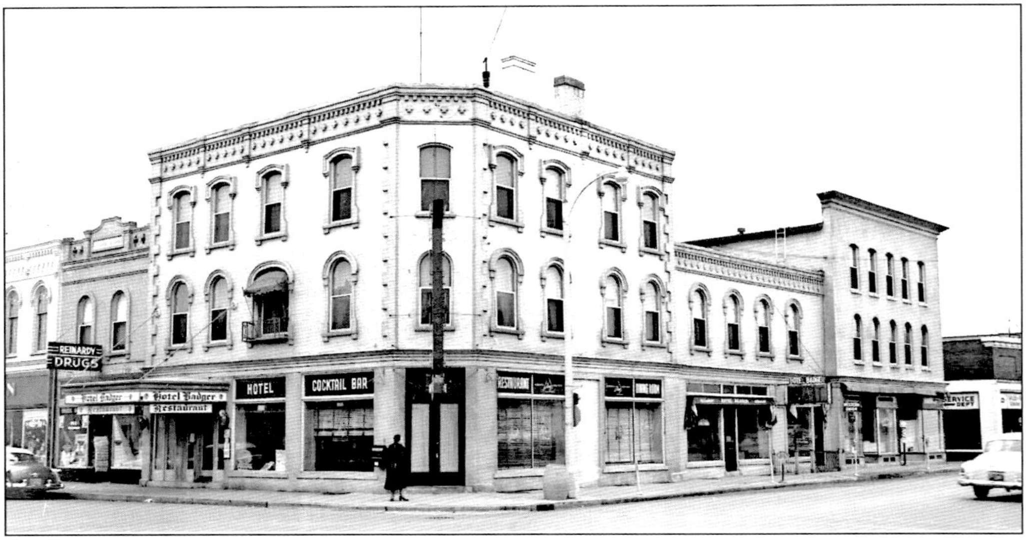

Fred Oberg bought the Jones House hotel at Chestnut and Geneva (now Milwaukee Avenue) Streets from Charles A. Jones in 1915. Selling an interest to his brother-in-law Charles Cote, the two named the place the Fritz-Karl Hotel. In 1918, they changed the name to the Hotel Badger because of the war with Germany. Oberg sold the hotel business in 1946, but retained ownership of the building, which is pictured in November 1953.

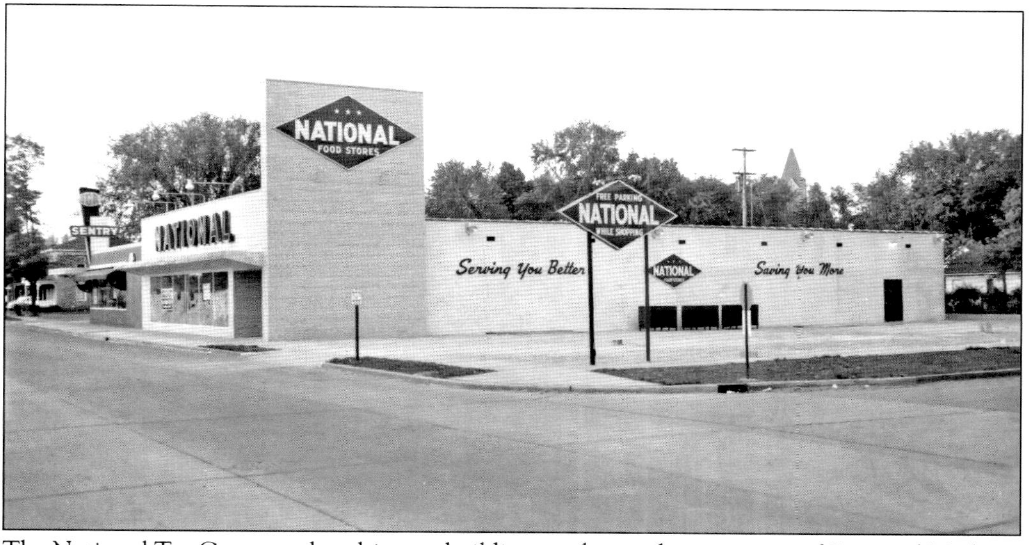

The National Tea Co. moved to this new building on the southwest corner of Pine and Madison Streets in 1955. Previously, the corner had been occupied by the Charles B. and Pauline Cheeseman McCanna residence. National came to Burlington in 1922, buying Frank Mathews grocery stock and taking over his store on Pine Street north of Washington Street. After 16 years in this building, National closed the store in December 1971. The building has since been occupied by restaurants.

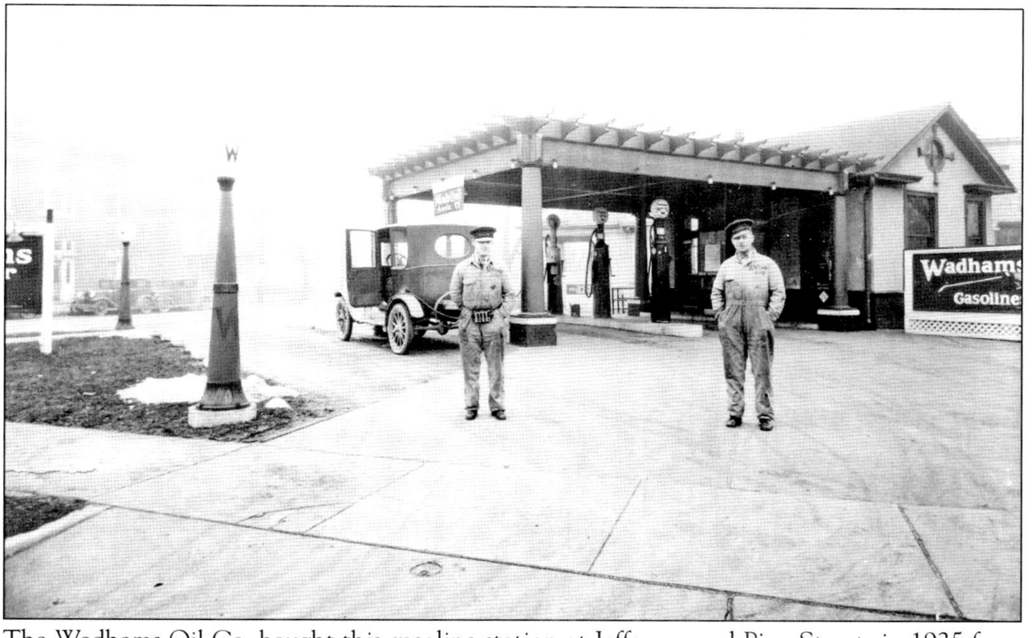

The Wadhams Oil Co. bought this gasoline station at Jefferson and Pine Streets in 1925 from the Burlington-Lockwood Oil Co. Burlington-Lockwood had built it in 1921, the first of this type of filling station in the city. Previously gasoline pumps were set on sidewalks in front of automobile garages and dealers. In 1931, Wadhams built a modern enclosed building, which replaced this one. City hall and the Charles B. Wagner house are at the left.

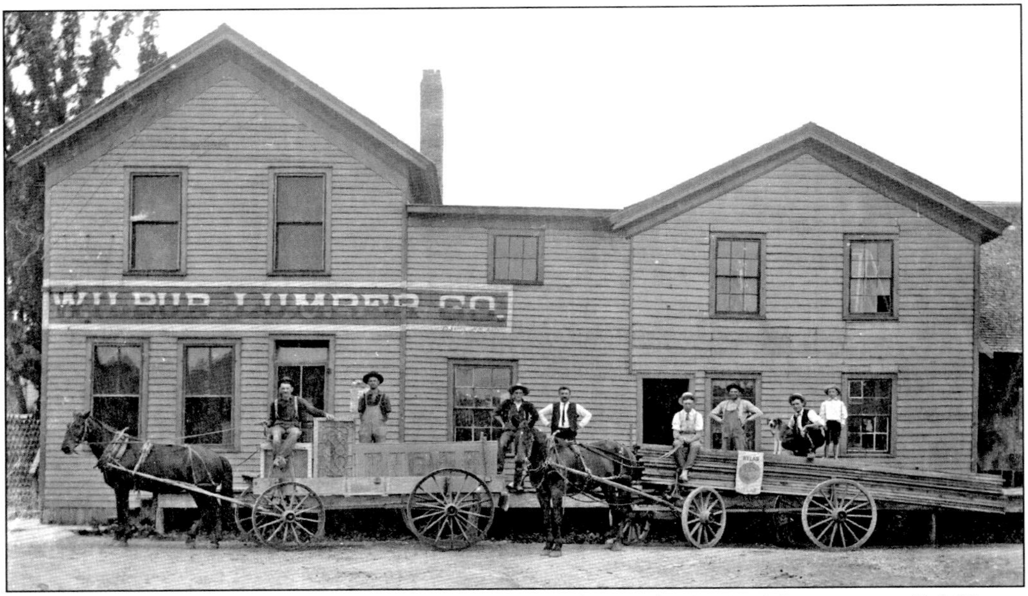

In 1885, George Wilbur, who conducted a lumber yard near the St. Paul depot west of McHenry Street, bought the Perkins homestead, which extended from Geneva Street (now Milwaukee Avenue) opposite Teutonia Hall to Conkey Street, and moved the lumber yard to part of the property. The office building, seen here *c.* 1900, was erected in 1886 next to Anton Zwiebel's machine shop on Chestnut Street. Moved back in the lumber yard in 1891, the building was still in use when the company closed in 1970.

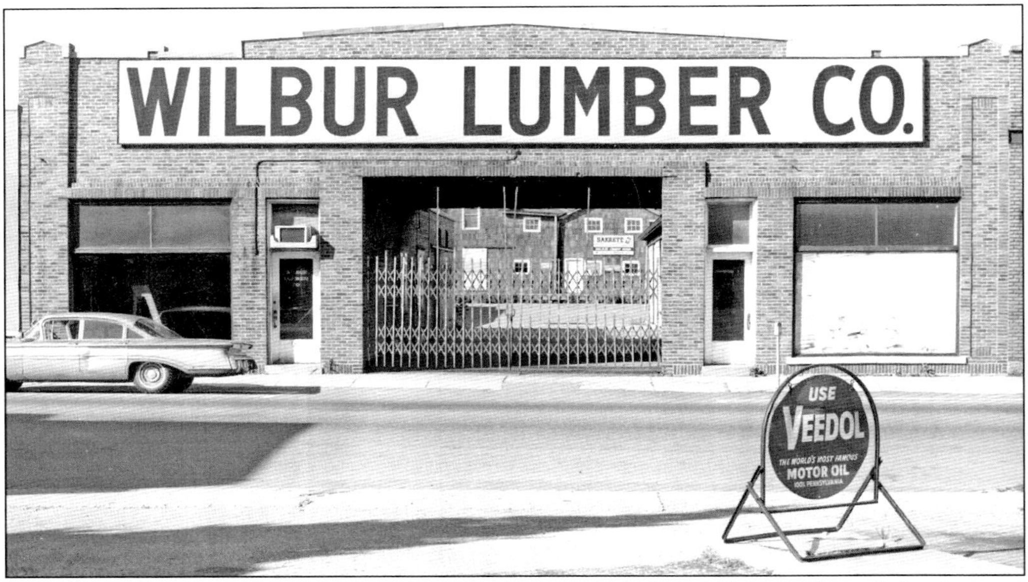

The Wilbur Lumber Co. grew out of T. H. Judd & Co., which established a branch lumber yard managed by George Wilbur near the St. Paul depot in 1875. Moving to a downtown site in 1885, the company was a Burlington mainstay until closing in May 1970. The company's building on Chestnut Street west of Milwaukee Avenue is shown in July 1970. Portions of the former office building can be seen behind the entrance fence. The property is now a parking lot.

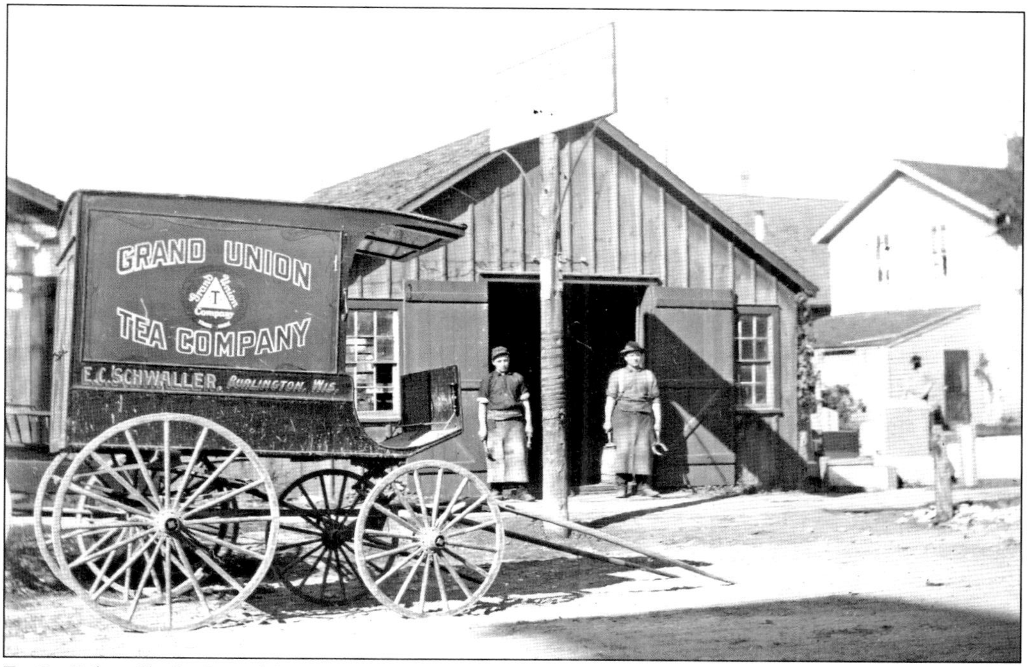

E. C. Schwaller's Grand Union Tea Co. wagon stands outside Louis F. Wanasek's blacksmith shop on the north side of Washington Street between Pine and Dodge Streets *c.* 1910. Wanasek came to Burlington in 1903, working in the Rein blacksmith shop until 1906 when he bought E. B. Stone's blacksmith business. In 1918, Wanasek moved his business across Washington Street, remaining there until 1924, when he built a brick shop adjacent to his residence on Dodge Street.

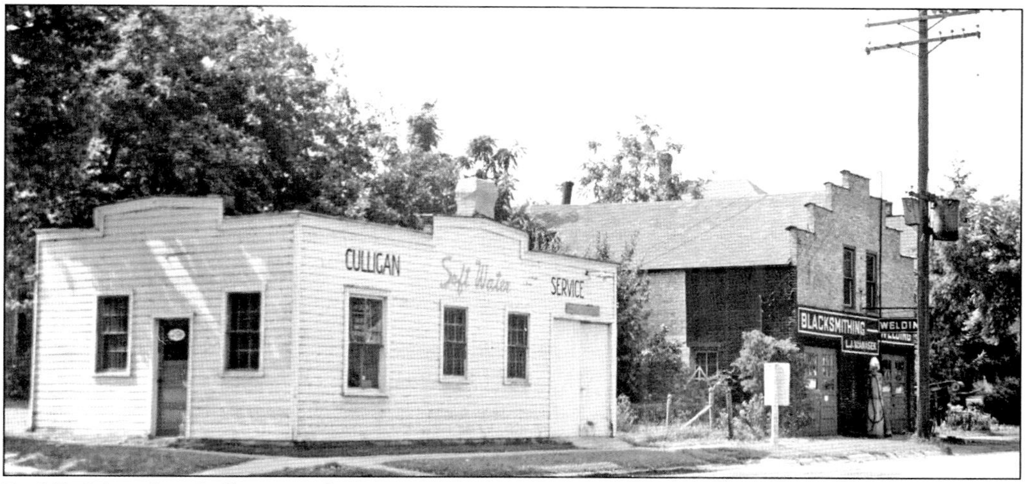

Earl Delahoyde's Culligan Soft Water Service occupies the Dodge and Madison Street corner next to Louis J. Wanasek's blacksmith and welding shop *c.* 1950. George Weithaus put up the corner building in 1920 as a blacksmith shop, which he later sold to Louis Rehberg. In 1922, Edwin James opened a battery service station there. Wanasek, whose father built the brick building in 1924, changed primarily to farm repair and welding in 1941 and to excavating in 1951. The Wanasek building was torn down in 1964.

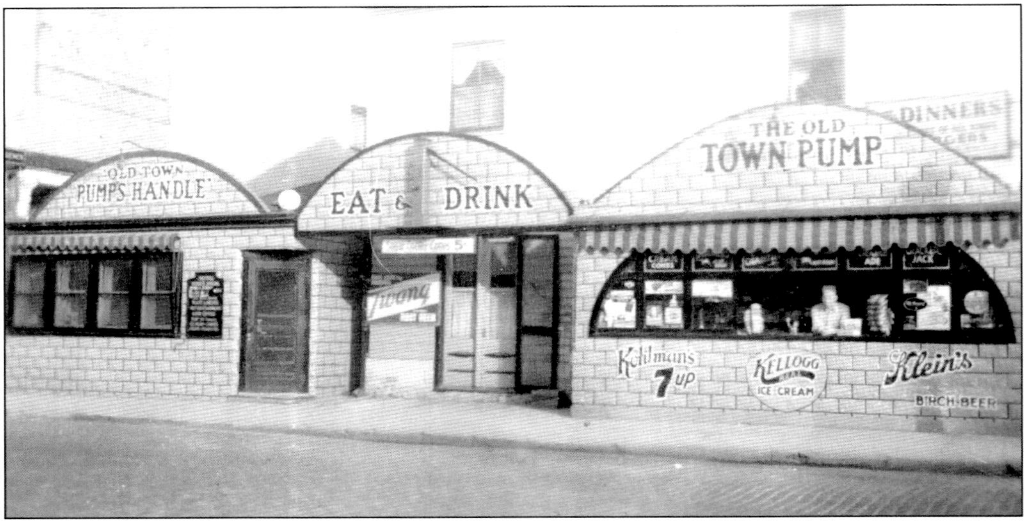

Roman Erdman and Floyd McCormack erected an orange hut on the side of George May's meat market at Chestnut and Geneva (now Milwaukee Avenue) Streets in 1929. Calling it the Old Town Pump, they served orange drinks, lunches, and refreshments. Erdman bought McCormack's interest in 1931 and added an adjoining lunch room, called Old Town Pump's Handle. John and Wilma Callen bought the business in 1940, and in 1942 sold it to Perry and Pearl Wiesenthal Fell. The restaurant operated into the 1960s; the sidewalk stand was torn down in 1968.

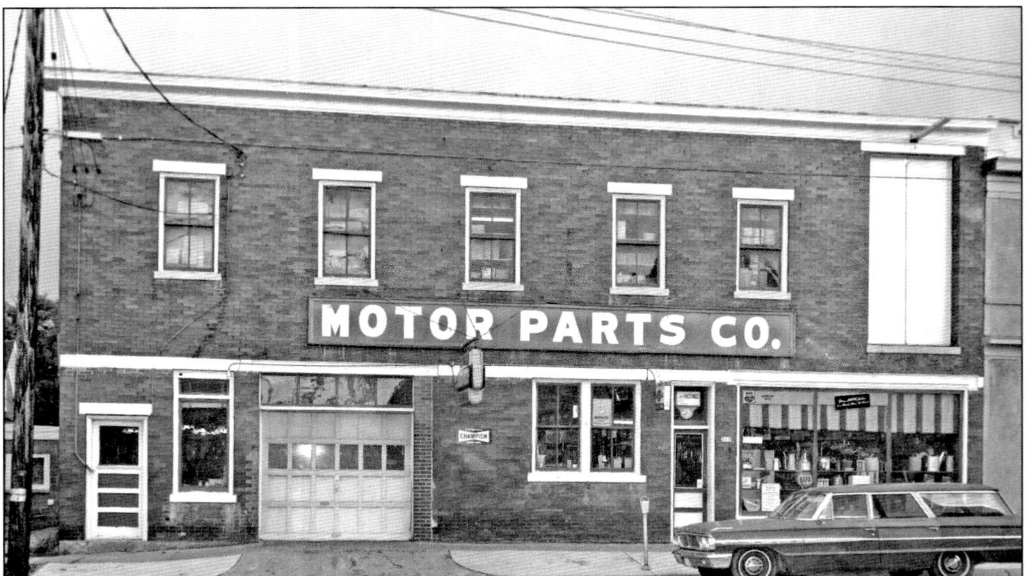

Motor Parts Co. moved to this Mill Street building in 1958, when owner Louis Behen bought Auto Electric Service, the building's occupant since the mid-1940s. The building, pictured in 1971, was erected by William Gill as a livery barn in 1909, replacing Jacob Gill's frame livery barn built in 1887. From 1916 to 1929, automobile dealers—first a Ford agency and then Knerien Chevrolet—leased the building. After Knerien vacated, Hansen Oil Co. had its office and repair shop here until 1944.

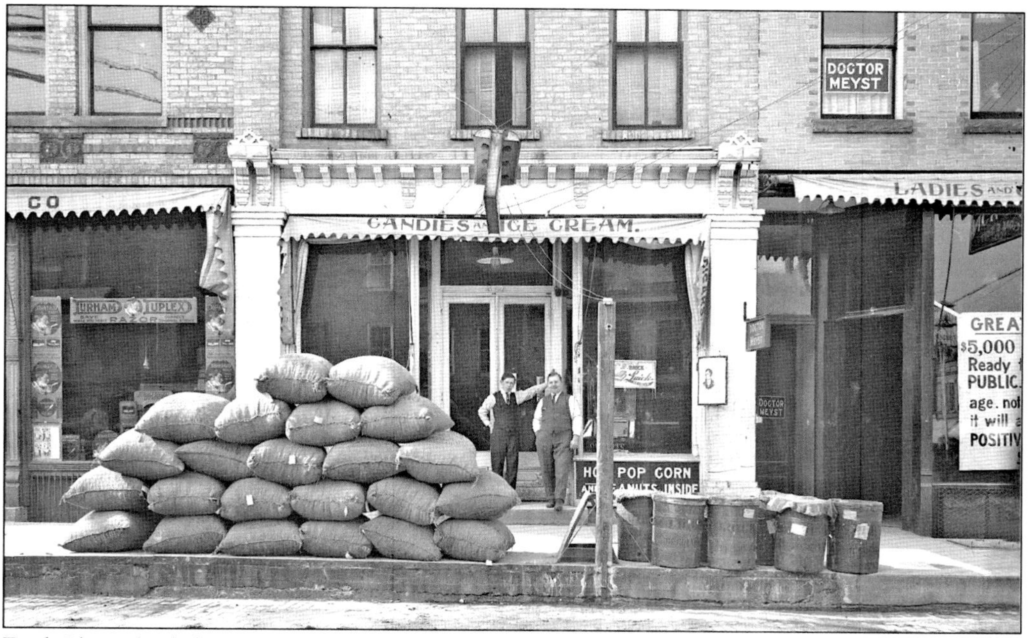

Fred Oberg (right) opened a confectionery store, called The Palace of Sweets, in this building on Chestnut Street in 1910. The building was previously occupied by S. M. Reinardy's drug store. Oberg had earlier had a popcorn, candy, and refreshment stand in the basement of a nearby building and had operated a popcorn and peanuts wagon on the street. Oberg closed this business in 1916 after he bought the Jones House hotel.

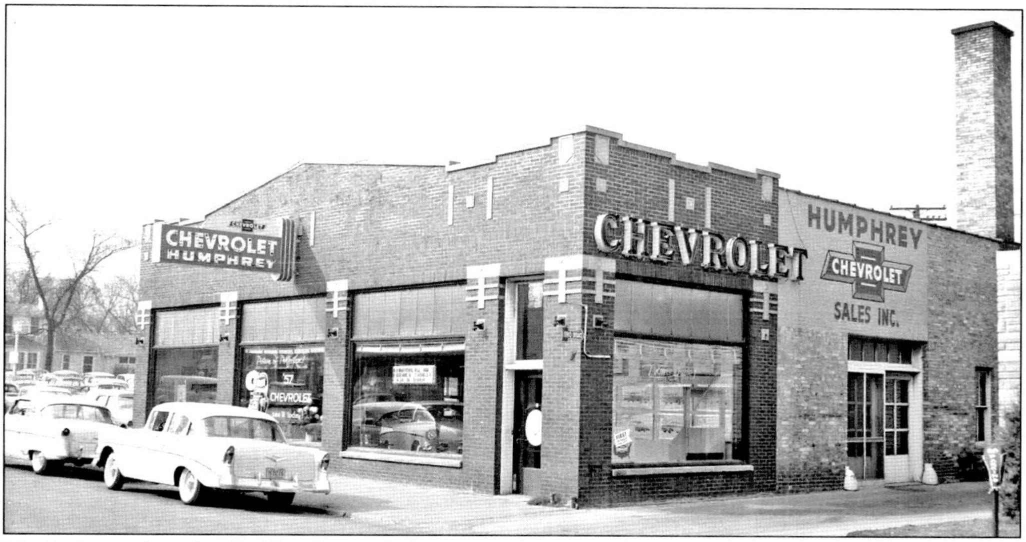

Hugh Agner bought the Frank Zwiebel property on Geneva Street (now Milwaukee Avenue) in 1927, moved the house to West Geneva Street (now West State Street), and built this garage building for his Studebaker agency. In 1929, Union Chevrolet Co., owned by Bryan Roberts and Howard Peterson, bought the building and moved their business here. In 1955, Roberts sold the company to Humphrey Chevrolet Sales, Inc. Humphrey sold the building to Harry Bigelow Sr. in 1960.

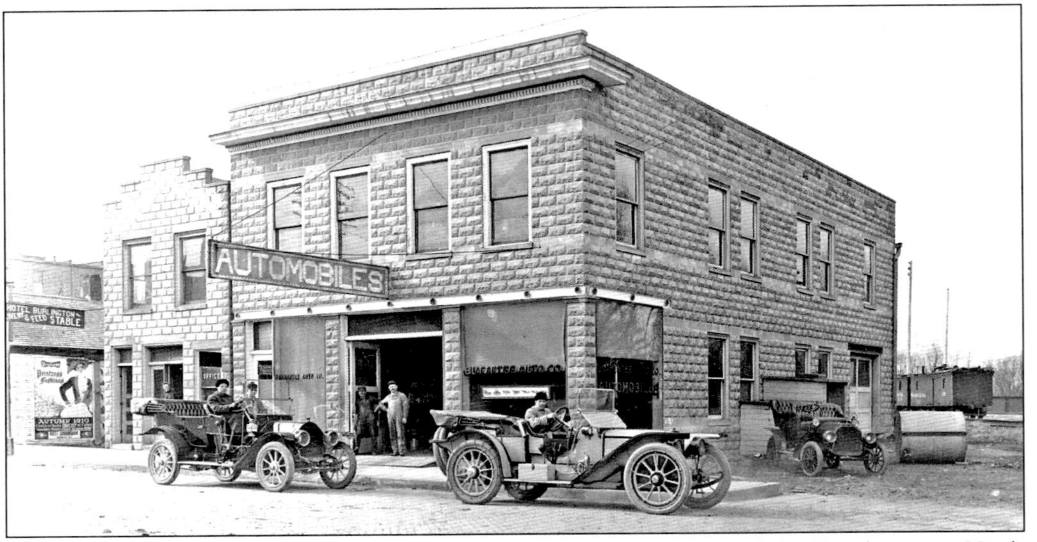

The Guarantee Auto Co. building, pictured in 1910, was erected by Buick agent Hugh Agner in 1909 on the north side of Chestnut Street near the intersection with Dodge Street. Agner later added Studebaker, Maxwell, and other makes. C. Roy McCanna's American is at lower center. Cunningham Bros., handling Buick and Overland cars, was here from 1917 to 1927. Subsequent occupants included Runkel-Newell auto company, L. F. Koch's implement company, Topel Nash, Reineman's plumbing and heating, and a video store.

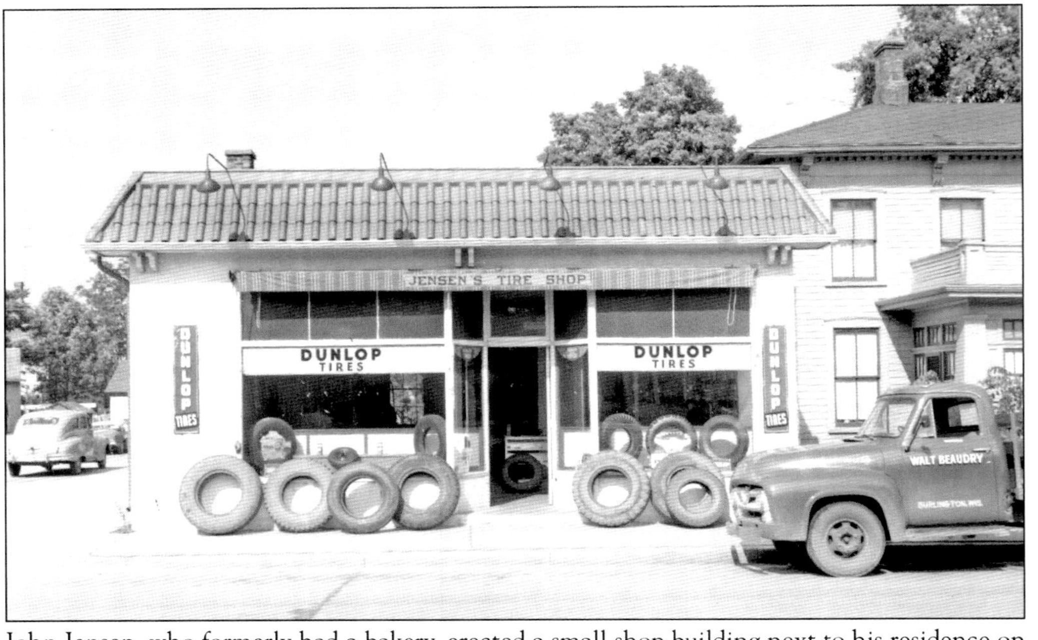

John Jensen, who formerly had a bakery, erected a small shop building next to his residence on Pine Street near Madison Street in 1917 and opened a tire repair shop. In 1921, he applied to install sidewalk gasoline pumps. The building was enlarged in 1929 and a Spanish-style front was added. John's son Clarence bought John's interest in 1933 and operated the tire shop into the 1950s. In 1957, Luigi Petracchi opened a restaurant in the building.

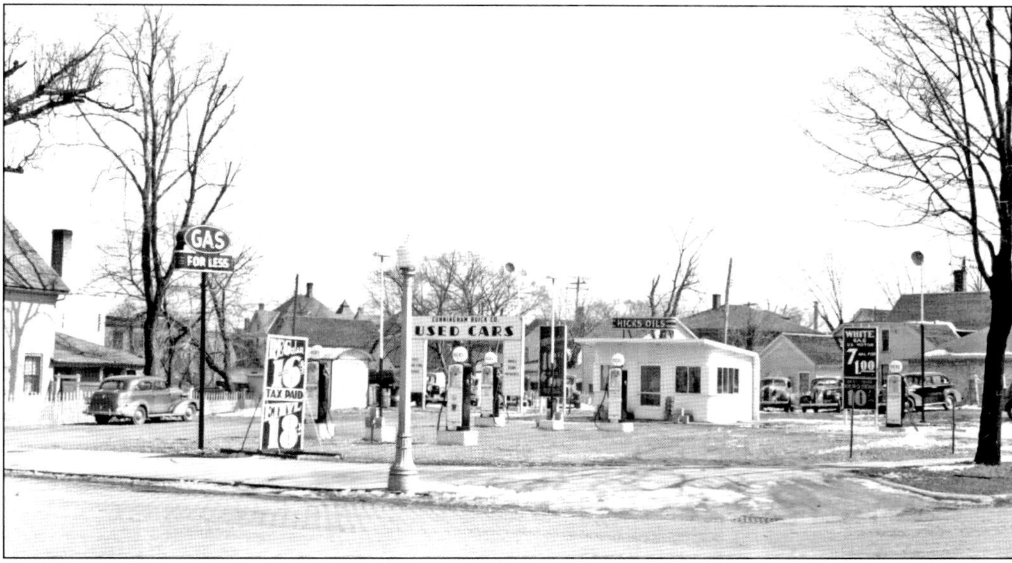

The Hicks Oil Co. filling station, operated by J. Harold Hicks, was built by Claus Ficken in 1939 on the corner of Geneva and Dyer Streets (now Milwaukee Avenue and North Kane Street). The corner had been vacant since 1930, when fire destroyed the Orpheum Theatre, known earlier as Teutonia Hall and the Opera House. This corner has since been occupied by various gasoline stations. The Cunningham Buick Co.'s used car lot is also seen in this early 1940s picture.

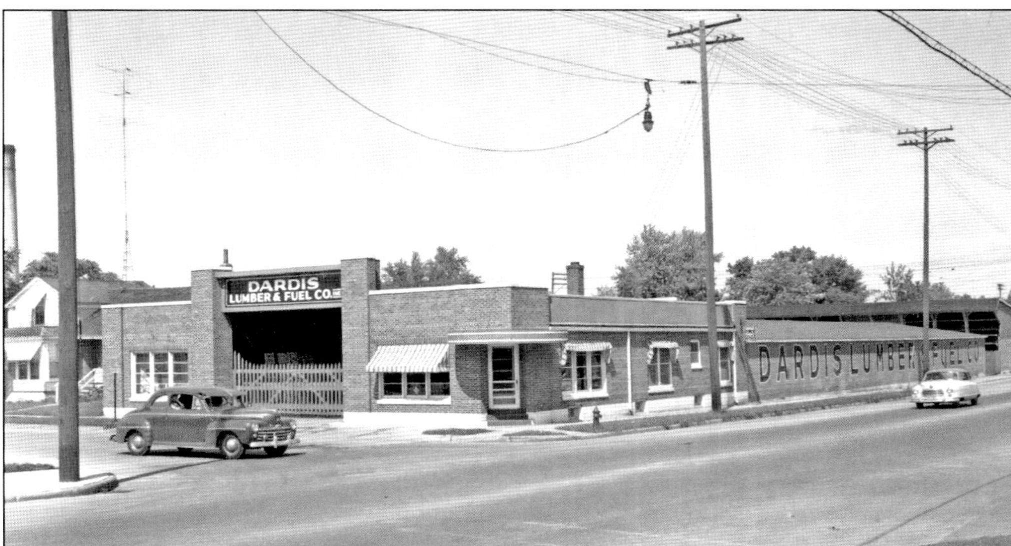

Dardis Lumber & Fuel Co. started in 1898 as Home Lumber Co. with yards on Jefferson Street adjoining the railroad tracks. After changing the firm name in 1908, Dardis added a large warehouse, coal elevator, and flour and feed store. In 1920, Dardis built an office building and a two-story lumber shed at Jefferson and Dodge Streets. Destroyed in a March 1944 fire, the office building and other facilities were replaced. Shown here in 1952, Dardis continued in the lumber business until 1964.

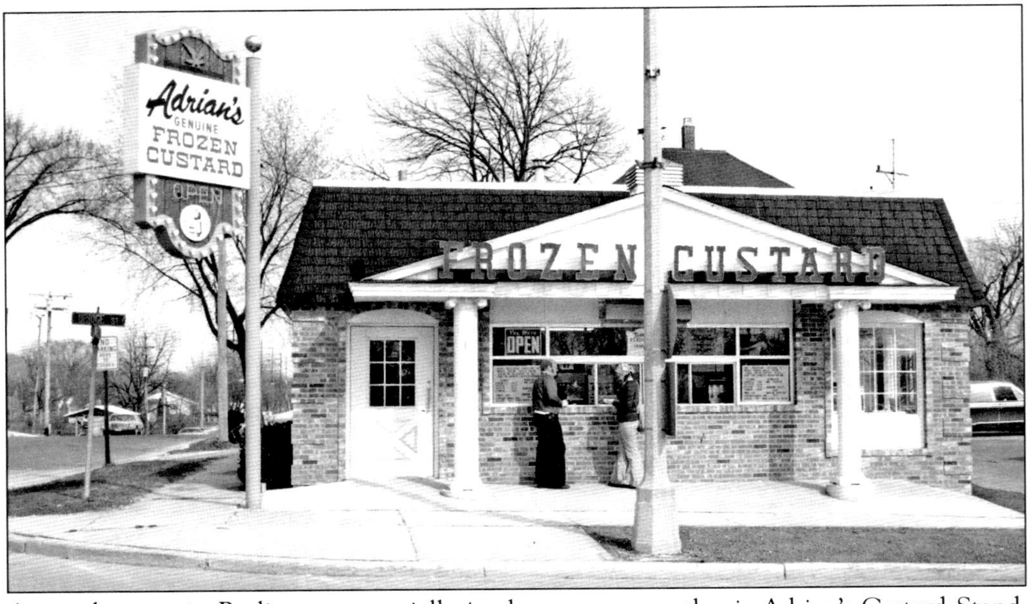

A popular stop in Burlington, especially in the warmer months, is Adrian's Custard Stand, pictured shortly after it was built in 1976. Jim and Darlene Adrian built the stand on the corner of Bridge and Congress Streets, near Echo Park, after the previous refreshment stand was razed. In 1989, the house on Congress Street next to the custard stand was demolished to provide more parking room.

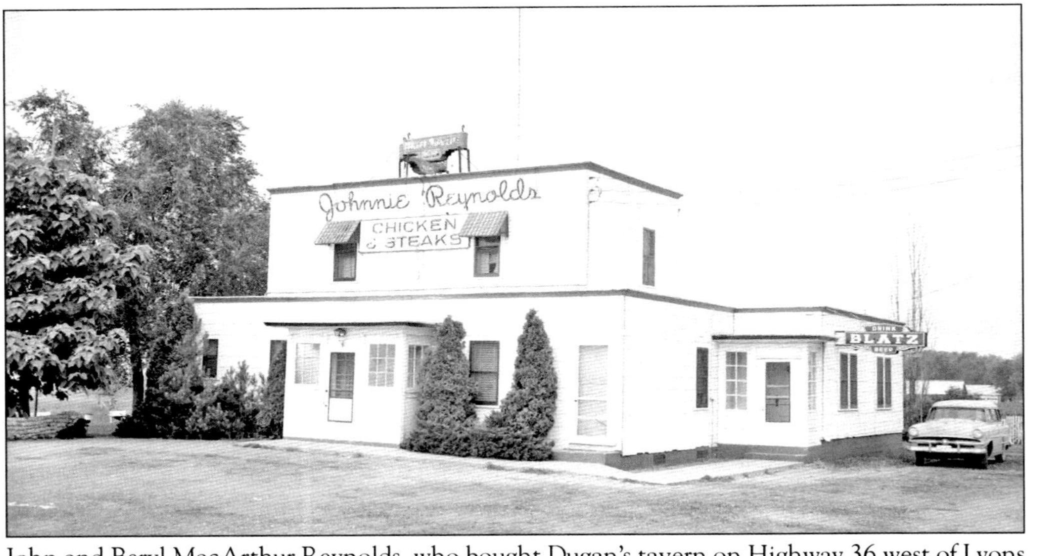

John and Beryl MacArthur Reynolds, who bought Dugan's tavern on Highway 36 west of Lyons in 1946, turned the business into a noted area restaurant called Johnnie Reynolds Supper Club. In 1960, after this picture was taken, the Reynolds did extensive indoor and exterior remodeling and redecorating. A new barroom, kitchen, two dining rooms, and an upstairs cocktail lounge were added. The restaurant later belonged to the Ken Solofra family.

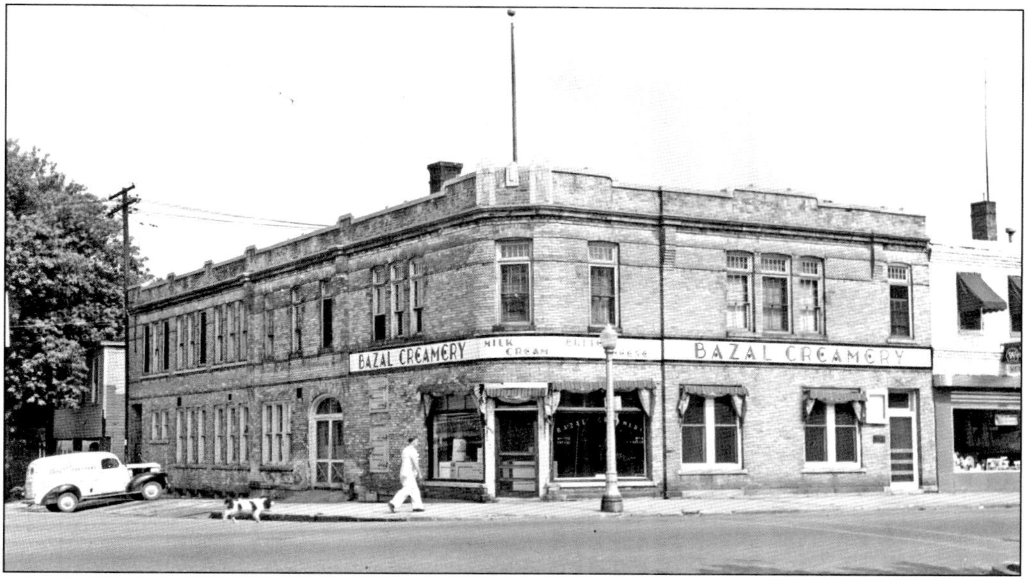

Joseph Bazal, who had been buttermaker at the High Street Creamery in Wheatland and the Badger Dairy Co. in Burlington, bought the former city and town hall building at Pine and Washington Streets in 1926. He remodeled the building into a creamery, removing all parts above the second floor. In 1949 (when this picture was taken), Bazal sold an interest to the Weber brothers, and in 1950, he retired. The business moved to the corner of Pine and State Streets in 1951.

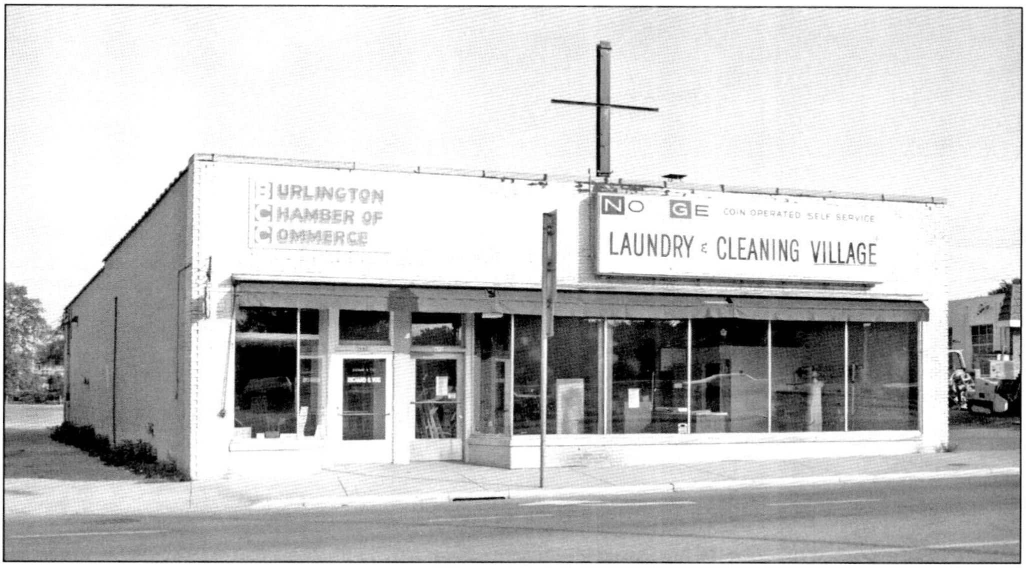

In 1949, the Kroger Grocery company bought the "Badger Annex" property (the former Verhalen and Halberstadt residence) between the Plaza Theatre and Lehr gasoline station on Geneva Street (now Milwaukee Avenue), had the house demolished, built this building, and moved its grocery store here. Since Kroger left Burlington in 1956, occupants of the building, pictured in 1976, have included a laundry and cleaning business, the Burlington Chamber of Commerce, and law and accounting firms.

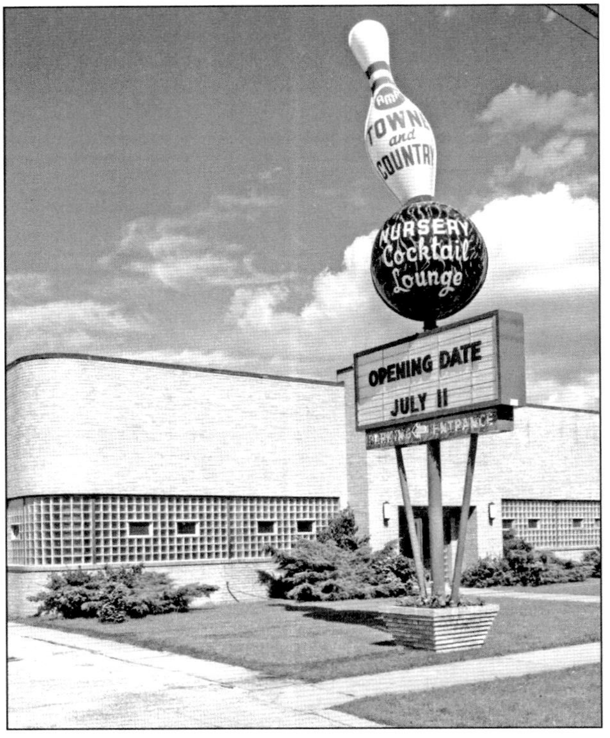

Clyde and Evelyn Anderson, Vincent Lois, and Edward Rueter opened the Towne and Country bowling lanes in this Wilmot Avenue (now South Pine Street) building in 1958. The building was originally constructed in 1948 to house Coopers, Inc. of Kenosha, makers of "Midway" and "Jockey" underwear. Coopers left Burlington in 1951, and in 1952, Torrent Manufacturing Co., maker of medicinal swabs for hospitals and institutions, occupied the building.

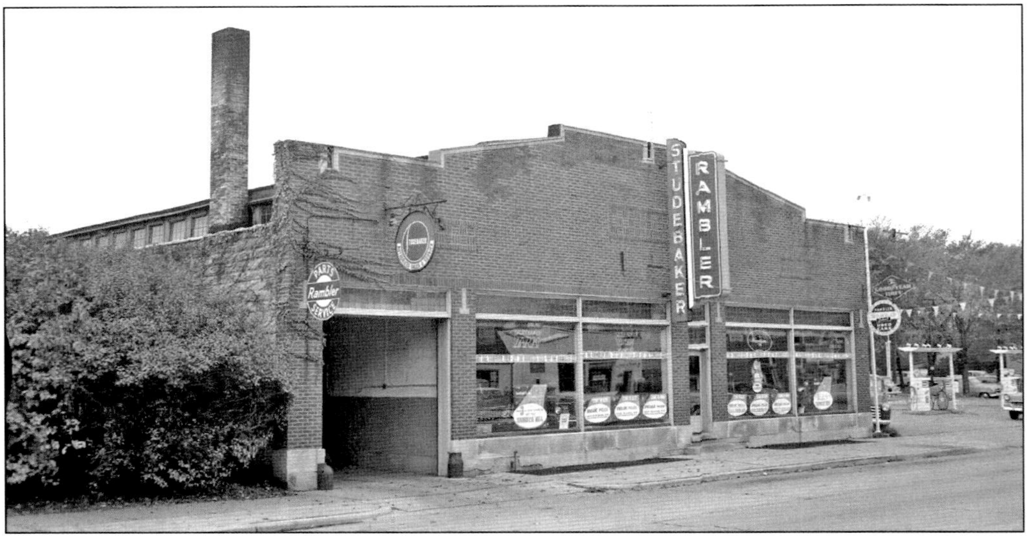

John Luke bought the Appleyard property on Pine Street near Madison Street in 1921, razed the pink-colored grout house, and built this garage building. The first tenant, Burlington Motor Car Co., a Ford dealer, was succeeded in 1938 by another Ford agency, Coughlin-Turner, Inc. In 1940, Champion Motor Co. moved to the building, and automobile dealers occupied the building until the early 1970s. Thereafter, the building housed sport facilities and restaurants. The building, which also housed other businesses over the years, burned in 1983. Another building has replaced it.

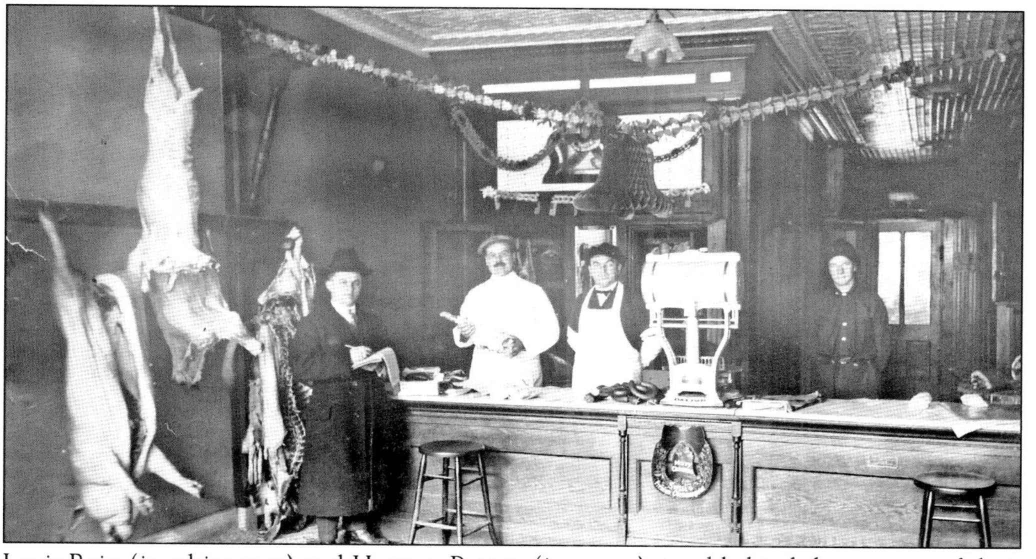

Louis Rein (in white coat) and Herman Potratz (in apron) stand behind the counter of their Pine Street meat market c. 1910. Others are unidentified. The building later housed a tire and appliance store, an infants' and children's wear store, an exercise studio, and a tanning salon. Rein, who later served on Burlington's park board, owned the business until 1929. In 1921, the meat market was the first in the city to install a refrigerating machine.

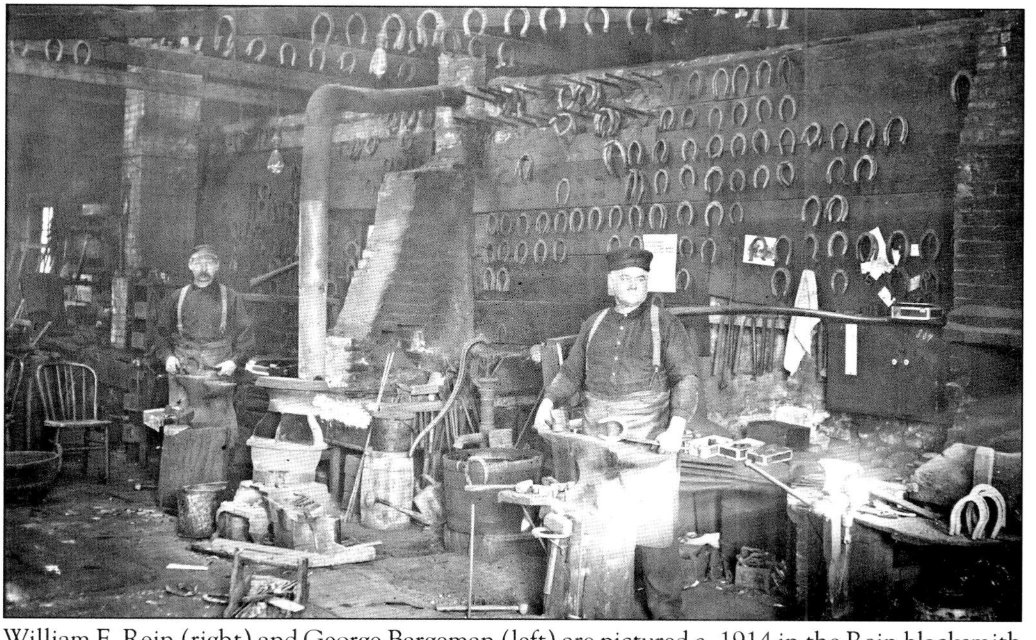

William E. Rein (right) and George Bargeman (left) are pictured c. 1914 in the Rein blacksmith shop which stood on Pine (now Commerce) Street northwest of the intersection with what is now Milwaukee Avenue. The building, which later housed Battery Service Station, was razed in 1953, together with its neighboring theatre building, to make way for a parking lot. The blacksmith shop, started by Rein's father, William B., before 1860, closed its doors in 1920.

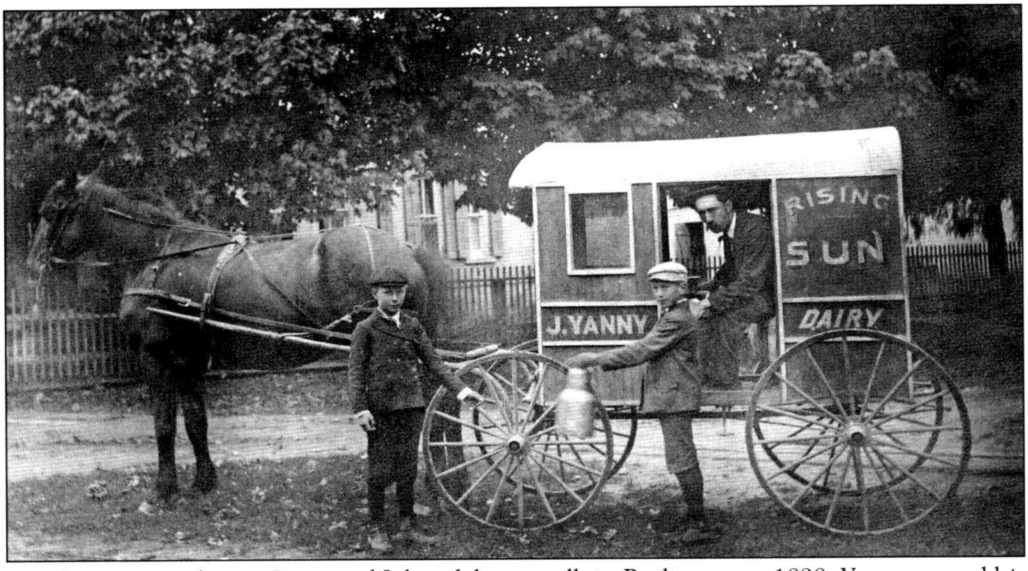

Joseph Yanny, with sons Peter and John, delivers milk in Burlington *c.* 1898. Yanny started his milk delivery business in 1890. In 1891, he bought up another milk route and a wagon, naming his business "Rising Sun Dairy." In 1893, he presented each customer with free milk on New Year's Day. Yanny bought the former Catholic school and convent building on the corner of Jefferson and McHenry Streets in 1895, and in 1896, opened a milk and cream depot and meat market there.

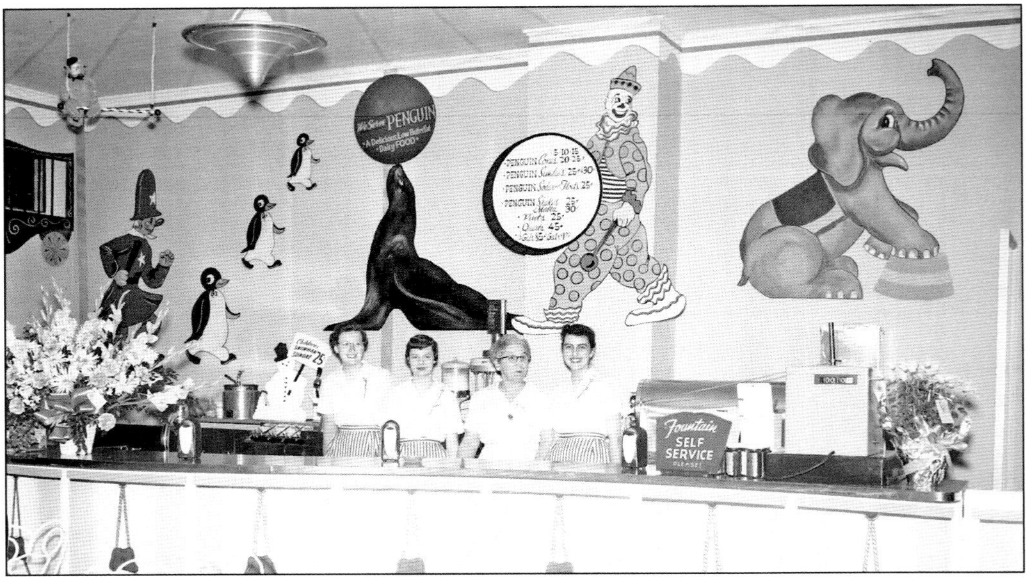

After Jackson Drug Store vacated the Oldenberg (formerly Hoch) building in 1952, C. B. McCanna rented the building, located just east of the "bend" on Chestnut Street, and opened a sweet shop called The Carousel. The shop featured cones, sodas, and sundaes made with "Penguin" frozen dairy food. Among the first employees were, left to right, Mary Eileen Vande Sand, Mary Lou Schmidtkamp, Angie Essman Martin, and Annette Van Bolhuis. The business operated for about 15 years.

Three

Manufacturing and Processing Plants

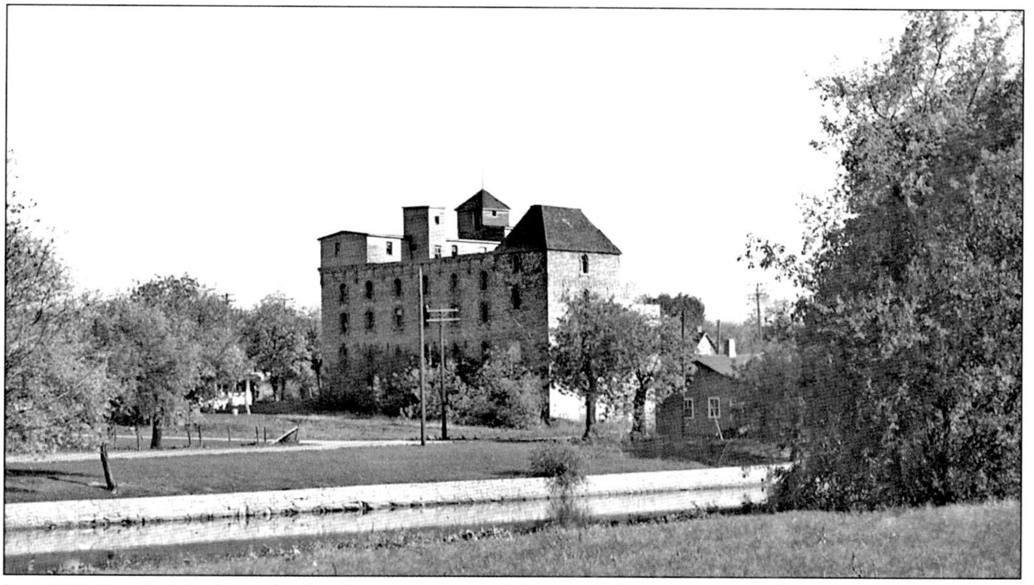

In 1868, Jacob Muth built the first portions of this malt house, pictured in the 1940s by John Zwiebel, on the east side of the Fox River. It replaced his frame brewery building erected in 1852. During the 10-month season, Muth would malt 60- to 80-thousand bushels of grain. Succeeding owners of the malt house included Chauncy Hall and Maurice L. Ayers in 1879, Mathew Petrie in 1898, and the Finke-Uhen Brewing Co. in 1900. After Prohibition ended, the Old Dutch Brewing Co. bought the building, but it was sold at a sheriff's sale in 1934. In 1943, it was sold again for delinquent taxes. At that time, the Haylofters, Burlington's little theatre group, bought the building, removed the parts that could not be used for their theatre and were too expensive to repair and maintain, and remodeled the remainder into the 100-seat Malt House Theatre. The theatre, dedicated in October 1947, is still used by the Haylofters.

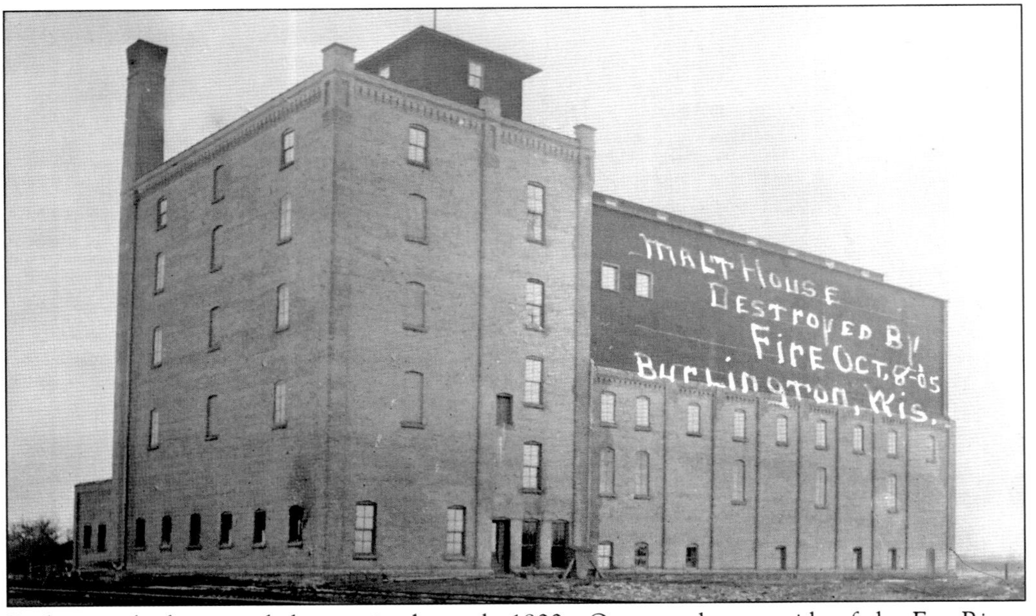

Burlington had two malt houses in the early 1900s. One, on the east side of the Fox River, is still used by Burlington's little theatre group, the Haylofters. The other, pictured here, was built by the Burlington Malting Co. on the west side of the Fox River near the Wainwright Avenue intersection with Pine Street, and dedicated in February 1900. The 70-foot-high plant, of brick on a stone foundation with steel construction throughout, was fireproof, according to newspaper reports, with the only wood of any account being the system of elevators. However, in October 1902 (not 1905 as the picture shows), the building was destroyed when a grain dust explosion caused the most disastrous fire in the city up to that time.

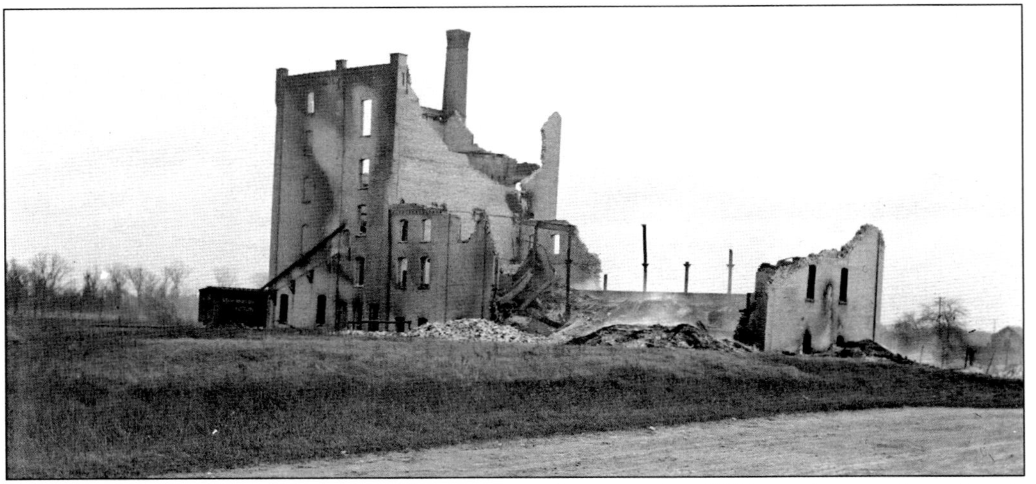

The ruins of the Burlington Malting Co. plant on the east side of Wilmot Avenue (now South Pine Street) are pictured in October 1902 following the most disastrous fire in Burlington to that time. The building, dedicated in February 1900, and equipment were valued at $75,000 and the malt at $40,000. In 1919, John J. Wolf built a pickle and sauerkraut factory here, which operated until 1949, when Leland F. Koch bought the buildings and property for his farm implement business.

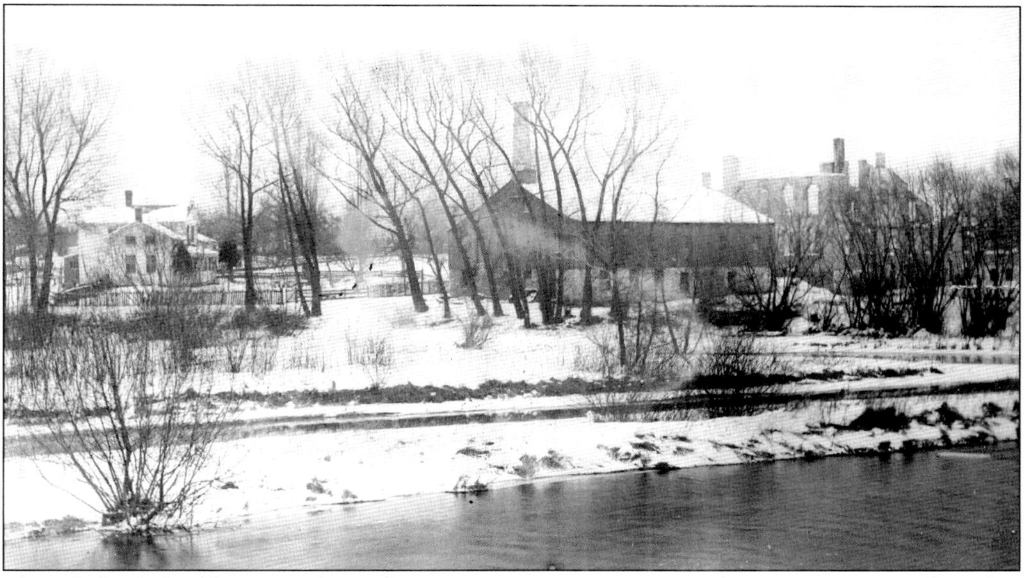

The "skeletal" building at right in this *c.* 1890 picture was once a large water-powered woolen mill that Pliny Perkins built in 1843 and leased to James Catton and others. The mill made the first roll of cloth turned out in Wisconsin and, during the Civil War, made cloth for Union uniforms. It operated, with some interruptions, until 1880, when a fire destroyed much of the building and took the life of its superintendent. The building at center is a former tannery.

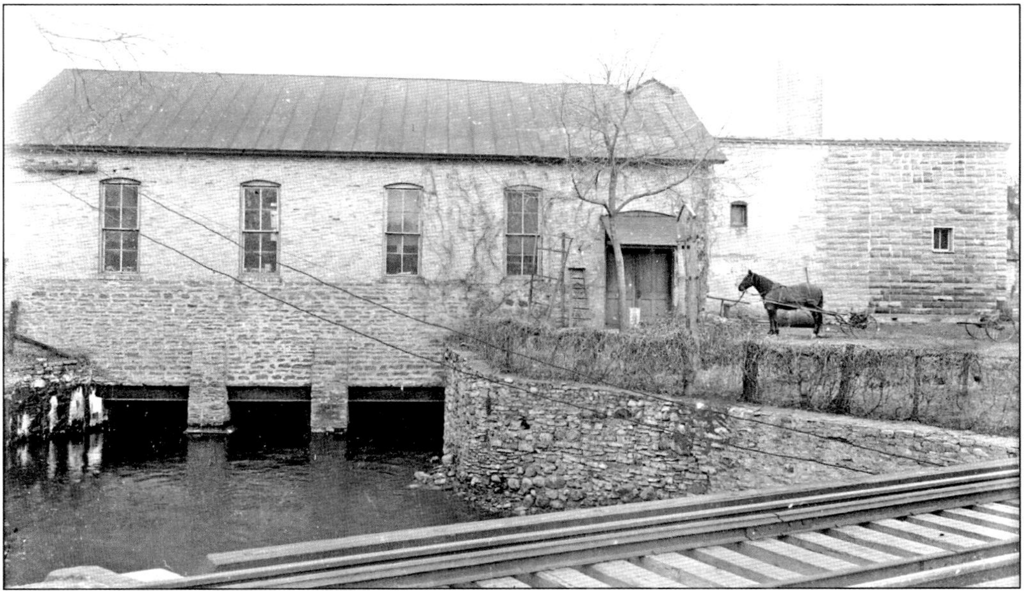

In 1894, the Hall & Smith Electric Company bought the former woolen mill property, with the sluice, flume, and wheel chamber still in fair condition; put up a building on the old foundation; and installed new water wheels to drive the generators. To back up the sometimes erratic water power, boilers and a steam engine were also installed. The plant, pictured *c.* 1910, supplied some electric power until 1933, when the water wheels were shut down. The Veteran Memorial building now occupies the area. The interurban railcar tracks are in the foreground.

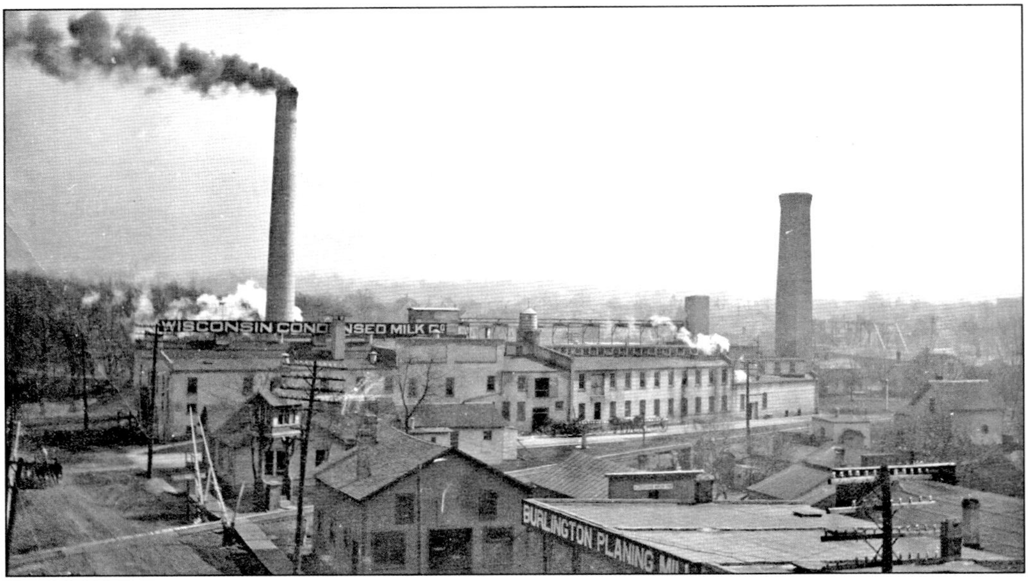

The Wisconsin Condensed Milk Co., incorporated by Charles B. McCanna, Robert G. Fraser, and Louis Rohr in 1898, grew out of the cheese and butter business that McCanna had started in Burlington with a cheese factory in 1882. The company's buildings, pictured in 1913 near the White and Fox Rivers, were added incrementally as the business grew, with a tin can factory built in 1901, a cold storage plant in 1902, and a 2-story, 233-foot brick warehouse in 1906.

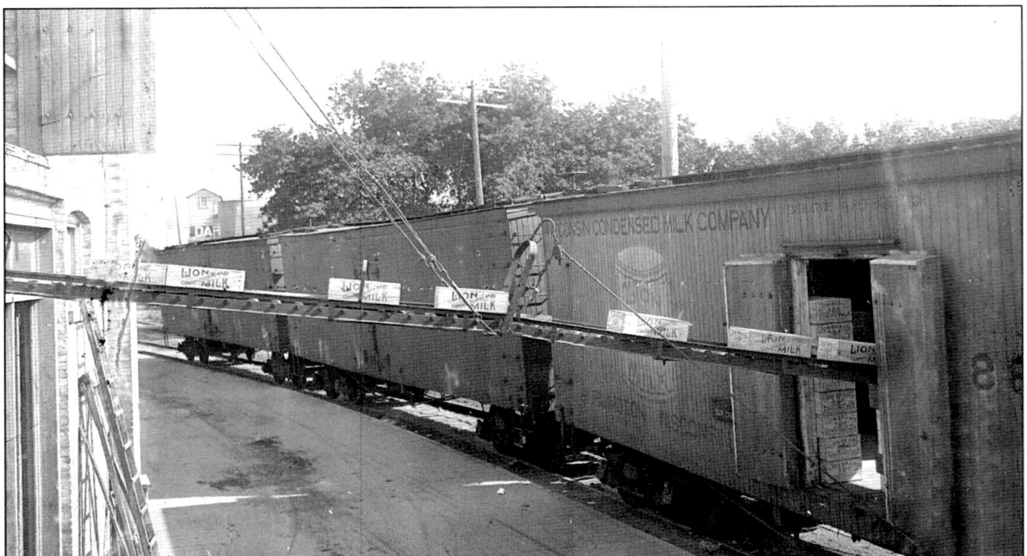

The Wisconsin Condensed Milk Co., the first and largest such company in Wisconsin, was a valuable industry for area dairy farmers. A 1903 report said that more milk was delivered in Burlington every morning than in any other Wisconsin city or village. The condensed milk, being loaded in railcars c. 1910, was sold worldwide under various names, mainly "Lion Brand." In 1913, the company placed an annual order for 25 million labels for just that brand. The company also operated three other condenseries.

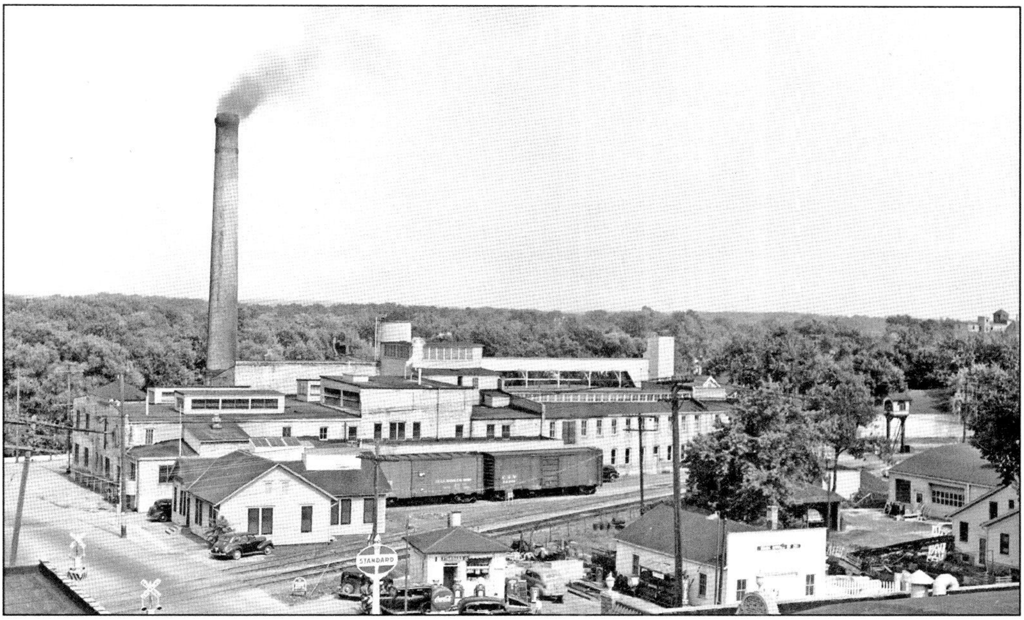

The Nestle' Food Co. bought the Wisconsin Condensed Milk Co. in 1919, took possession in 1920, and renamed it Nestle's Milk Products, Inc. Burlington became Nestle's Midwest division headquarters, and in 1922, the plant added powdered milk to its line. During World War II, the plant supplied the armed forces with canned and powdered milk. After the war and as the South developed a dairying industry, demand dropped. Nestle' closed the milk plant in 1950 and sold the can shop in 1959.

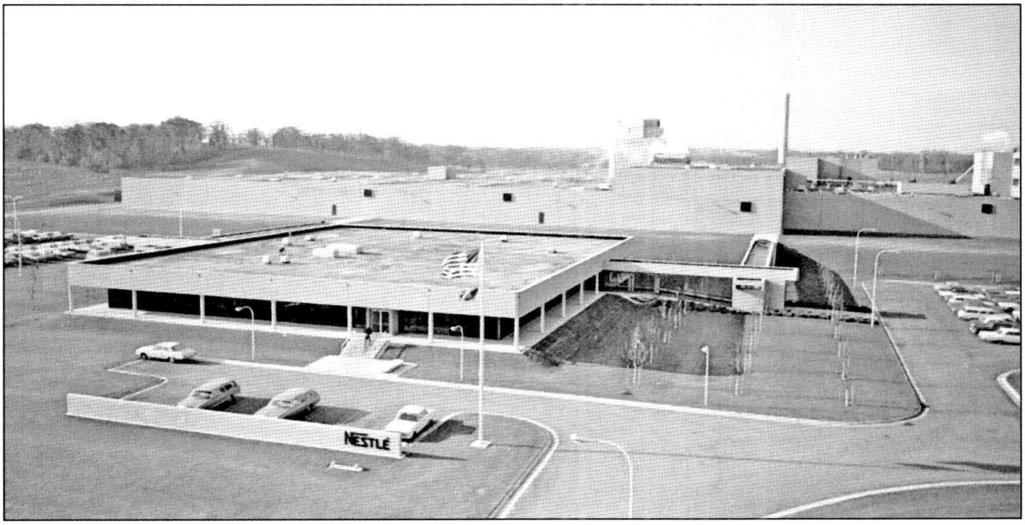

In 1964, the Nestle' Food Co. returned to Burlington, breaking ground for a chocolate plant on South Pine Street, which opened in 1966. The plant, pictured in 1985, has become one of Burlington's largest employers, just as Nestle's Milk Products, Inc. was one of the city's largest employers in its day. In 1987, the Governor proclaimed Burlington as Chocolate Capital of Wisconsin, and in May of that year, Burlington held its first Chocolate Festival, which has become an annual event.

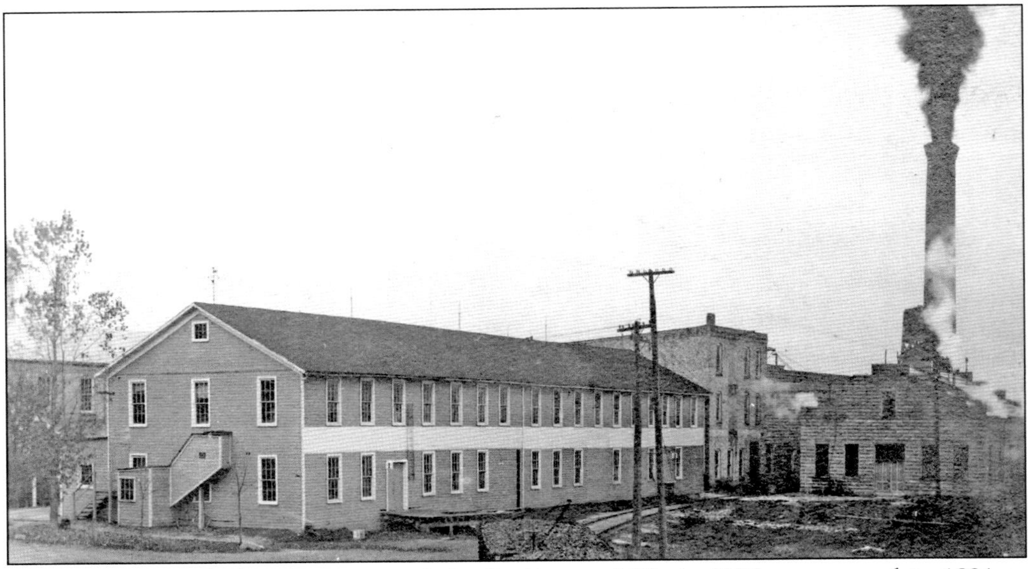

The Burlington Blanket Co., renamed the Burlington Mills in 1933, was started in 1891 to manufacture Albert Ransom's Stay-On horse blankets. By 1905, the company was making over a million blankets a year, selling them countrywide and overseas. The company later made other fabric products and, during wartimes, a variety of military-related materials. One of Burlington's largest employers, it was sold in 1967, with the operations being moved to Kentucky, where the factory closed a few years later.

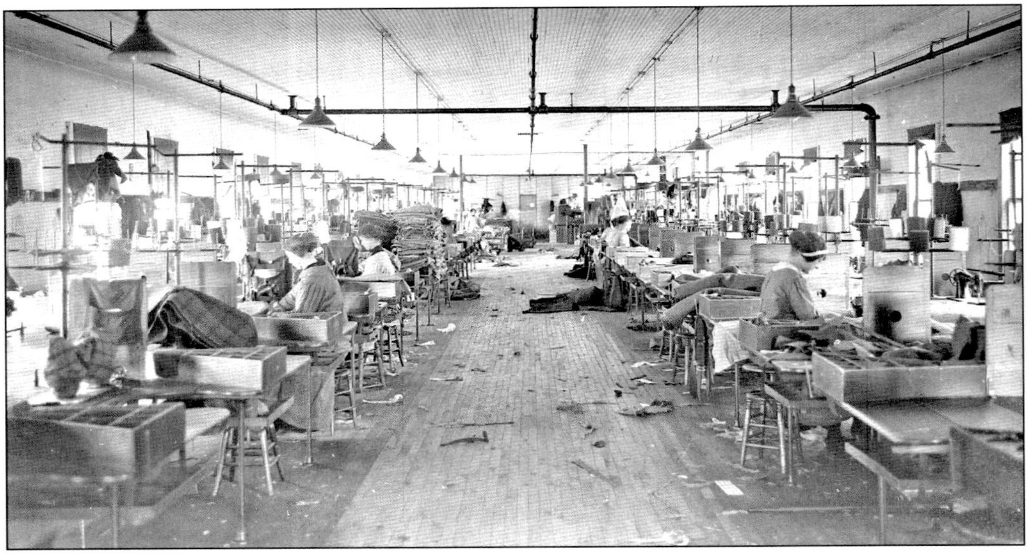

Women operate the Burlington Blanket Co.'s sewing machines in this *c.* 1907 picture. The company was one where women could find work. As times changed, the company added new products: linings for Mackinaw coats, saddle pads, felted carpeting, linings for automobile trunks, and sound-absorbing and insulation material. The company made horse blankets and collar and saddle pads for the government in World War I and cartridge and pistol belts, canteen covers, and camouflage material in World War II.

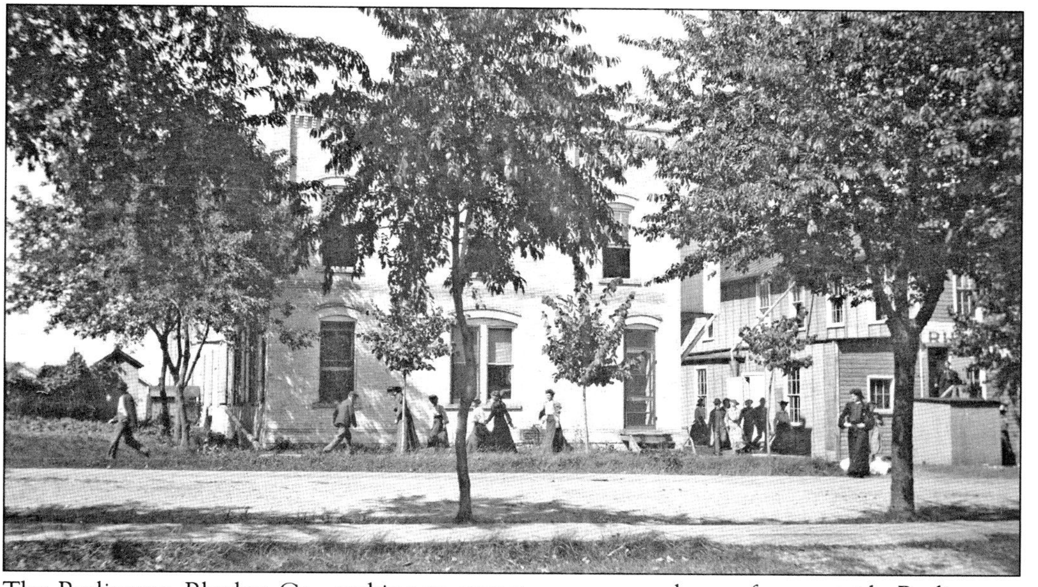

The Burlington Blanket Co., seeking to attract women employees from outside Burlington, built a two-story brick dormitory in 1920 for about 40 occupants. However, occupancy did not meet expectations and the dormitory was changed in 1921 to a hotel named the Riverview. Among the hotel operators were Mr. and Mrs. Chris Peterson, Mr. and Mrs. Seymour White, Mr. and Mrs. William Schmaling, and Mrs. Rose Kortendick Lohaus. In 1937, the building was sold to the Burlington Mills for use as an office.

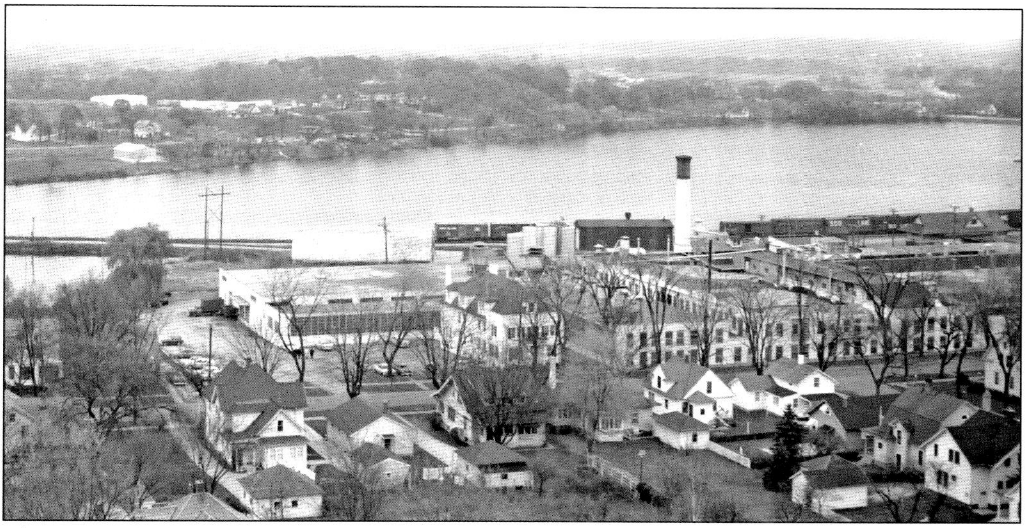

The main facilities of the Burlington Mills, successor to the Burlington Blanket Co., are pictured along West Chestnut Street in 1960. The company's offices were in the former dormitory building (center), with manufacturing, warehouse, and other operations in the buildings stretching back toward the railroad tracks and Echo Lake. After the company moved to Kentucky in 1967, the buildings were used for warehousing and other purposes. The entire complex, some of which was seriously dilapidated, was demolished in 2002.

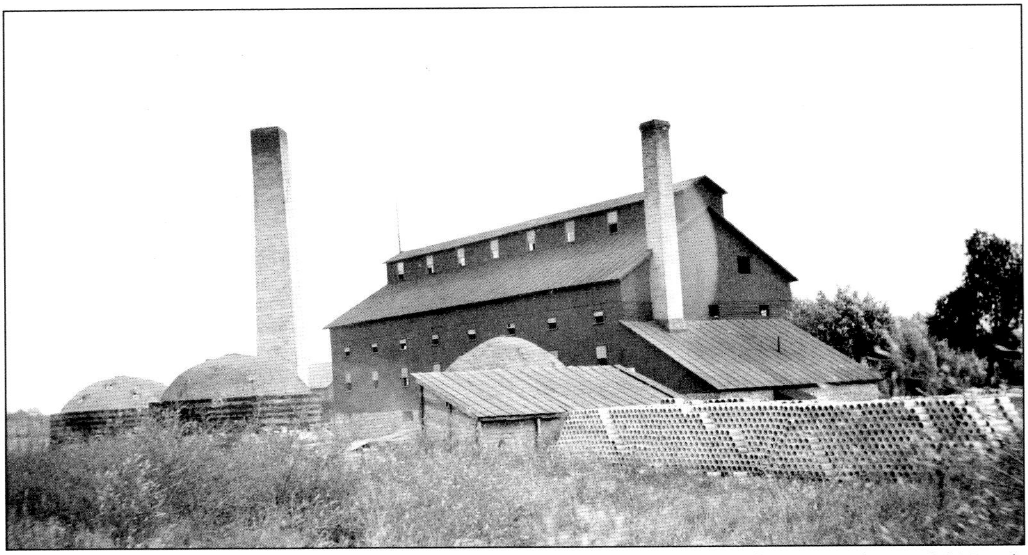

The Burlington Brick & Tile Co., pictured *c.* 1900, was near Echo Lake on Highway 36 North and Grove Street. Its main product—tile for draining wetlands to increase crop-growing acreage —was in demand both locally and in surrounding states. Brick was a secondary, but still important, product. The company started turning out tile and bricks in 1887 and operated until about 1925. In 1928, the Burlington Clay Products Co. leased the facilities for three years. In 1931, the property was sold and the facilities demolished.

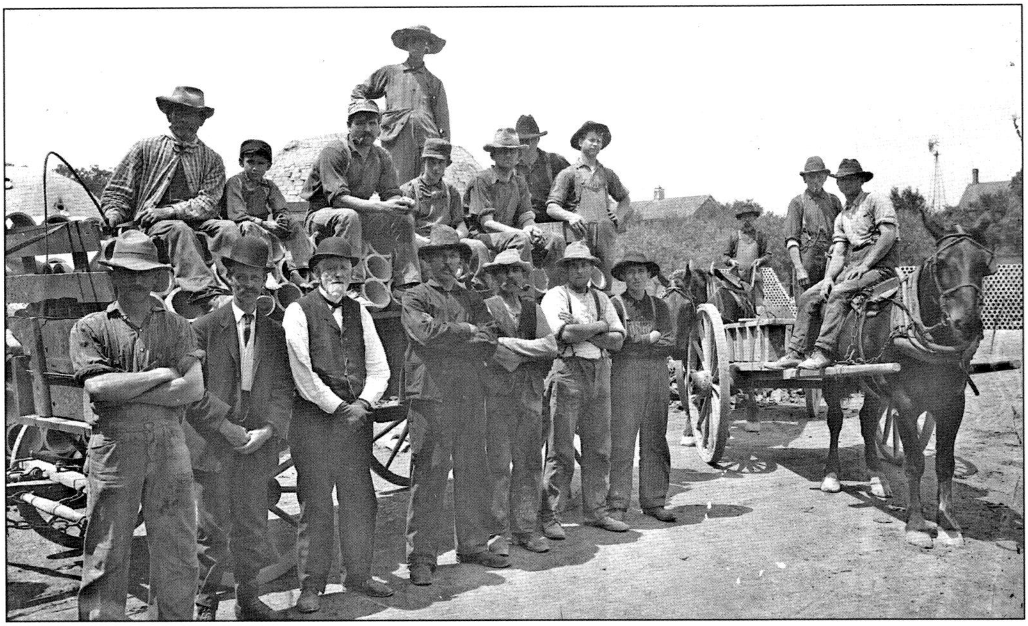

The work crew of the Burlington Brick & Tile Co. poses *c.* 1915 with general manager William Meadows, standing third from left. Meadows served as general manager for 34 years, retiring in 1920. Much of the clay for making the drainage tile and bricks was dug from the clay beds across Highway 36 from the factory in the area that is now a baseball field. The young boys in the crew helped to dig the clay.

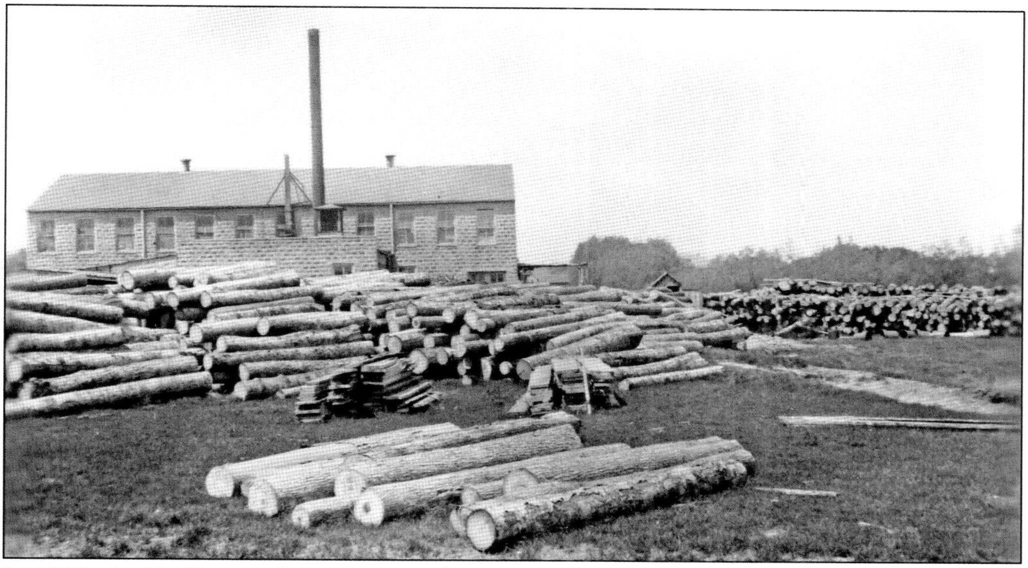

In 1907, the Burlington Advancement Association bought five acres between the Wisconsin Central tracks and the Fox River, including the old canning factory site, and built a two-story brick factory, a boiler house, and a storage building, where the Badger Basket and Veneer Co. was started in 1908. In the ensuing years, several additions were built. The basket factory, pictured *c.* 1910, made a variety of high-quality wooden baskets and, at its peak, employed over 70 men and women. The factory closed in 1926.

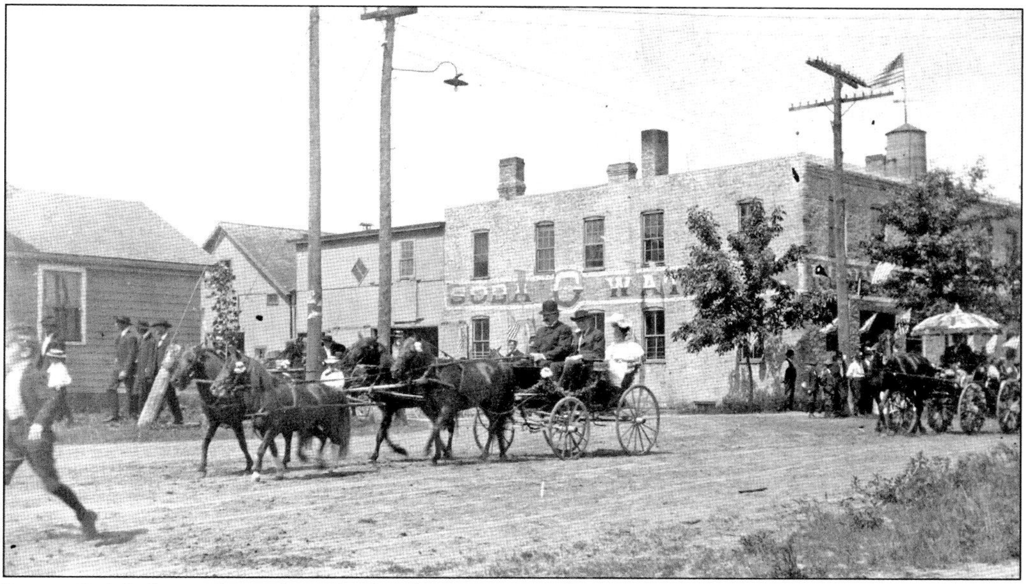

James G. Mathews drives his Shetland ponies near the F. G. Klein Co.'s bottling works at Pine (now Commerce) and Mill Streets on July 4, 1907. Klein came to Burlington in 1865, opening a foundry and machine shop with an uncle and later engaging in manufacturing agricultural implements. In 1886, Klein joined a soft drink manufacturing firm, and in 1889 became owner. In 1891, the company moved to this building, and the business remained in the Klein family into the 1930s.

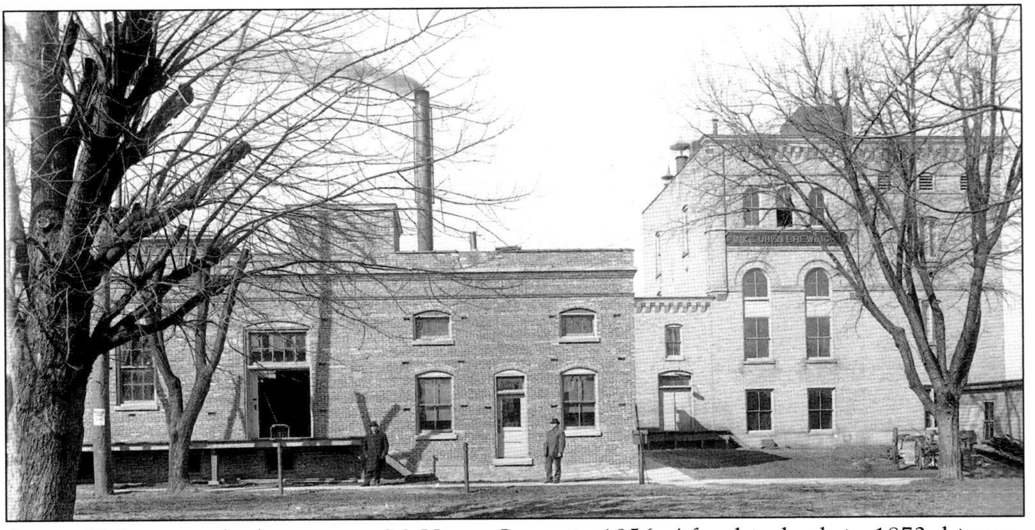

Anton Finke started a brewery on McHenry Street in 1856. After his death in 1873, his son, William, took over. In 1896, William and brother-in-law John H. Uhen incorporated as the Finke-Uhen Brewing Co. The company's horse-drawn beer wagons were a familiar sight in Burlington and surrounding towns and villages where the company owned some taverns and sold its product to others. Closed by Prohibition in 1918, the brewery, pictured *c.* 1910, was sold in 1923 to a firm which made malt cereal products and "near beer." After Prohibition ended in 1933, Chicago interests headed by A. C. Kettler bought the brewery and operated it into the 1950s as the Burlington Brewing Co.

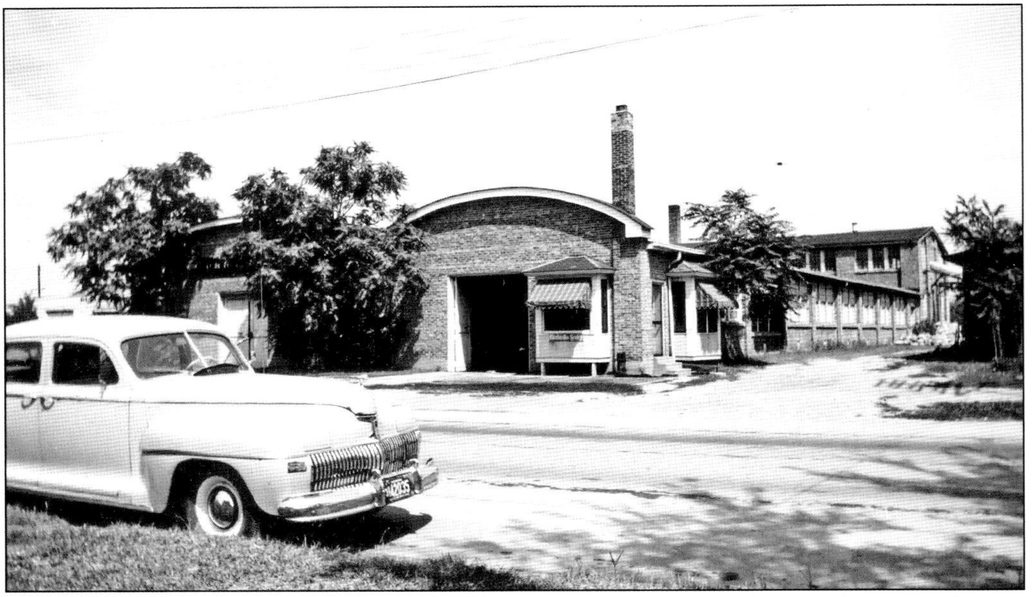

John J. Wolf started his sauerkraut and pickle factory on Wilmot Avenue (now South Pine Street) in two buildings he put up in 1919 on the site of the former malt house that had burned in 1902. Sauerkraut production, which totaled about 725 tons in 1920, grew to about 2,000 tons a year (except for drought years) in the 1930s and 1940s. The kraut was shipped to canners around the country, with some sold under the "Burlington" label. The plant closed in 1949.

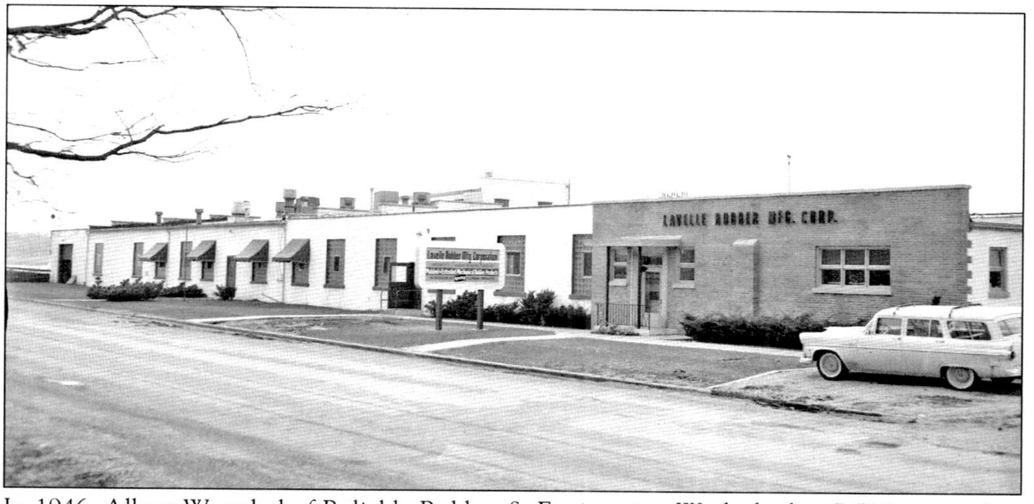

In 1946, Albert Westphal of Reliable Rubber & Engineering Works built a 7,500-square-foot building on McHenry Street south of the St. Paul railroad depot to manufacture molded, extruded, and die-cut rubber products. In 1947, Robert Sullivan Sr. and Mike Weidert bought the company; in 1955, the name was changed to Lavelle Rubber Manufacturing Corp. By 1985, Lavelle had grown to a 110,000-square-foot complex employing 125 people full-time, with the original building still part of the complex.

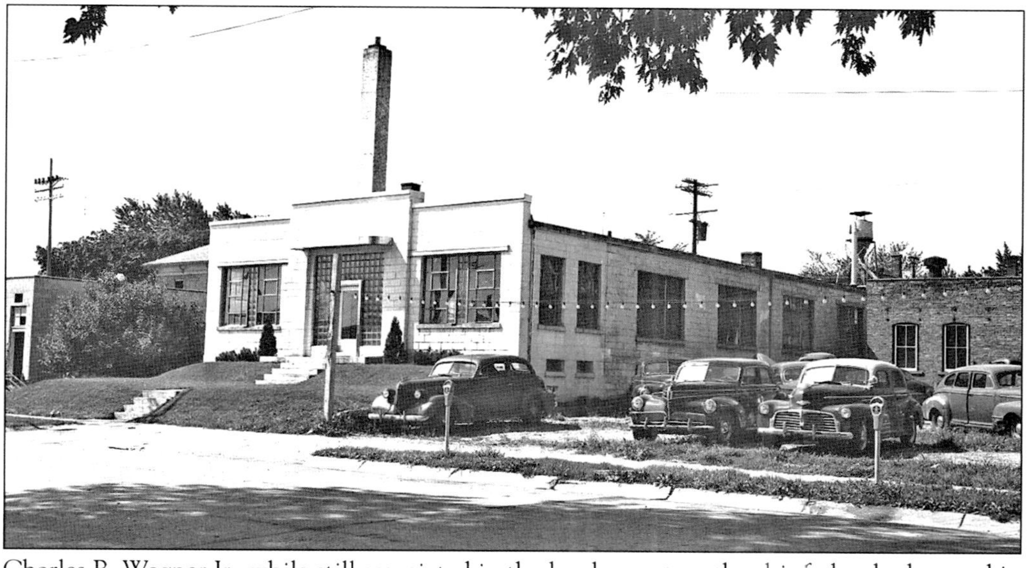

Charles B. Wagner Jr., while still associated in the hardware store that his father had started in 1869, patented and started to sell various hardware items, such as bull rings, calf weaners, and a tail clip for cows. As the demand grew, he installed manufacturing equipment in a building on Dodge Street behind the family's Jefferson Street home. His sons, Paul and Charles, later joined the business, known as the Wagner Specialty Co. The building is pictured *c.* 1951.

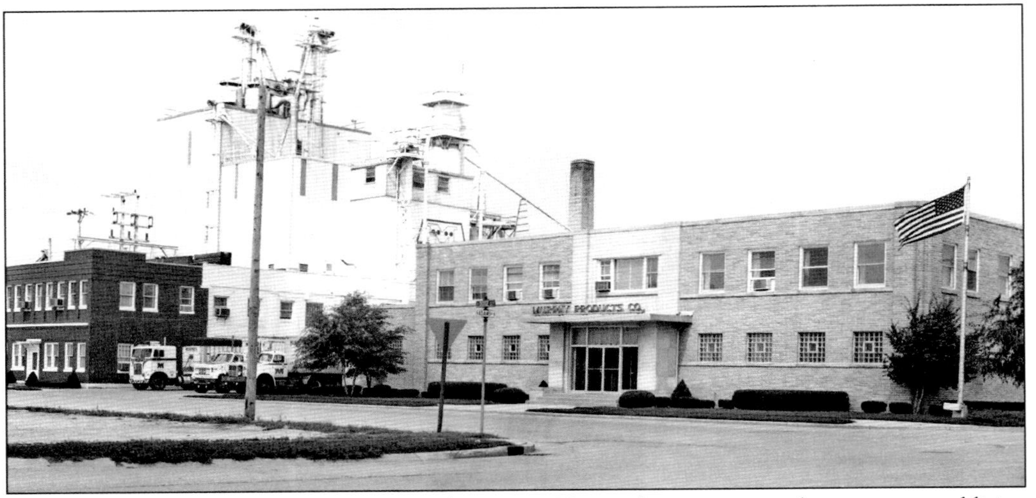

Murphy Products Co., which started in Delavan in 1921 producing a mineral concentrate additive for livestock feed, moved to Burlington in 1925, taking over the Badger Dairy Co. building (left) on Dodge Street. The product line and plant grew and, in 1936, the company decided to advertise heavily on radio, sponsoring the barn dance on Chicago's WLS. A 1951 fire led to a new, more-advanced automated plant. In 1971, the company was sold to the Schlitz Brewing Co.

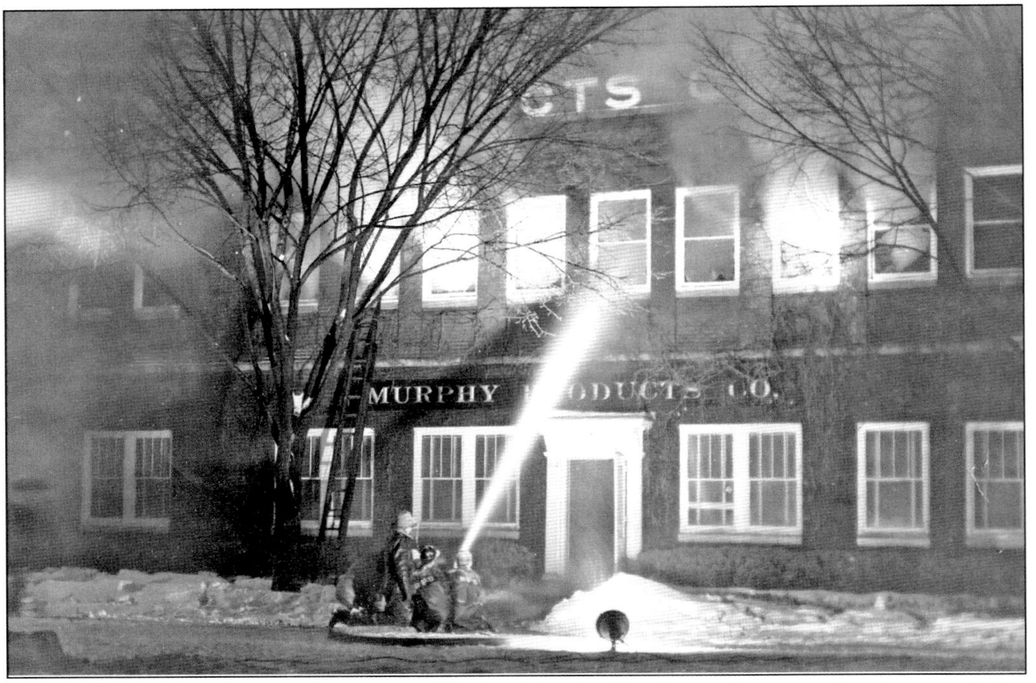

On Christmas Eve 1951, disaster struck the Murphy Products Co. as a fire destroyed the manufacturing plant and a part of the warehouse facilities. Using borrowed equipment, milling resumed at an Illinois location until a new automated plant arose. In the 1960s, the company grew, establishing plants in North Carolina, Mississippi, Texas, and California. Since the Schlitz Brewing Co. bought Murphy Products in 1971, the facilities, now owned by Maple Leaf Farms, have changed hands a couple of times.

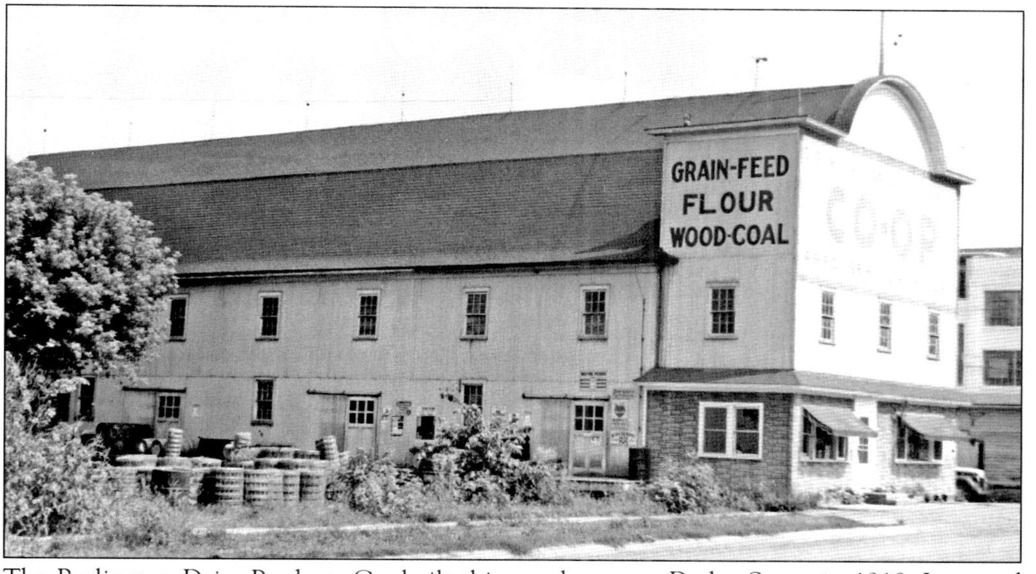

The Burlington Dairy Products Co. built this warehouse on Dodge Street in 1918. It started operations in 1919, selling flour, corn meal, dairy feed, salt, hay, straw, and dry wood, and exchanging wheat for flour. It added coal sales and a new feed grinding mill in 1920, and changed its name to Farmers Feed & Fuel Co. Burlington Consumers Co-op bought the plant in 1943, and later added feed storage tanks. In 1987, the Co-op built a new feed mill in a Burlington industrial park.

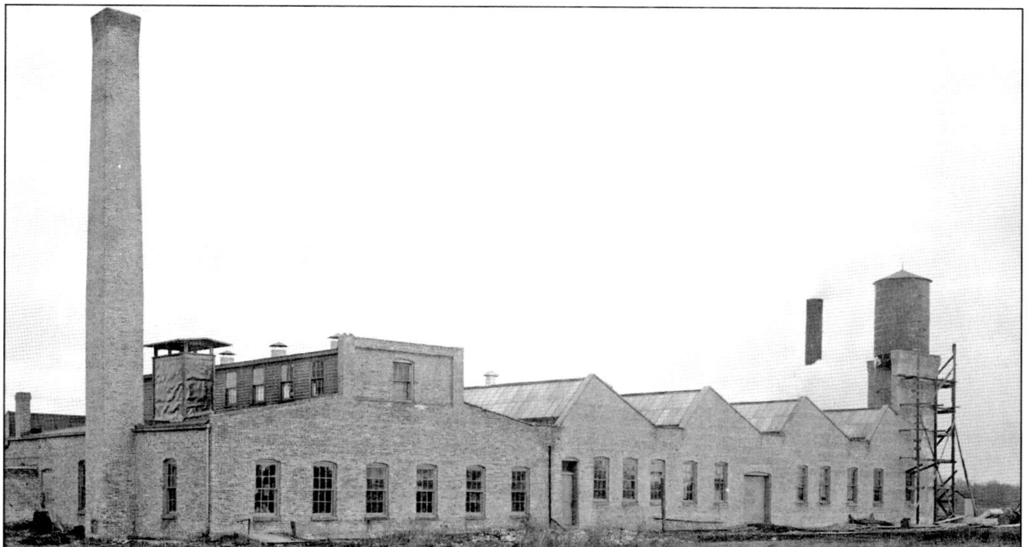

The Burlington Brass Works, pictured *c.* 1908, started in 1902 when Ole O. Storle developed an industrial steam valve and, with John Gill, built a small factory on Wilmot Avenue (now South Pine Street). In 1906, C. B. McCanna and son bought the business, added products such as the "Kant-Leak" valve for sink faucets, and started plating and polishing departments. In the 1920s, a new foundry was built to make bearings, hub caps, and other automobile parts. During World War II, the company made shells, detonator parts, and engine bushings. Sold in 1975, the plant closed in phases in 1979.

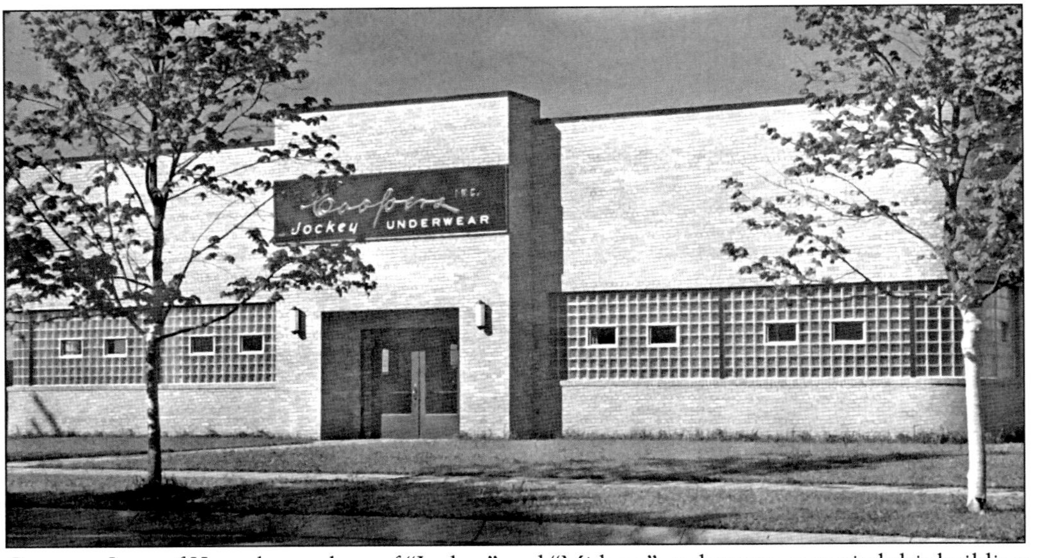

Coopers, Inc., of Kenosha, makers of "Jockey" and "Midway" underwear, occupied this building from its construction in 1948 until 1951. Coopers first opened a branch plant in Burlington in 1946, above the Ben Franklin and Gamble stores on Chestnut Street, before moving here. At its peak, Coopers employed about 110 women and turned out about 5,000-dozen shorts a week. In 1952, Torrent Manufacturing Co., maker of medicinal swabs, moved to the building. After Torrent left, Towne & Country Lanes opened a bowling center in 1958.

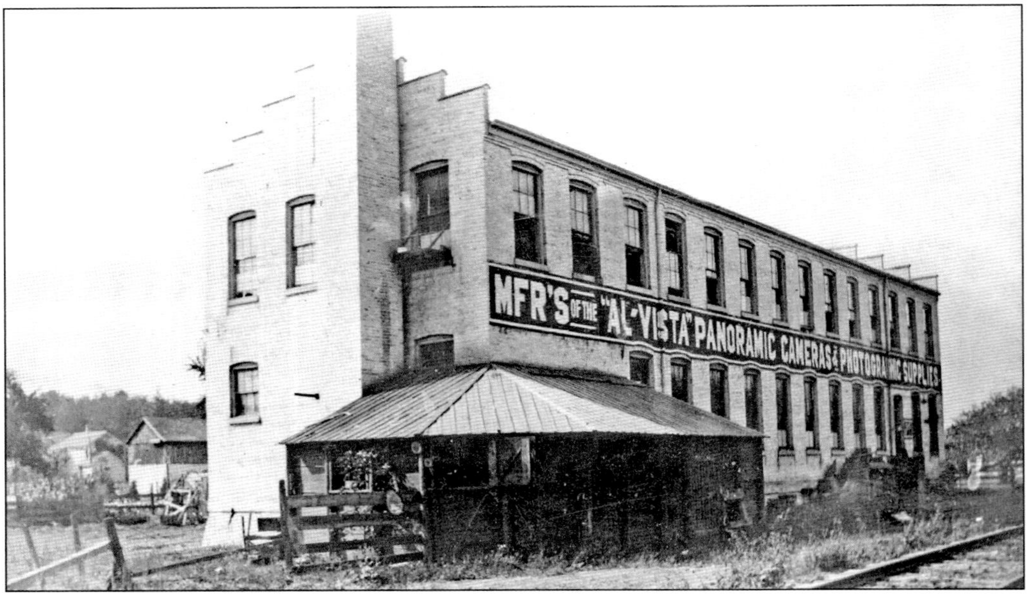

The Multiscope and Film Co., maker of the Al-Vista Panoramic camera invented by Peter Angsten, started production in 1897 in the vacant Union (now Lincoln) School building. In 1900, the Burlington Advancement Association built this brick factory south of Jefferson Street near the railroad tracks. The plant, pictured in 1905, produced thousands of cameras between 1897 and 1908. Verstraete & Fyfe Co., an automobile parts maker, bought the company in 1908 and contracted to make the cameras, but the plant burned in 1909.

Four

Houses–from Humble to Grand

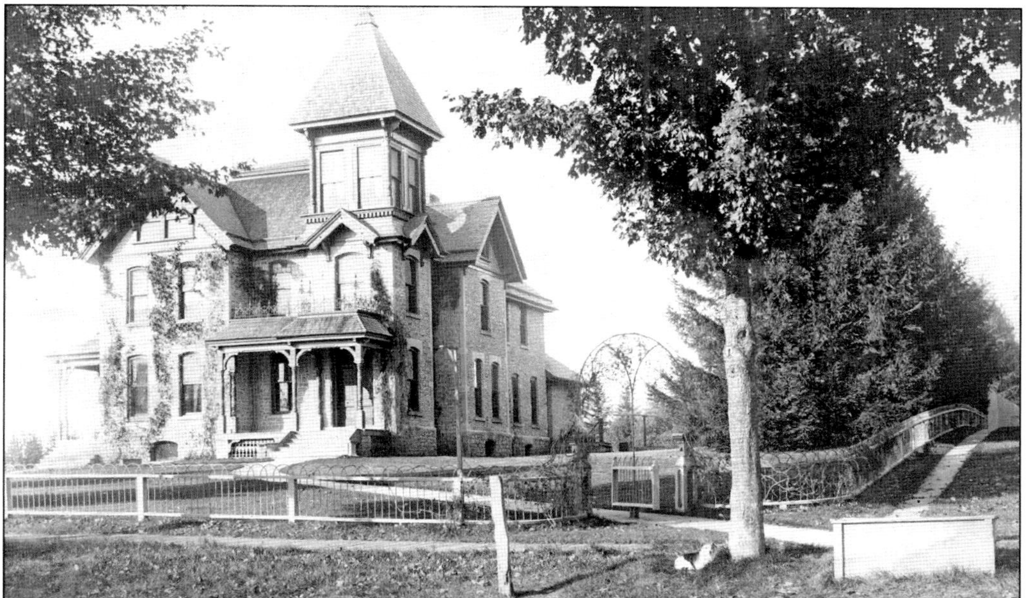

The Meinhardt house on Kane Street, considered the showplace of Burlington, originally was surrounded by 15 acres of landscaped grounds, an orchard, a pasture, a pine grove, fountains, and a tennis court. Completed in 1883 by Anthony and Eliza Riel Meinhardt, the house, pictured *c.* 1900, was occupied by Meinhardt family members until 1963. Daughter Antoinette (Mrs. William A. Fulton) was the last of the Meinhardts to live here. In 1963, the house was sold to Donald and Dorothy Johnston, and in 1971, to Cecil and Jeannie Everett.

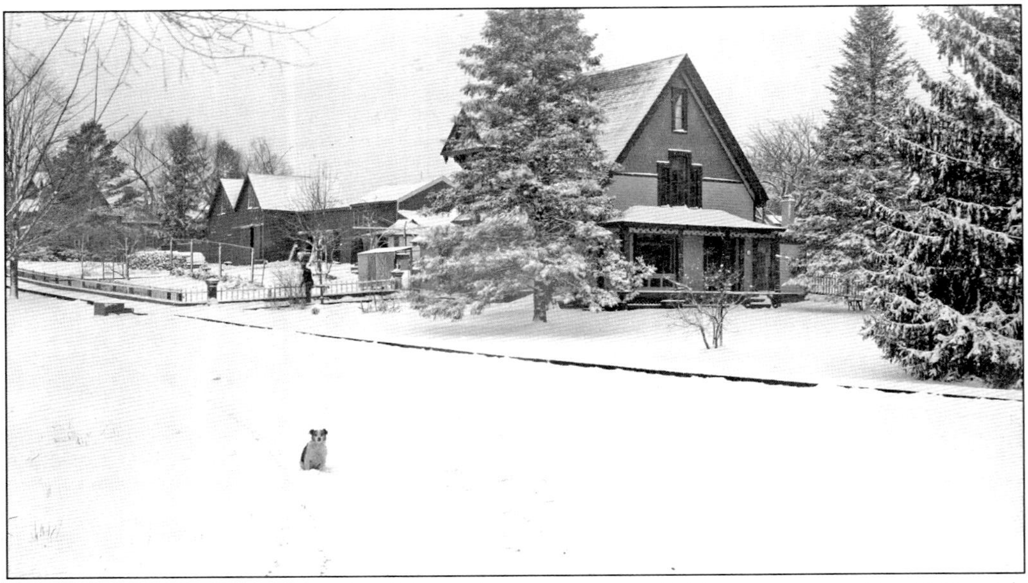

This house on Kane Street south of State Street, shown c. 1895, was separated in 1907, with one part moved to the adjoining lot. The Anthony and Eliza Meinhardt family lived here before moving to their new Victorian home farther south on Kane Street in 1883. Eliza's brother, Theodore Riel, and his family then moved in. In 1897, Riel built an addition for his daughter Carrie and her husband, Frederick Buell. The Buells sold the house to Henry Siehoff in 1907.

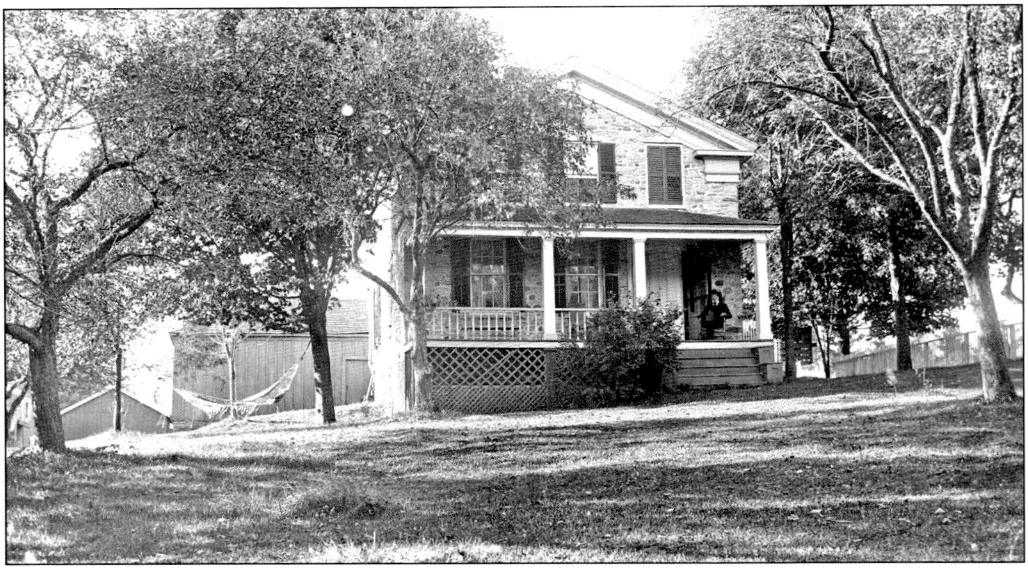

The Durgin-Schwaller house on State Street was built in sections starting about 1848. When Trueworthy Durgin bought the property in 1854, he completed the partially finished stone house that was there. The front block is a fieldstone structure, with the porch added later. On the rear is a square block with a hipped roof. The Frank Schwaller family lived here from 1901 into the 1950s. In 1911, Schwaller built a new porch with the steps in the center.

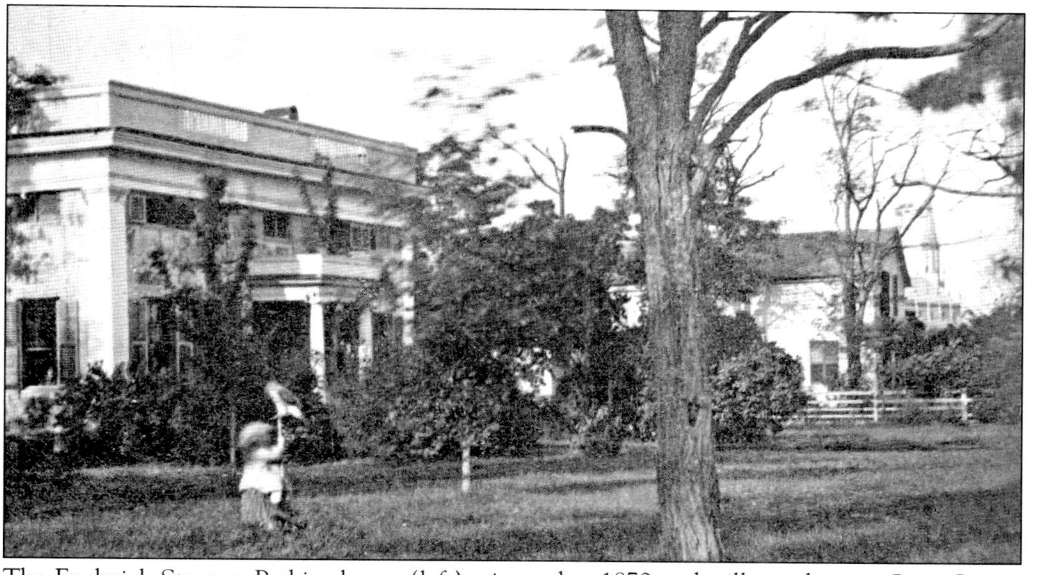

The Frederick Stanton Perkins house (left), pictured *c.* 1870 and still standing on State Street, was built by his parents, Origen and Julia Dyer Perkins, in 1846. Arriving in 1837, they first built a log house, then a frame dwelling, and finally this residence. At right is the house of Dr. Edward G. and Ann Eliza Morse Dyer. He was Burlington's first physician. Their house was moved off the site about 1915. Both the Perkins and Dyer houses were Underground Railroad shelters.

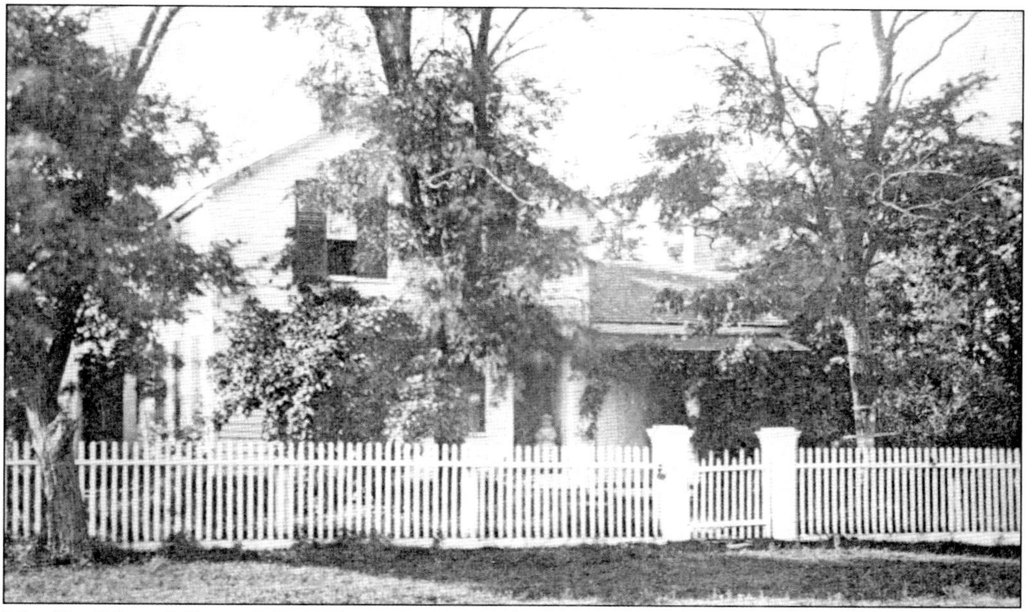

The Dr. Edward G. and Ann Eliza Morse Dyer house, pictured *c.* 1870, was built on the south side of State Street east of Kane Street about 1840. Dr. Dyer, an ardent abolitionist, gave Liberty Street (now part of State Street) its name. In 1876, the house was sold to deputy sheriff John Pennington and Maria Brierly Mather. Mather had been proprietor of the Exchange Hotel on Pine Street and a circus owner. About 1915, the house was moved, and in 1917, C. Roy McCanna bought the property.

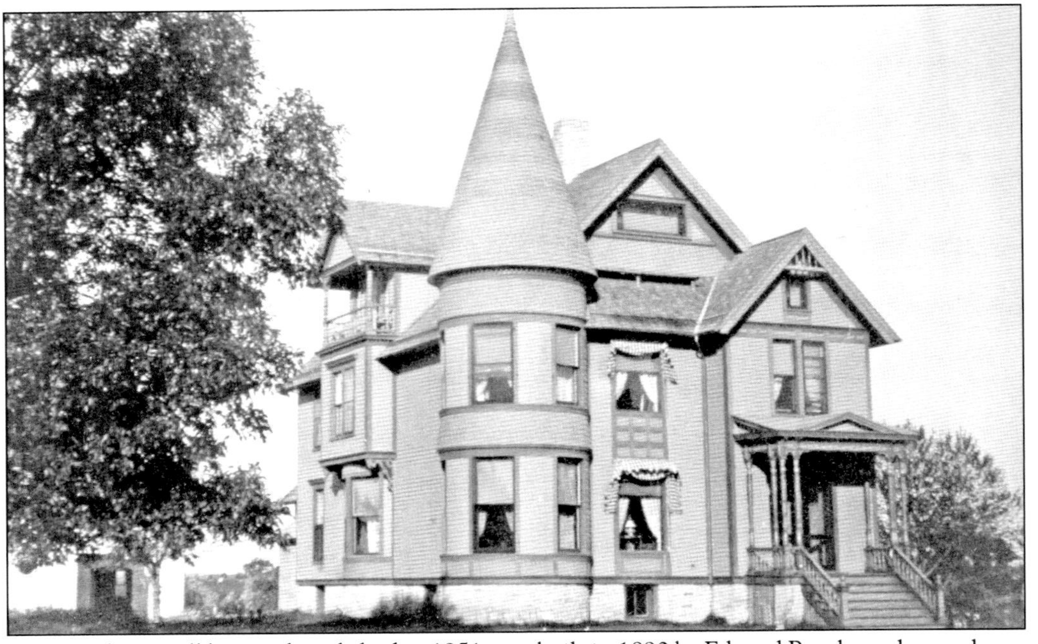

The Brook-Newell house, demolished in 1951, was built in 1890 by Edward Brook on the southeast corner of Pine and State Streets, now site of the Burlington Post Office. In 1931, Brooks' daughter, Edith, and her husband, Howard Newell, offered a new "little theatre" group the use of the loft of the barn, lower left, where Howard kept trotting horses. The group, which used the loft to review scripts, plan productions, and rehearse, adopted the name "Haylofters" in its honor.

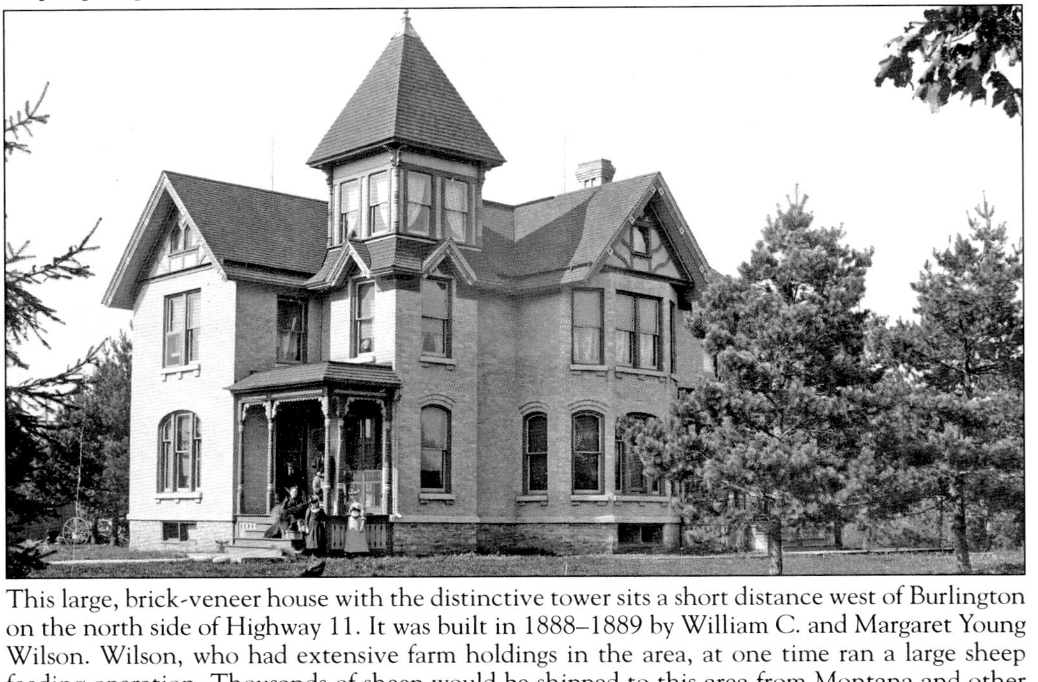

This large, brick-veneer house with the distinctive tower sits a short distance west of Burlington on the north side of Highway 11. It was built in 1888–1889 by William C. and Margaret Young Wilson. Wilson, who had extensive farm holdings in the area, at one time ran a large sheep feeding operation. Thousands of sheep would be shipped to this area from Montana and other western states for fattening up before being sent to the Chicago packing plants.

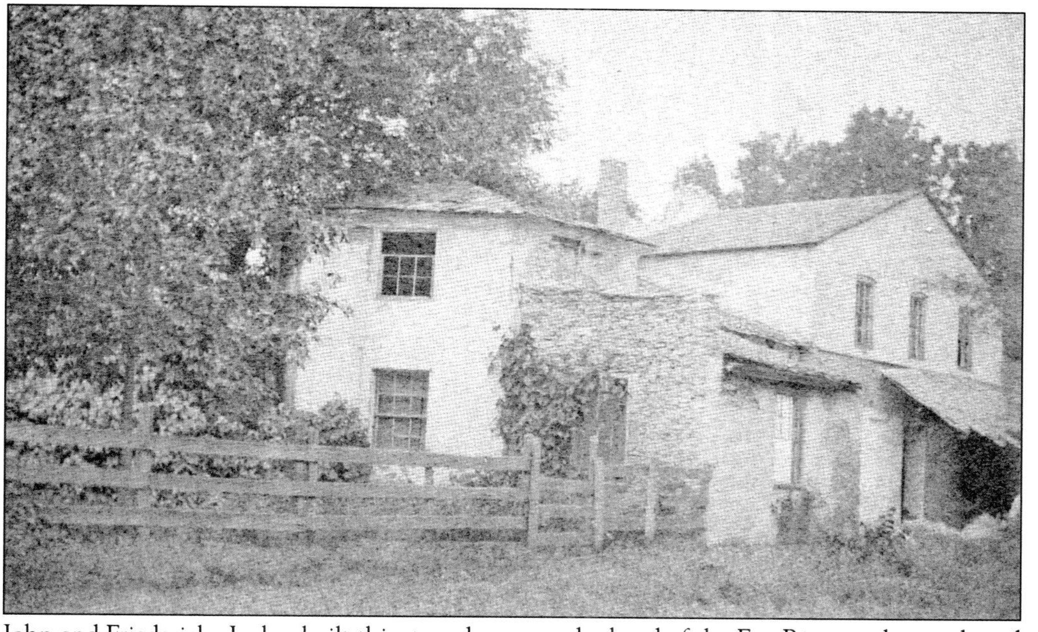

John and Friedericka Jucker built this stone house on the bend of the Fox River at the north end of what is now Main Street in the 1840s. It was near here that Burlington's earliest settlers—Moses and Lemuel Smith, William Whiting, and Benjamin Perce—built a shelter to use while exploring the area in 1835–1836. Daughter Emma Jucker married Eugene Wehmhoff in 1869. The Wehmhoff family donated the Jucker property to the City in 1953 for Wehmhoff-Jucker Park.

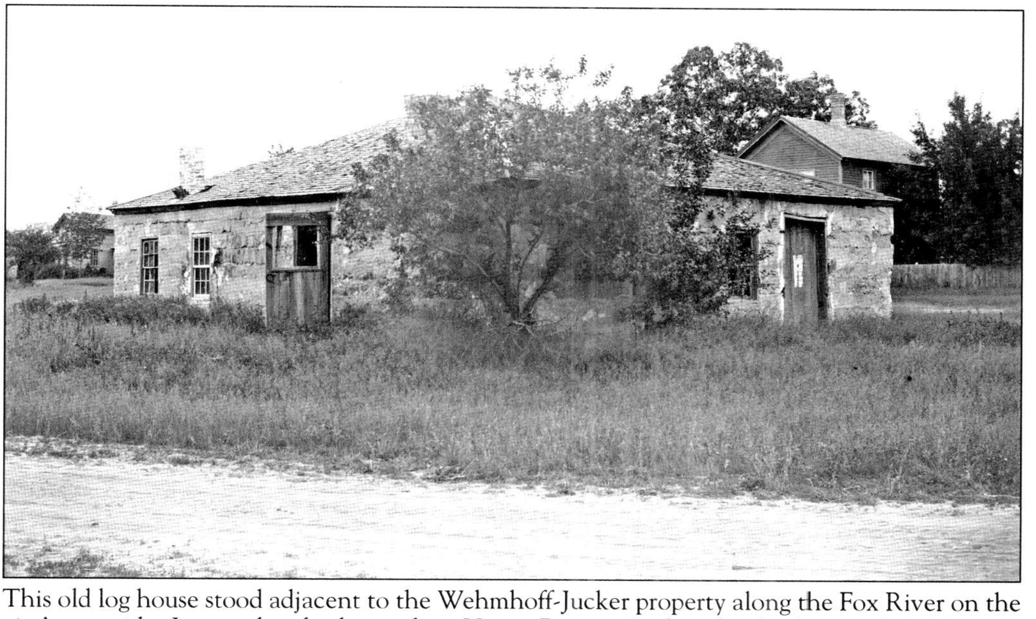

This old log house stood adjacent to the Wehmhoff-Jucker property along the Fox River on the city's east side. It was already there when Henry Benson Sr. bought the lot in 1848. His son, Henry, who was born in the log house and lived there about 75 years, was one of Burlington's quaint characters, keeping a cow in a back room. Albert Meinhardt bought the property in 1928 and presented it to the City for a campsite.

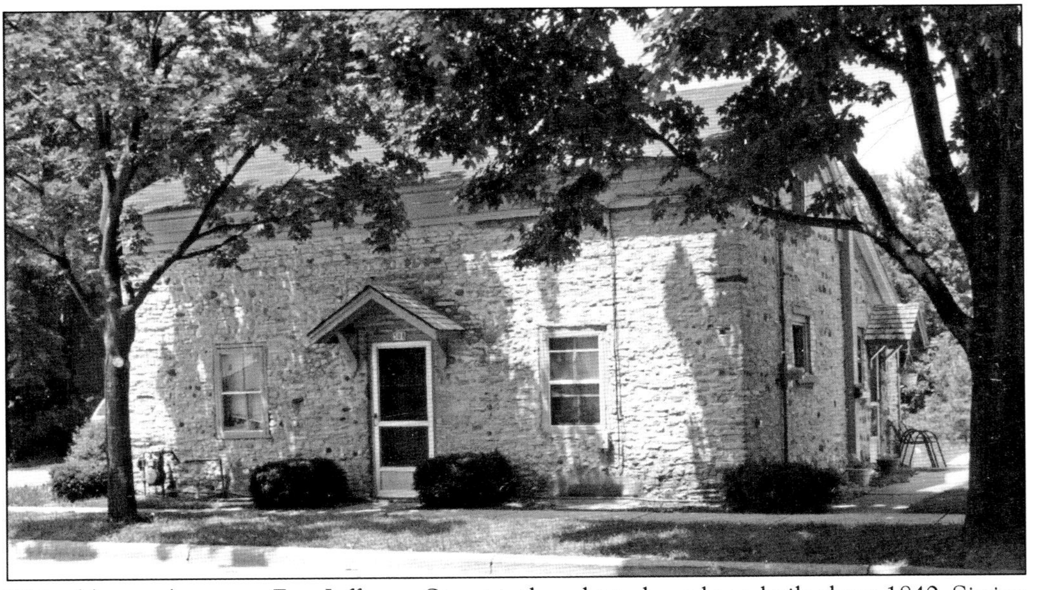

This old stone house on East Jefferson Street is thought to have been built about 1840. Sitting close to the street in a fashion typical at that time, it is one of the city's oldest existing houses. The stone walls are laid with alternating horizontal courses of cobblestones and thin limestone rubble. Wilhelm and Maria Riel lived here in the 1850s. Richard Weygand, a building and sign painter after whom Weygand's Peninsula at Brown's Lake is named, later lived here.

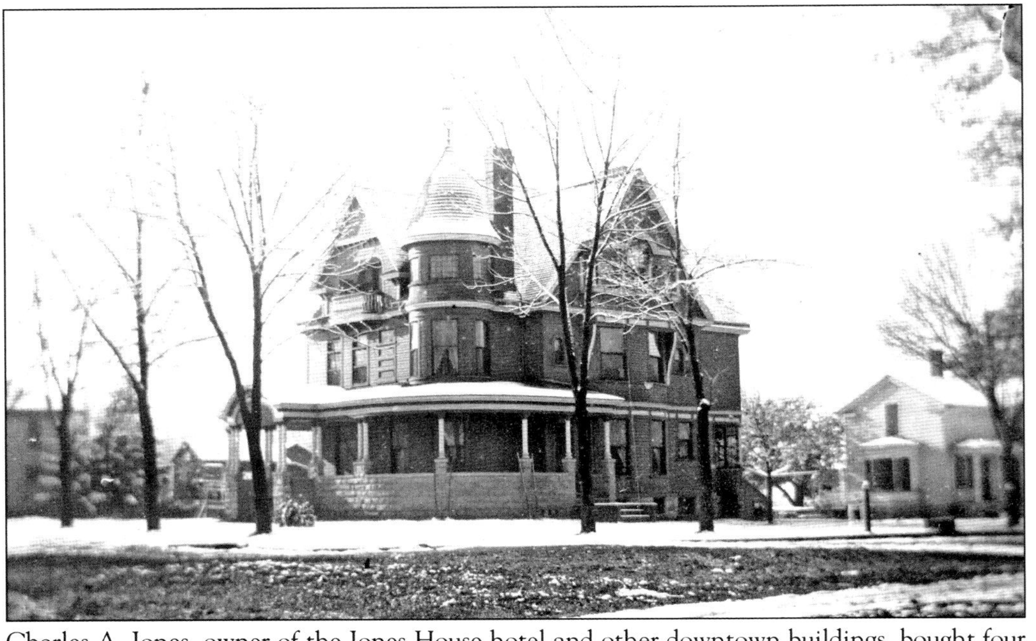

Charles A. Jones, owner of the Jones House hotel and other downtown buildings, bought four lots on the corner of Jefferson and Dyer (now Kane) Streets from the Billings estate in 1895. He moved the old Billings house to a lot on Washington Street and built this house, pictured c. 1900. A garage was built on the property in 1921. In 1927, William A. Trost bought the house, and there have been other owners since. A rear addition was recently completed.

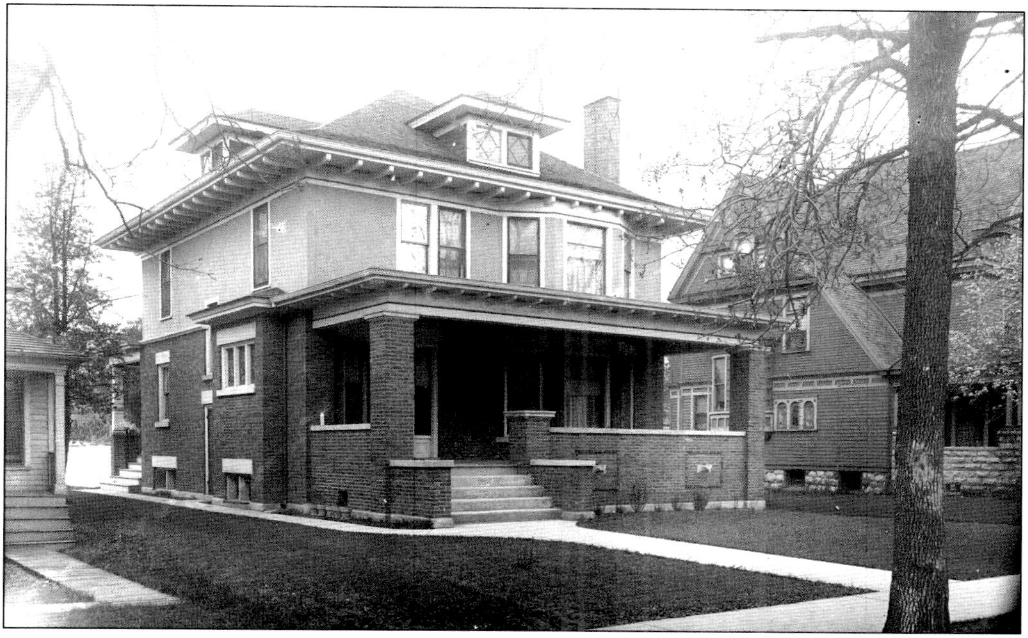

In 1912, Hugh Agner bought property on Dyer (now Kane) Street between the Charles A. Jones residence on the corner of Jefferson Street and the Jackson residence (both partially visible in this c. 1913 picture). Agner completed this house in 1913, and moved in. In 1928, David E. Peck bought the residence, which he sold to John F. "Jack" and Altana "Babe" Ayers Hansen in 1929. The Hansens occupied the house until their deaths, his in 1954 and hers in 1984.

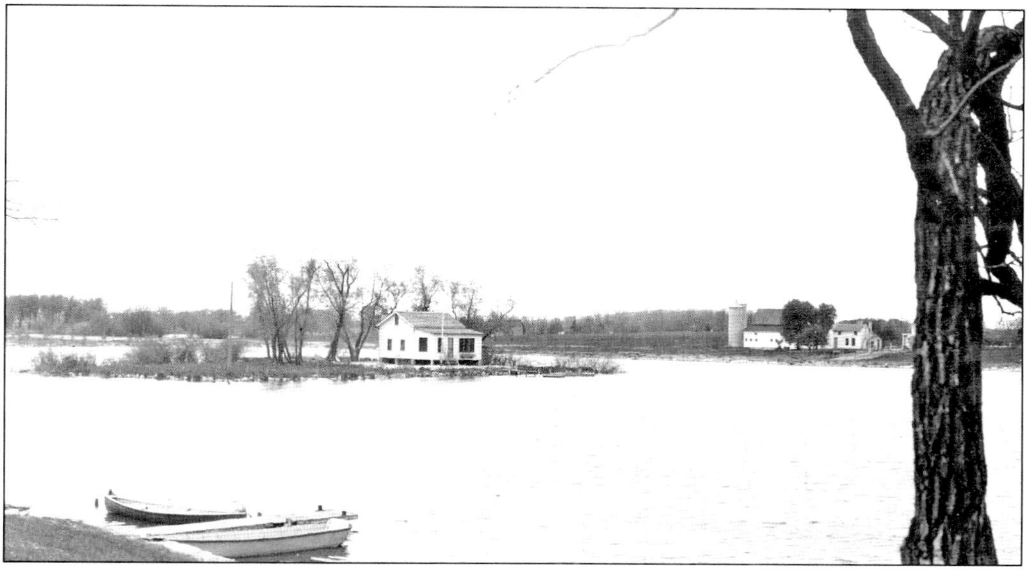

Albert Zechel bought an island, about 200 by 150 feet, in the mill pond in 1928. The island was created after Pliny Perkins secured a government charter in 1837 to flood a low portion of his land adjacent to the White River and to dam it. By this charter, the bottom of the mill pond remained private property. Starting in 1929, the Zechels built this hunting cabin and summer cottage. The building is no longer standing. The farm at right is now owned by Roger and Joy Bieneman.

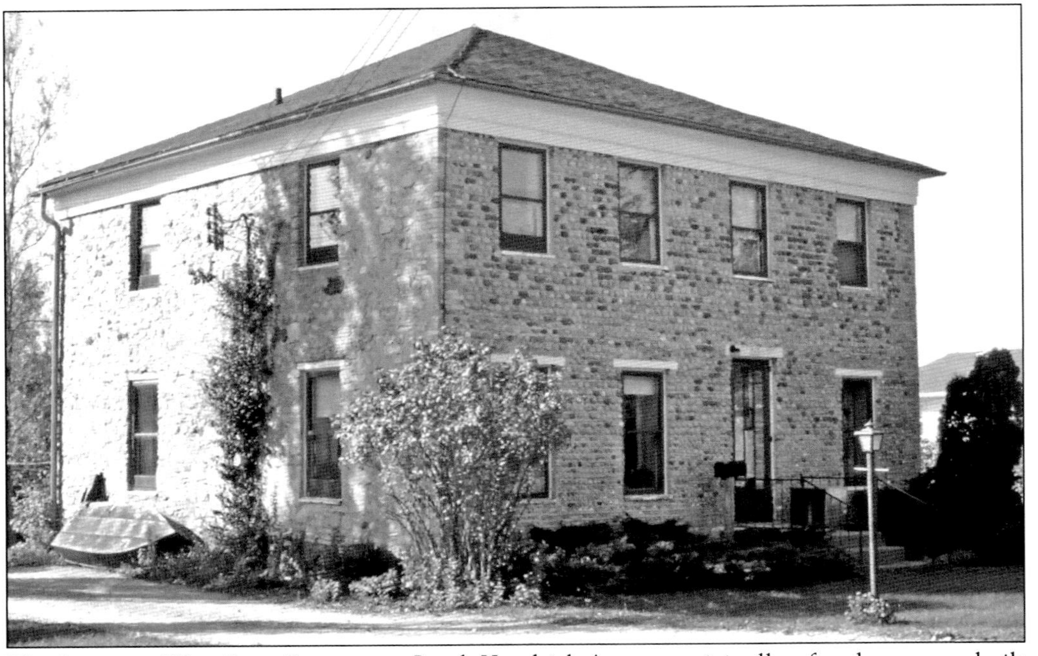

This house on West State Street near South Kendrick Avenue, originally a farmhouse, was built in the 1840s by Pliny Perkins on a foundation believed to have been laid by John Acken. Three of the walls are coarse masonry, but the front is finished in cobblestones that are graded from the smallest at the bottom to the largest at the top. John Prasch bought the farm in 1869, and the house was in the Prasch family for 90 years.

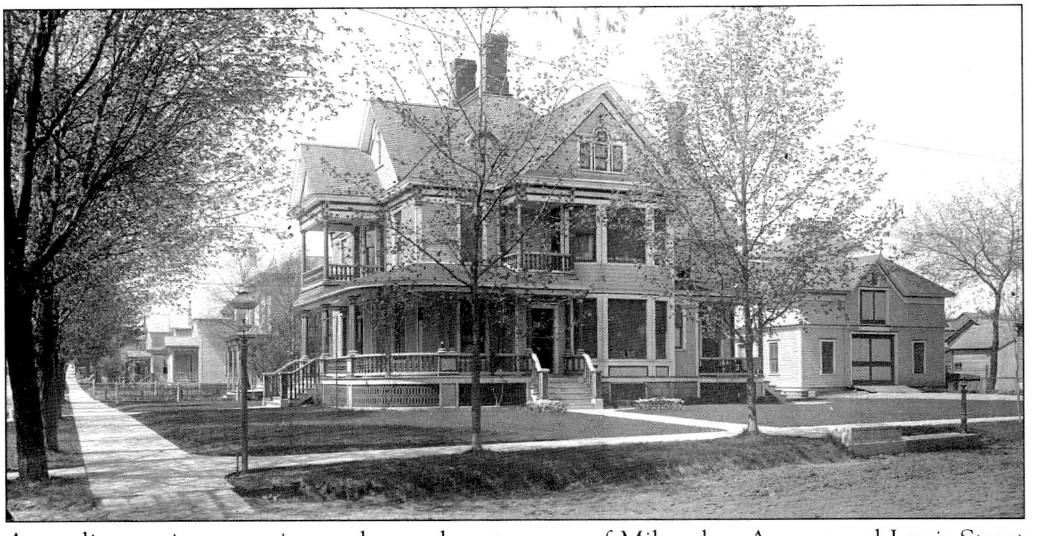

A gasoline station now sits on the southwest corner of Milwaukee Avenue and Lewis Street where this house stood from 1896 to 1957. The house, pictured c. 1907, was built by John H. and Frances Finke Uhen after an earlier stone house, which had been the residence of Henry and Christina Arndt Kerkman, was moved south to the opposite side of Milwaukee Avenue where it still stands near the intersection with Washington Street. Uhen was a partner in the Finke-Uhen Brewing Co.

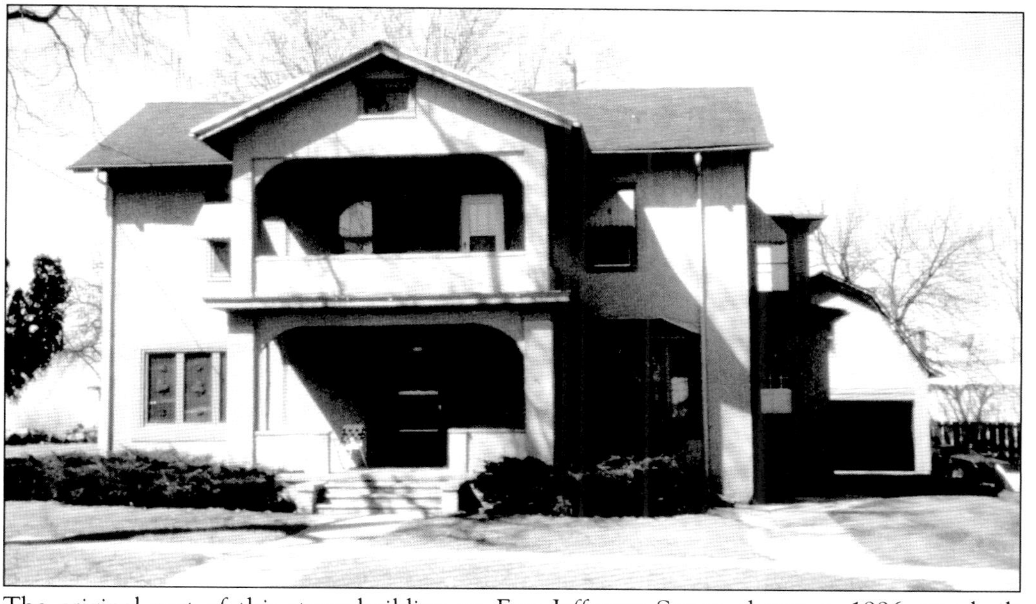

The original part of this stone building on East Jefferson Street, shown c. 1996, was built in 1844 to house the Burlington Academy, a private school incorporated by the territorial legislature. The academy lasted into the 1850s, after which the building became a residence. About 1920, Jacob Wien bought the property, intending to erect a new residence. Instead, he had the rear part torn down and the two-story front remodeled, adding some rooms and a sun porch and pebble-dashing the exterior.

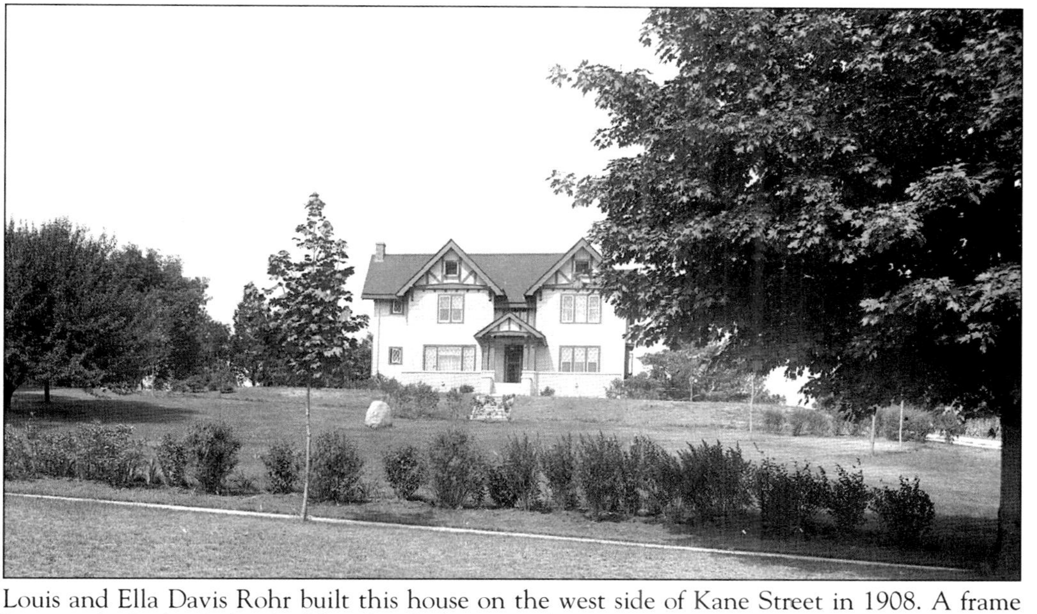

Louis and Ella Davis Rohr built this house on the west side of Kane Street in 1908. A frame house, which the Rohrs had lived in before completing this one, was moved off the property. The large stone on the lawn reportedly marks the burial place of Old Major, a favorite horse of Henry Devereux, who had earlier owned the property. The Lee and Ruth Barney family owned the property from 1944 to 1965, when Dr. Robert Wheaton bought it.

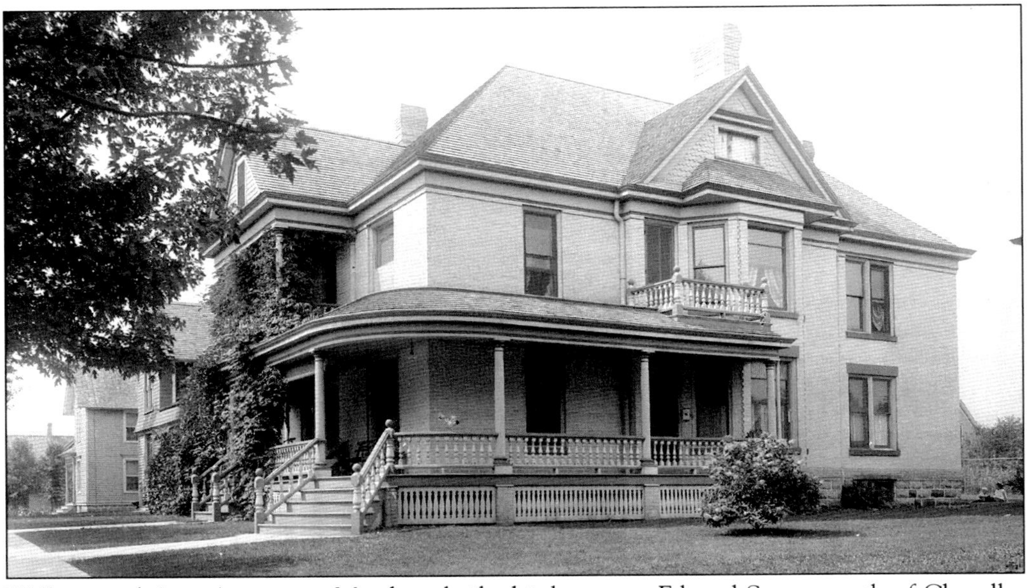

William and Ann Armstrong Meadows built this house on Edward Street, south of Chandler Boulevard, in 1898. Meadows had come to Burlington in 1850 with his parents and two brothers. After owning a farm near Norton's Lake where Burlington High School is now located, the family moved to Lyons township. William was general manager of the Burlington Brick and Tile Co. for 34 years, resigning shortly before his death in 1920. Subsequent owners divided the house into flats.

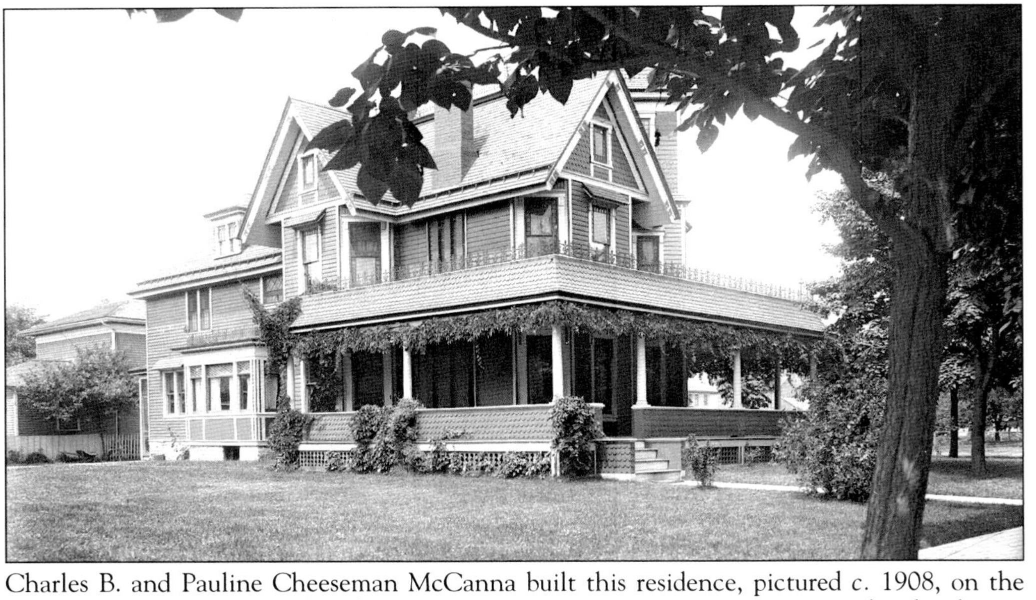

Charles B. and Pauline Cheeseman McCanna built this residence, pictured c. 1908, on the southwest corner of Pine and Madison Streets in 1886. McCanna was instrumental in developing the dairy farming industry in southeast Wisconsin and northern Illinois by establishing butter and cheese, and then condensed milk, factories in the region. The house was torn down after Mrs. McCanna's death in 1954, and a grocery store was built. Since the grocery store closed in 1971, restaurants have occupied the store building.

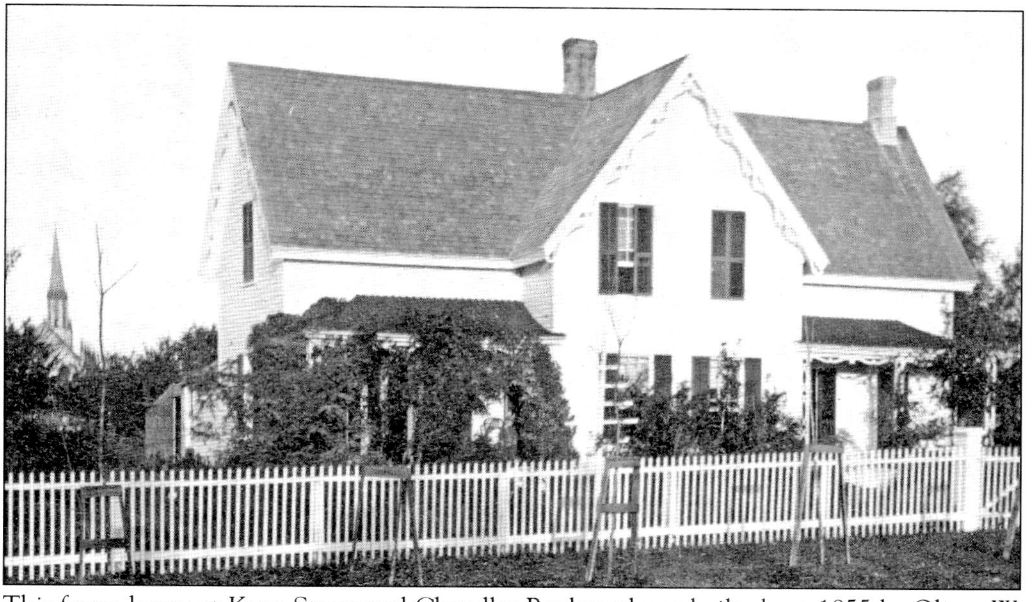

This frame house at Kane Street and Chandler Boulevard was built about 1855 by Oliver W. and Eunice Hess Chandler. He was a music dealer and piano agent. As pictured *c.* 1890, two porches originally flanked the entrance pavilion and a picket fence, later replaced by a chain strung between cast iron posts, made to look like pruned logs, surrounded the grounds. Later alterations included a rear addition and two dormers. After Chandler, his nephew Ernest Foltz and family, and later the Dr. Herbert Granzeau family, occupied the house.

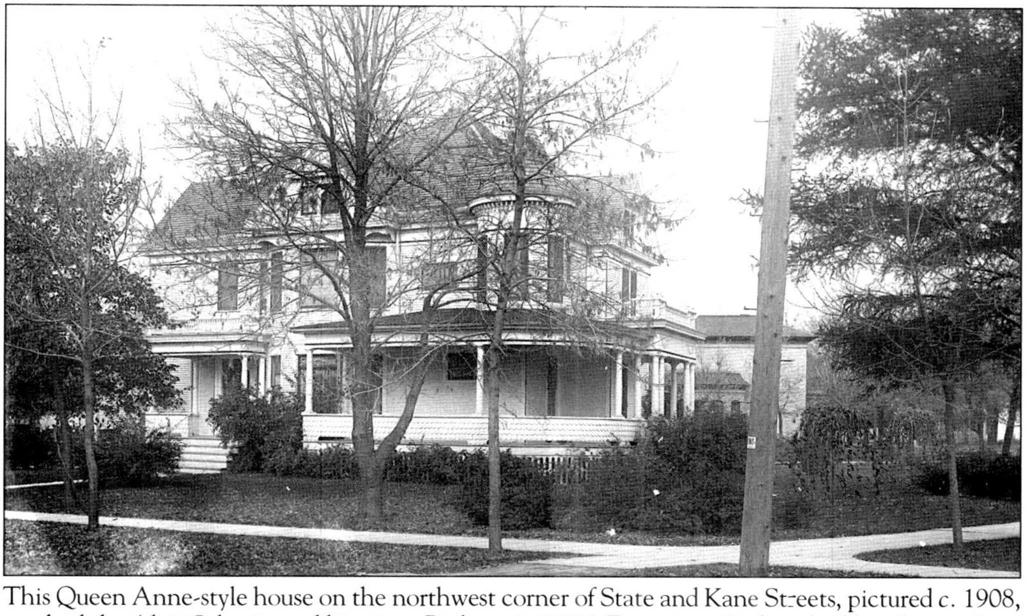

This Queen Anne-style house on the northwest corner of State and Kane Streets, pictured *c.* 1908, was built by Alois Schmitt and his sister, Barbara, in 1906. For a time, Barbara had her dressmaking parlors in the house. John and Laura May Cunningham bought the house in 1919. After a 1929 fire gutted the house, they essentially restored it except for eliminating the porch near the rear. For many years, the house has been divided into two apartments, upstairs and down.

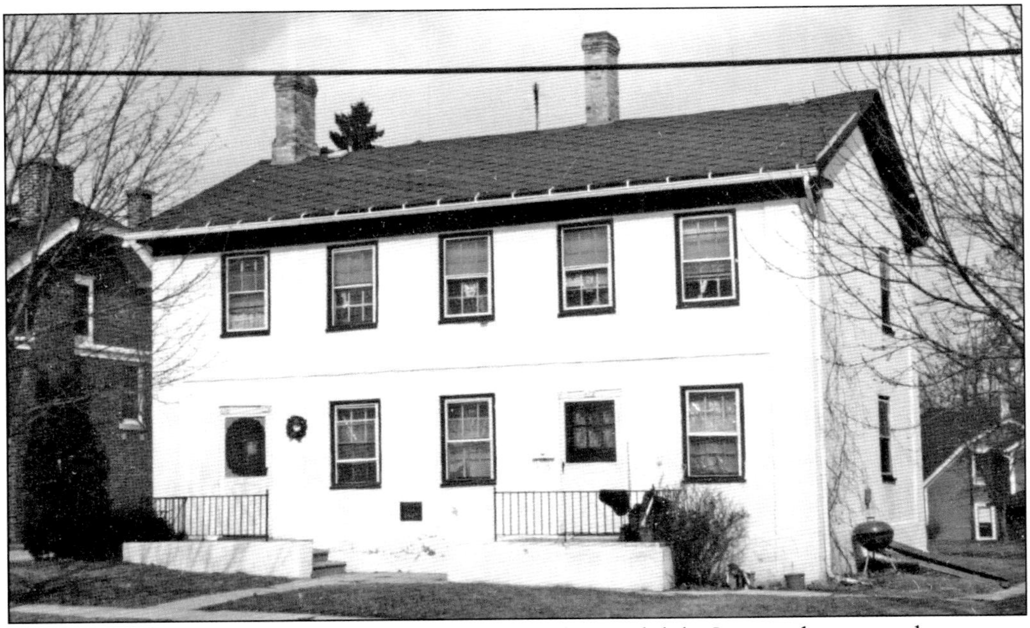

Sitting on State Street near the intersection with Randolph Street, this stone house was completed in 1847 by John Frank Rueter, a stone mason. Built as a multiple-family unit, Rueter used the parts aside from his family's living quarters to house other German immigrants until they could manage on their own. The house, which previously had no electricity or plumbing, was remodeled in 1933 into three apartments. Getting through the walls to install the wiring and pipes took much hard labor.

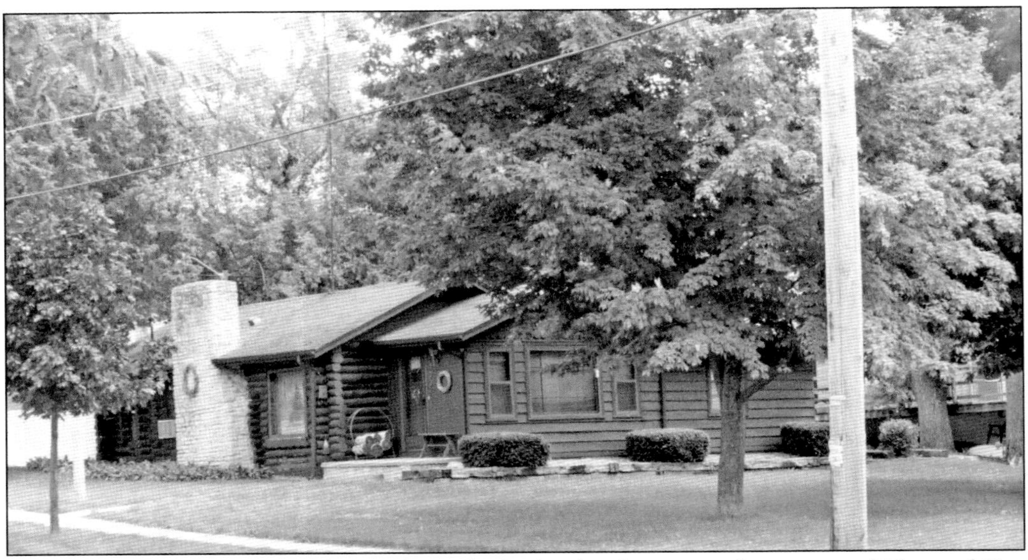

A full-blooded Chippewa, John Webster, built this log house on the corner of Elm and Fox River Streets (now Gardner Avenue and Hawthorn Street) in 1928 for Joseph "Jerry" Riefler and Thomas "Tom" Wall, who had a furniture repair and reupholstering business on Emerson Street. At that time, Burlington did not have a city park, so the two men also had Webster create a park on the property, including a fort and a stockade, for Burlington's children.

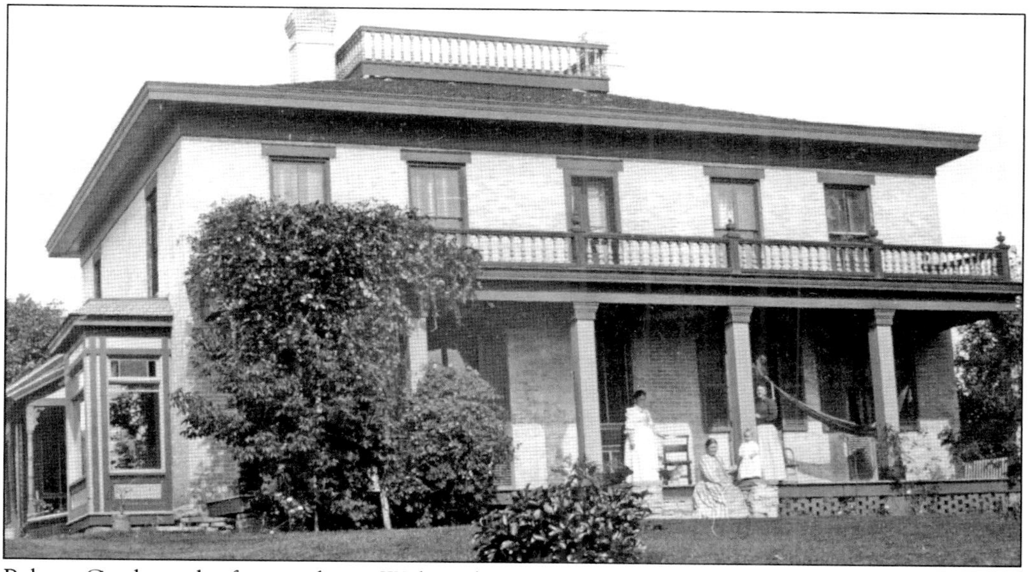

Palmer Gardner, the first settler in Walworth County, whose farm home still stands on County Trunk DD west of Burlington, and his wife, Margaret Williams, built this home on Kane Street in 1871. Margaret, however, died before she could move in. Gardner and his second wife moved here in 1872. At that time, there were few houses in this part of the village. In 1893, Andrew and Anna Wilson Patterson bought the house, pictured *c.* 1895, and later added a third story and Victorian tower.

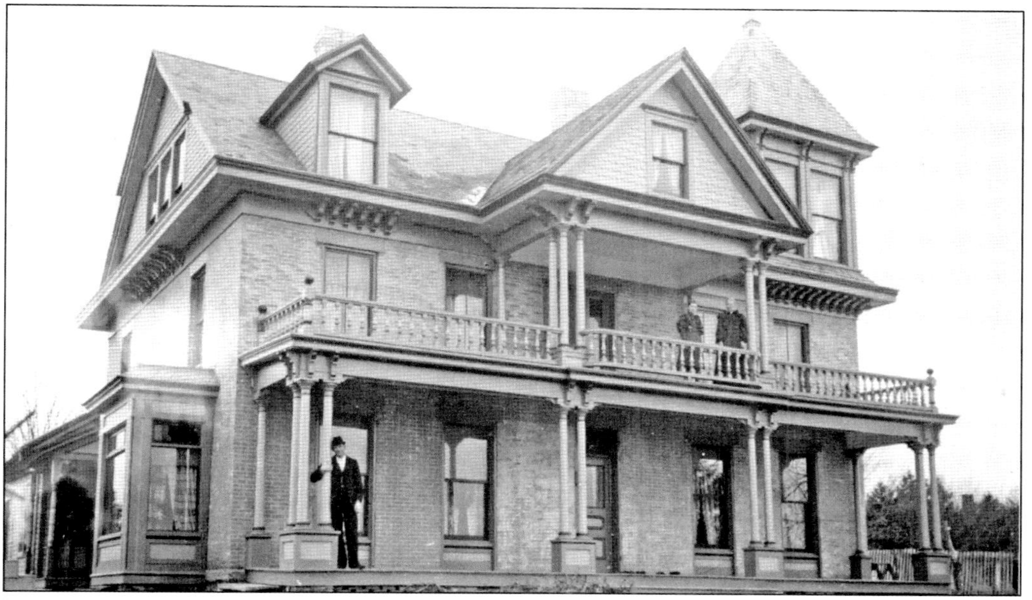

In 1920, attorney George W. Waller bought the Gardner-Patterson residence, pictured *c.* 1900 with the third story and tower, as a home for himself, his mother, Harriet, and his sister Annie. The house contained an impressive amount of woodwork, including a parquet floor; a circular staircase, which contained no nails; sliding parlor doors; and intricately carved moldings. The house, later owned by Our Savior Lutheran church, was moved in 1996 to the Shiloh Hills subdivision on the western edge of Burlington.

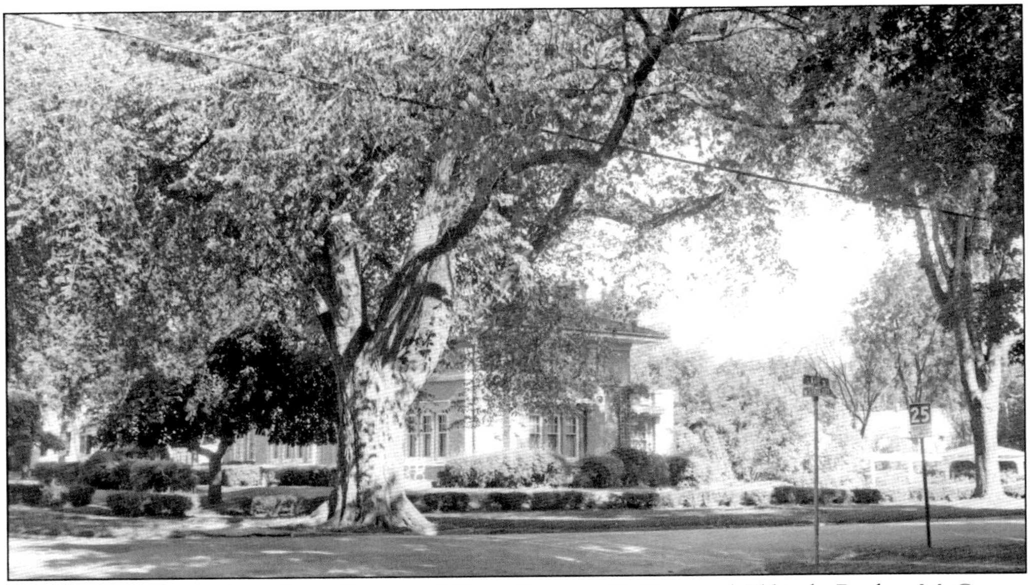

After buying seven lots along State and Kane Streets, C. Roy and Elfrieda Becker McCanna built this house, pictured c. 1970, completing it in June 1920. After Mr. McCanna's death in 1975, the McCarthy-Koenig Funeral Home acquired the property, adding a chapel and installing restrooms. Schuette and Daniels Funeral Service later bought the property and, in 1997, opened a furniture store. From 2001, when the furniture store closed, to 2004, a variety of businesses occupied the building.

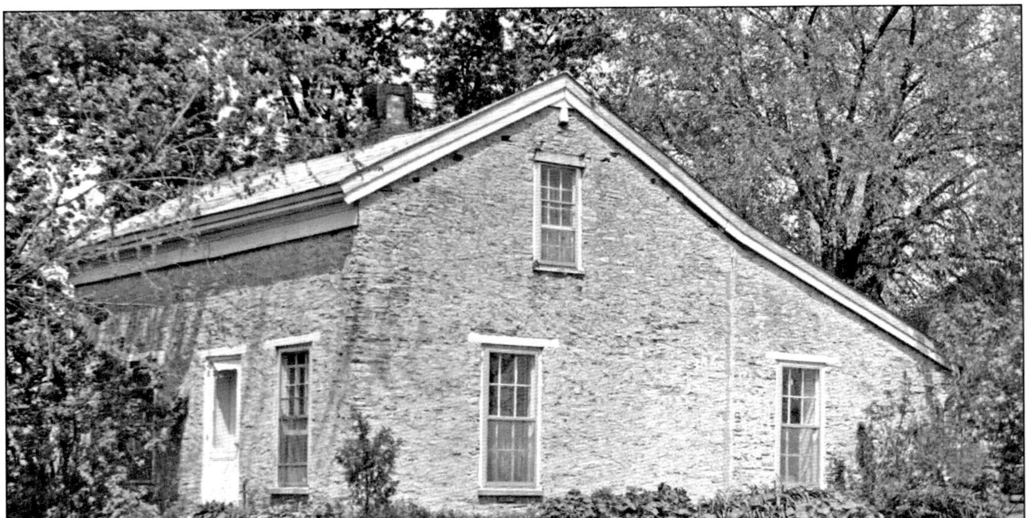

This house on Highway 11 west of Burlington near the White River is where James Jesse Strang, leader of one branch of Mormons, died in 1856 after being mortally wounded by two former followers at Beaver Island in Lake Michigan. Claiming to be Joseph Smith's successor, Strang had founded Voree, a Mormon community just west of Burlington, in 1844. In 1849, Strang led his followers to Beaver Island. After being shot, he was brought to this house, dying 19 days later.

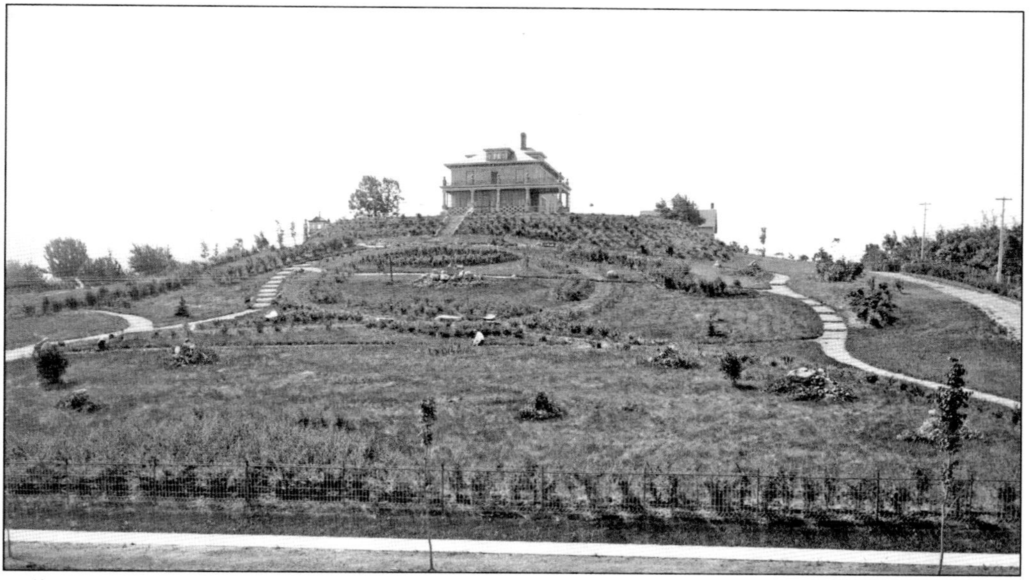

Hillcrest, built by Edwin and Lucille Perkins Caldwell in 1908, sits atop one of Burlington's highest points, providing a scenic seven-mile view on the Chestnut Street side that has changed little over the years. The hill was originally owned by Ephraim Perkins, whose protests against plans to run Chestnut Street directly over the hill led to the road being built around the base. Now called Hillcrest Inn and Carriage House, the residence is a bed-and-breakfast inn.

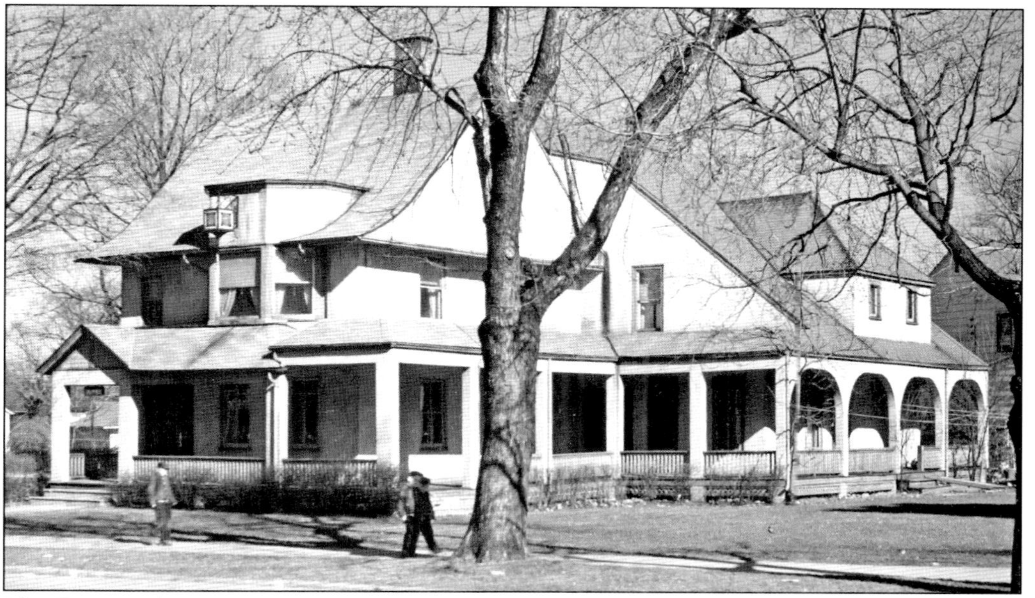

The First Banking Center now occupies the corner of Milwaukee Avenue and North Kane Street where this house once stood. Eugene and Florence Cooper Hall bought the former Peter Forbes residence in 1882, making extensive improvements both inside and out. After Eugene's death, Rev. Theodore Jacobs and then Anna C. Koller owned the property. In 1915, the Knights of Columbus bought the property, using the building as a clubroom. In 1957, the bank's predecessor bought the property and had the building razed.

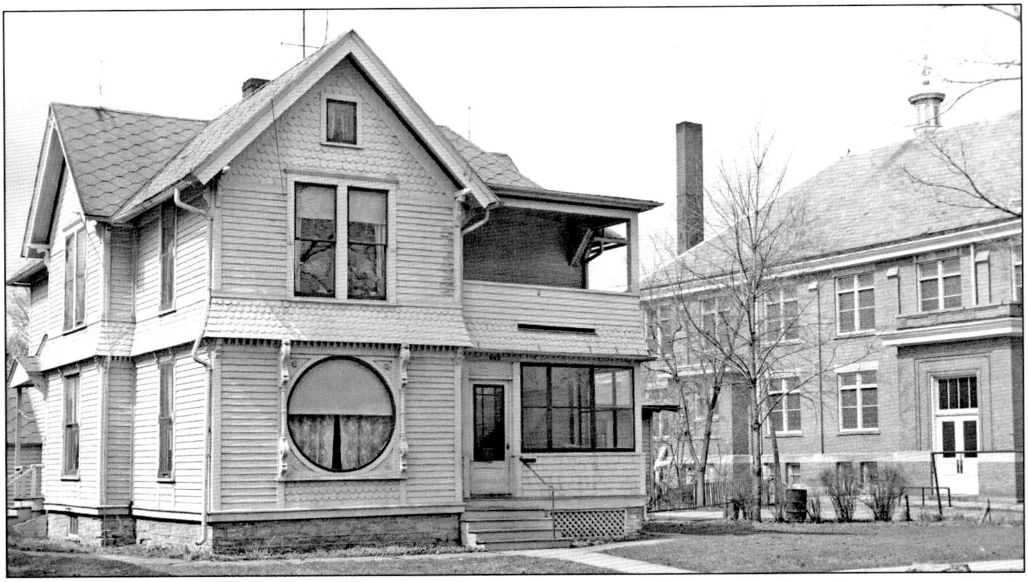

Gustave and Mathilda Geheb Rasch built this house in 1892 on Conkey Street near Lewis Street. The round-bevel, plate-glass parlor window, about six feet in diameter, was something new in Burlington. After Mr. Rasch's death in 1932, Edward Hinchliffe bought the house and remodeled it into two flats. St. Charles Borromeo Catholic Church (right), built in 1910, bought the property in 1956 and sold the house to Harry Bigelow, who moved it to a lot on Edward Street near Wainwright Avenue.

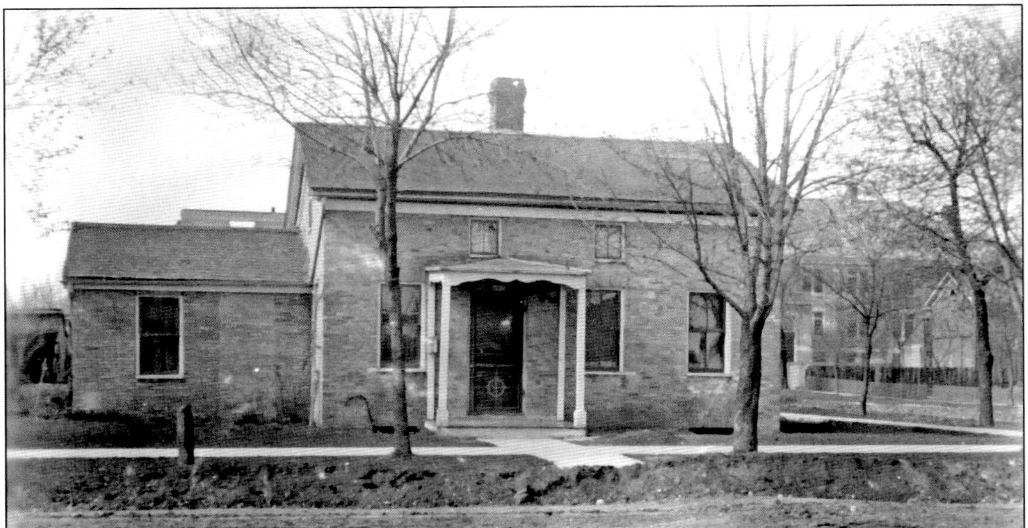

This house, pictured c. 1910 with St. Charles Borromeo Church in the background, stood on the corner of Chestnut and Conkey Streets for more than 125 years. Built by David and Cornelia Eddy Wells in 1844, the house was replaced in 1972 by a savings and loan building. Occupants over the years included George W. Stone, John and Dora Karcher, Sherman and Anna Gillespie, and Joseph and Josepha Block. For a time in the 1950s, the house served as Burlington's Greyhound bus station.

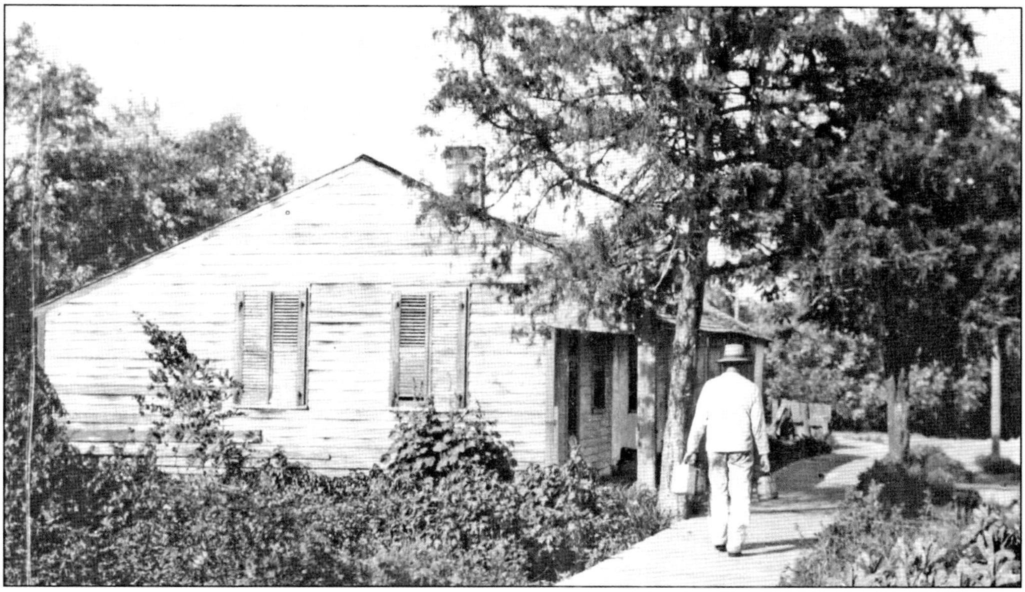

The John Davis house was on the north side of East Chestnut Street near the White River Bridge. The McCanna-Fraser Co. (later called the Wisconsin Condensed Milk Co.), whose offices were across the street, bought the property in 1899, removed the house, and built a cold storage warehouse. In 1909, the former Veteran's Saloon was moved to the property. That building served as a feed store, can plant, warehouse, and Hi-Liter Graphics headquarters until demolished in 2001.

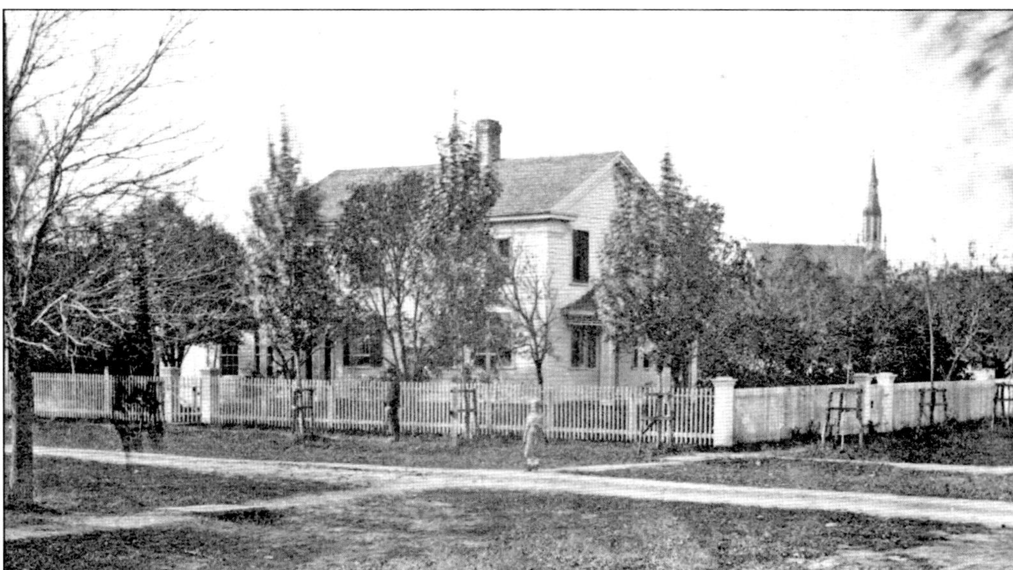

When Charles G. and Mary Ann Chandler Foltz wanted to build a new house in 1889, this house was moved south from the corner of Washington and Dyer (now North Kane) Streets to a lot next to Lincoln School where it still stands. The house that replaced it was torn down in 1928 to make way for the Masonic temple. The steeple of the Church of the Immaculate Conception (now St. Mary's school annex) is seen in the distance in this *c.* 1885 picture.

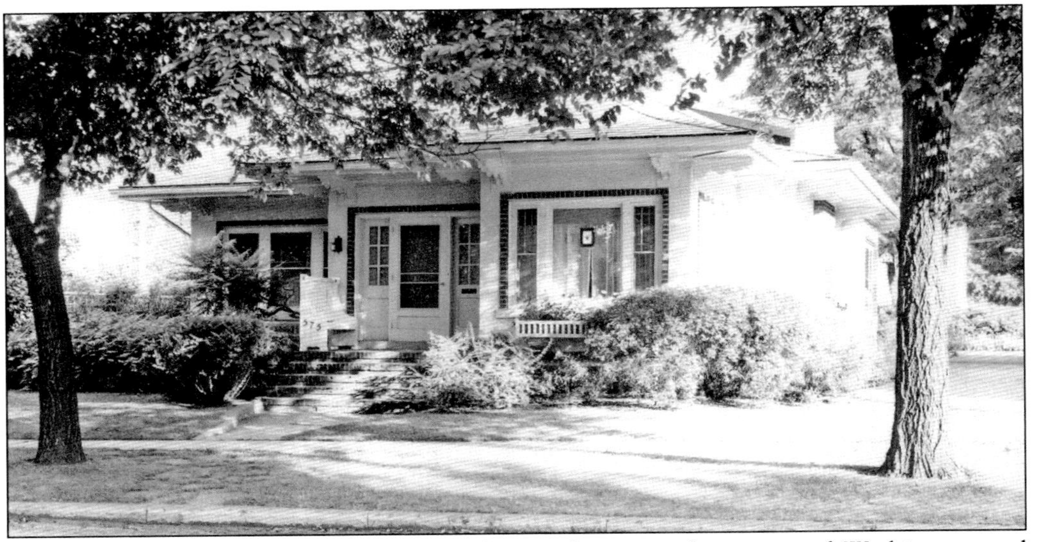

Gustave and Lettie Smith Luetten built this residence on the corner of Washington and Dyer (now Kane) Streets in 1924–1925 after the previous house had been razed. Luetten, a contractor, and partner Frank Schwartz built several houses in Burlington. In 1934, Ferd and Louise Roesing Robers bought this house, which they owned until their deaths, in 1986 and 1996, respectively. Robers had several businesses over the years, including excavating, trucking, and dredging. A title insurance company now occupies the building.

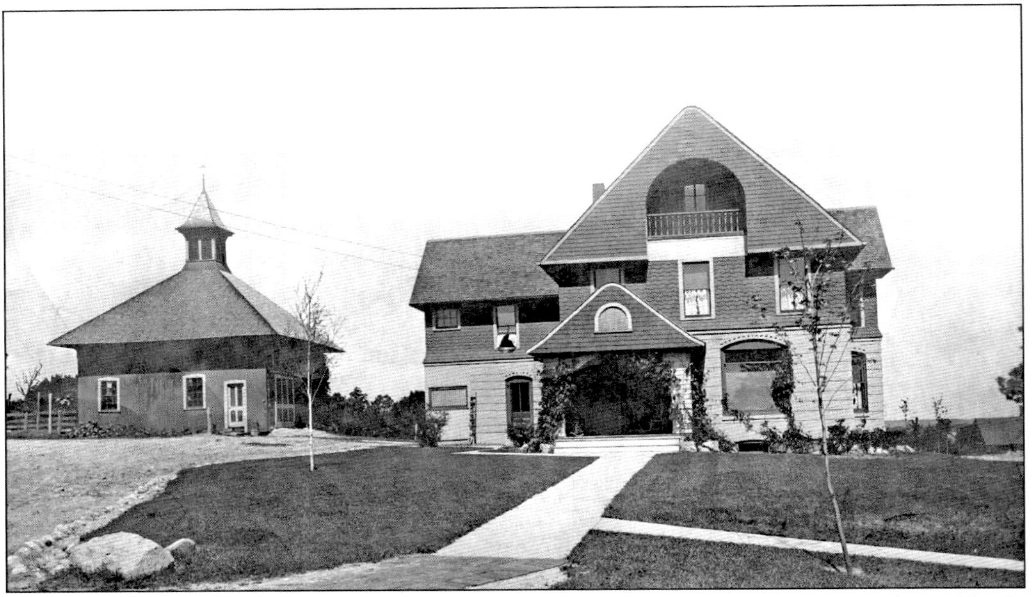

In 1893, Albert F. Ransom bought property at Storle Avenue and James Street from Ole O. Storle and built this house, moving in with his family in 1895. Ransom, who invented the Stay-On horse blanket, patented in 1891, helped found the Burlington Blanket Co. In 1904, newly married daughter Katherine and husband, Ernest H. Foltz, moved in, living here until 1920. In 1955, Mrs. Dorine Breske and father, Harry Boehne, started the Burlington Nursing Home here. The house is now an adult-care facility called Burlington Manor.

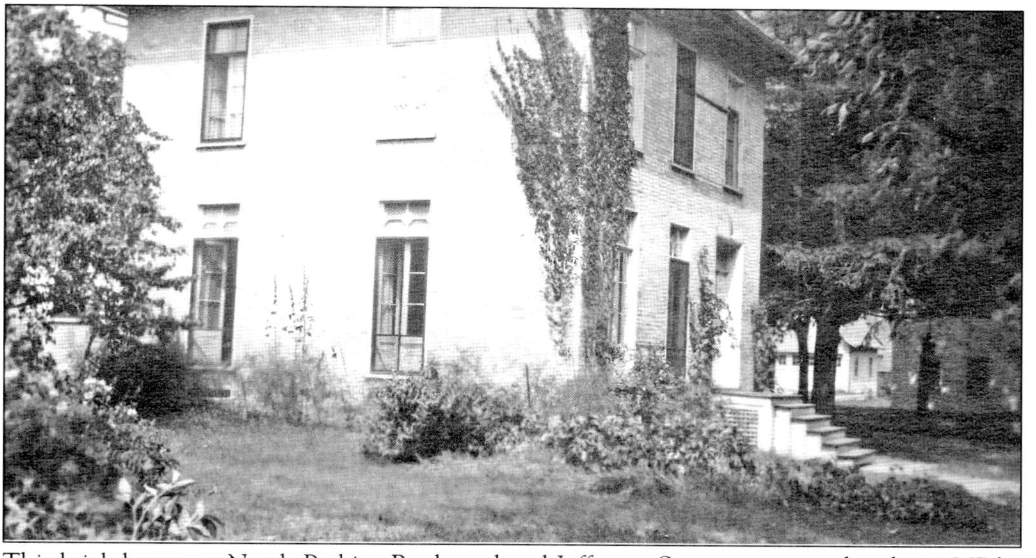

This brick house, at North Perkins Boulevard and Jefferson Street, was completed in 1867 by Henry Neuhaus, with woodwork handmade by John Heinrich Rueter. Neuhaus was a merchant, selling groceries, crockery, jewelry, and dry goods. His store building, later housing other businesses, including Lee Herrman's Jewelry, is now part of the Bank One building. Neuhaus was also a beekeeper. In the 1881 season, he reportedly produced more honey, according to the number of bees, than any other man in this country.

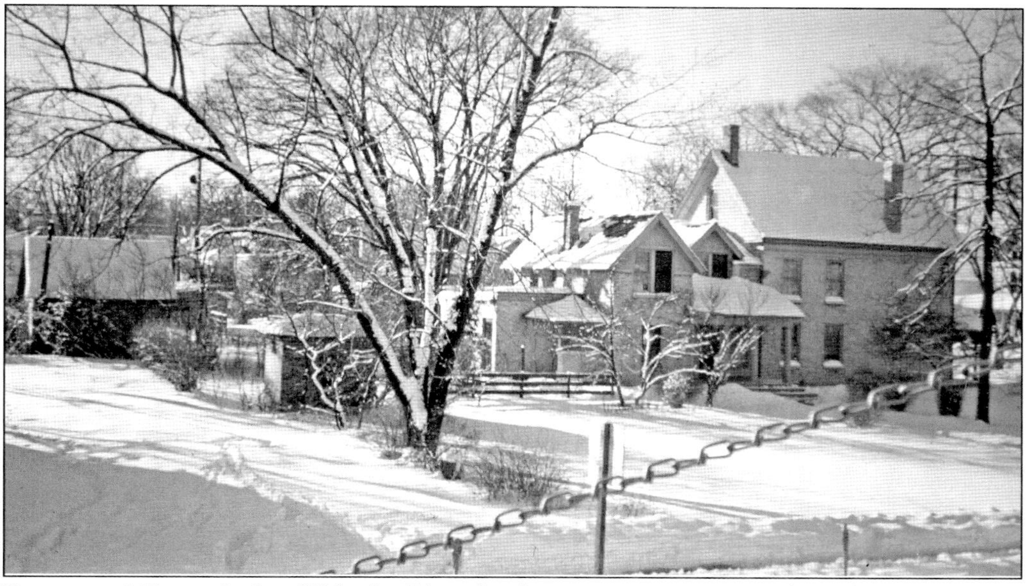

Eugene and Emma Jucker Wehmhoff bought this property at Pine and Washington Streets from the Caleb P. and Elizabeth Ann Eddy Barns estate in 1880. Barns was an early Burlington lawyer and banker. The Wehmhoffs, who owned a jewelry and millinery store, added to the house over the years. The Wehmhoff children bequeathed the property to the City for park purposes, and the house and other buildings were razed. Now called Wehmhoff Square, the park is home to the Burlington Historical Society's Pioneer Log Cabin.

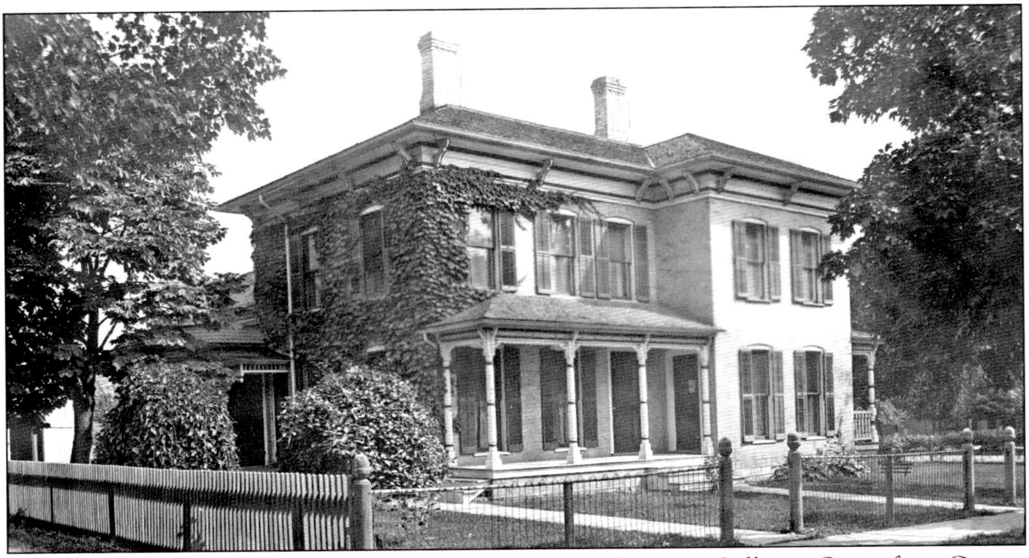

Charles B. and Elizabeth Borngesser Wagner bought this house on Jefferson Street from George W. French, a carpenter, in 1876. Wagner, who owned a hardware store, added a cornice, a frame addition to the rear, and later, a conservatory with bay, to the dining room. The City razed the house in 1976, after acquiring the property, which had been unoccupied for several years. The property is now occupied by the City's police and court building.

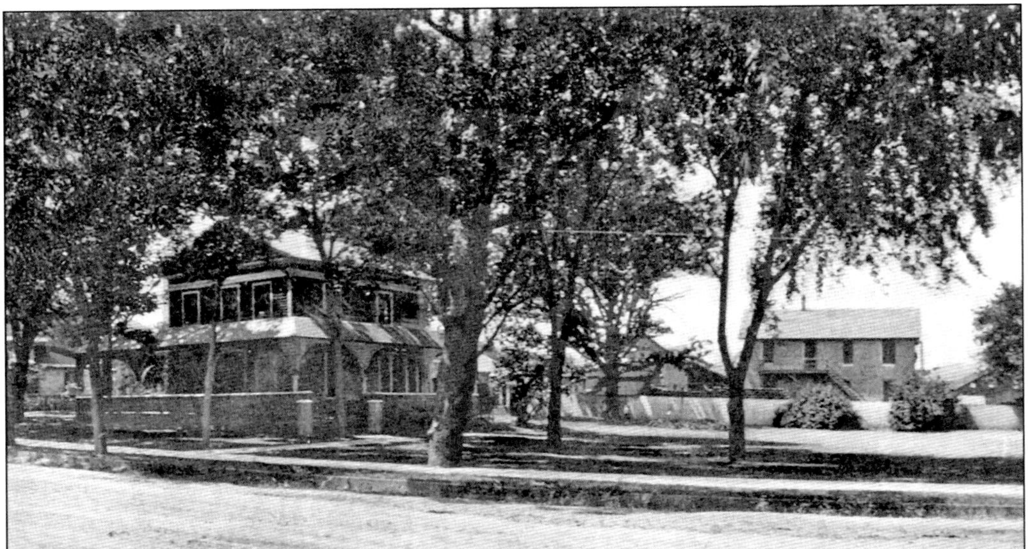

George Wilbur bought the Pliny and Ellen Conkey Perkins homestead on Geneva Street (now Milwaukee Avenue) in 1886, using part of the land for a lumber yard. In 1894, Robert G. Fraser, of the McCanna-Fraser cheese and butter company, bought the residence (left) and three lots and remodeled the house, adding a fireplace of large red, white, and blue granite boulders—all from this area. After Fraser moved, the house was rented by several parties, including the Business Men's Association. The main part of the house was moved near Bohner's Lake in 1939, where it has since been used as a tavern.

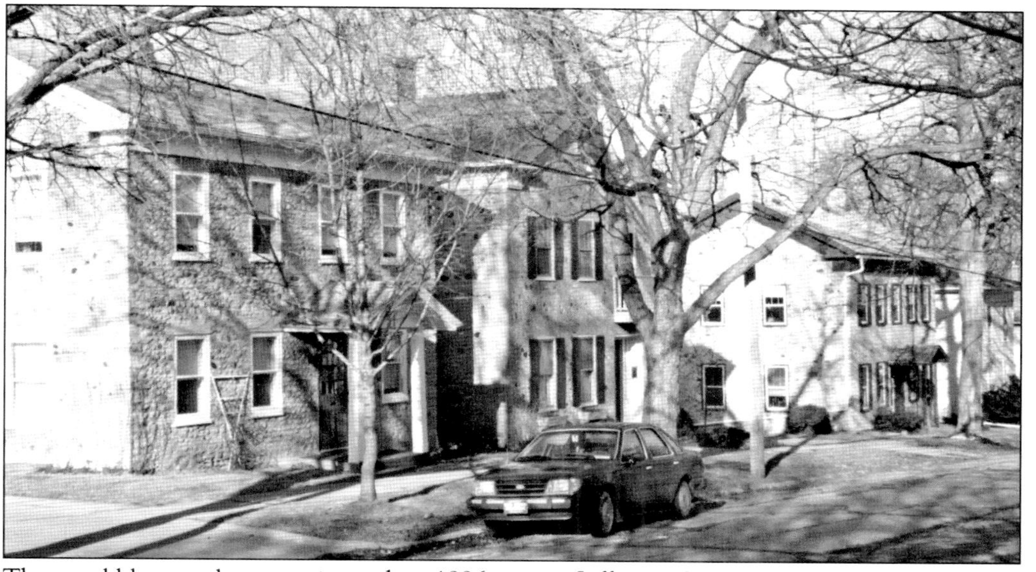

These cobblestone houses, pictured in 1996, sit on Jefferson Street just east of the Hillside. The middle house has its gable end to the street; the other two are set parallel. Joseph Thering bought the house at the left from the Ephraim Perkins estate in 1851. Two German carpenters, John Heinrich Rueter and John Heinrich Burhans, bought the center and right lots in 1851, gathered cobblestones while excavating the foundations, and completed their houses, which shared a common well on the lot line, in 1854.

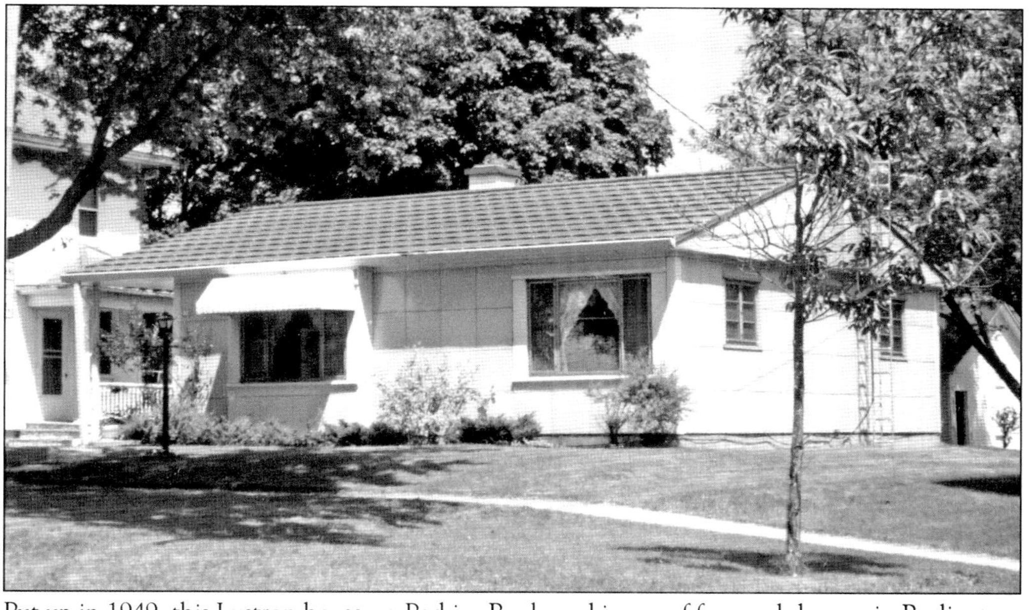

Put up in 1949, this Lustron house on Perkins Boulevard is one of four such houses in Burlington. Others are on Origen Street, Randolph Street, and McHenry Street. The pre-fabricated all-steel Lustron houses, conceived by Carl Strandlund as an answer to the housing shortage after World War II, were manufactured in a former airplane plant in Columbus, Ohio. Less than 3,000 Lustrons were made before the federal government foreclosed on the company in 1950.

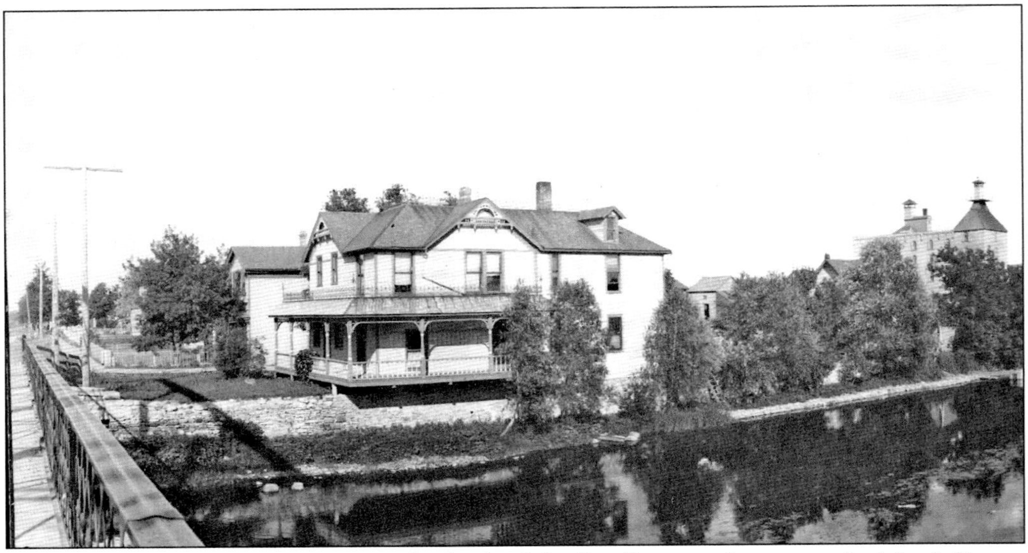

This house, pictured *c.* 1905, sat on the bank of the Fox River at the east end of the Jefferson Street Bridge (bridge railing at left) from 1892 until 1943, when the land was donated to the City for park purposes. The upper portion of the malt house is seen at right. The house, built by Mrs. Elise Diener and family, was also owned by Chris Oldenburg and Charles Beller before Albert and Eda Meinhardt bought the property and donated it to the City.

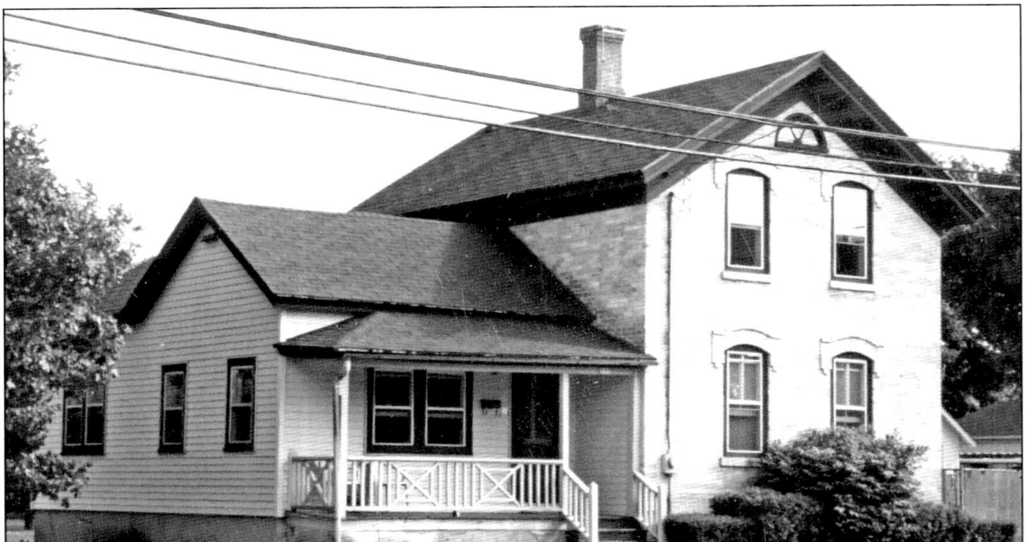

Sitting on East State Street opposite the intersection with Capital Street, this house, pictured in 1997, was built in 1882 by Gerhard and Gertrude Underberg Vande Sand, replacing a log house in which the first nine of their ten children were born. Following Gertrude's death in 1903 (Gerhard died in 1896), Arnold Hegeman bought the house. Subsequent owners included William and Ida Garnatz, William and Emilie Bartelt, Lillian Daberkow, Frank and Katie Zarneke, Emma Richter, Joel Richter, and Roger and Joy Richter Bieneman.

Five

Churches and Schools

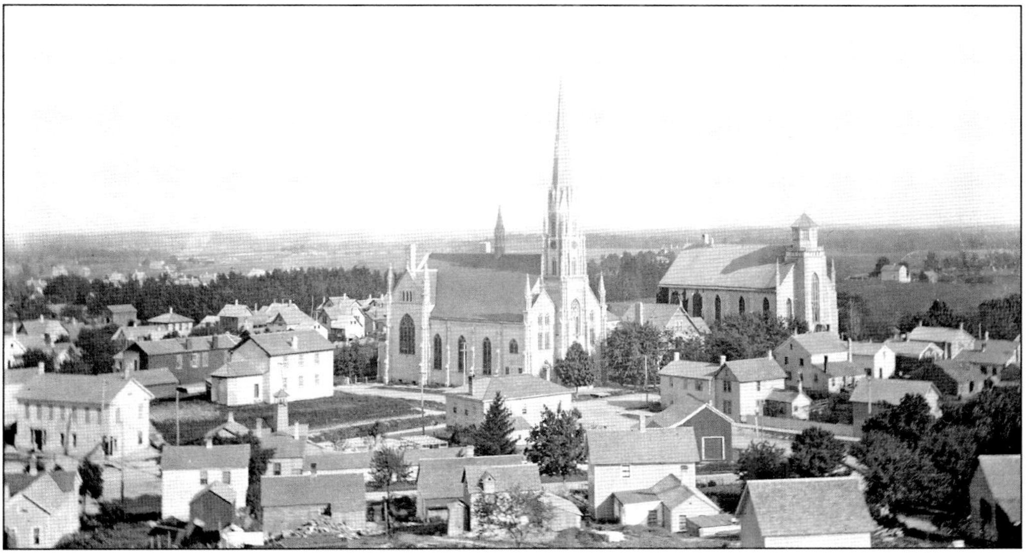

The first three Catholic Church buildings are shown *c.* 1900, looking southeast toward McHenry and Liberty (now State) Streets. St. Sebastian's, with the rear addition (left center), served from 1844 to 1859. The Church of the Immaculate Conception (right center), whose cornerstone was laid in 1855, served until 1891. St. Mary's (center) was dedicated in 1891 and rededicated in 1979 after a fire. Also shown are the Yanny building (lower left) on the Jefferson Street corner; the former Hillside hotel, which obscures some of the 1891 church; and the fire-bell tower on Wentker's wooden saloon building (the top of the tower appears near the base of the St. Sebastian's building).

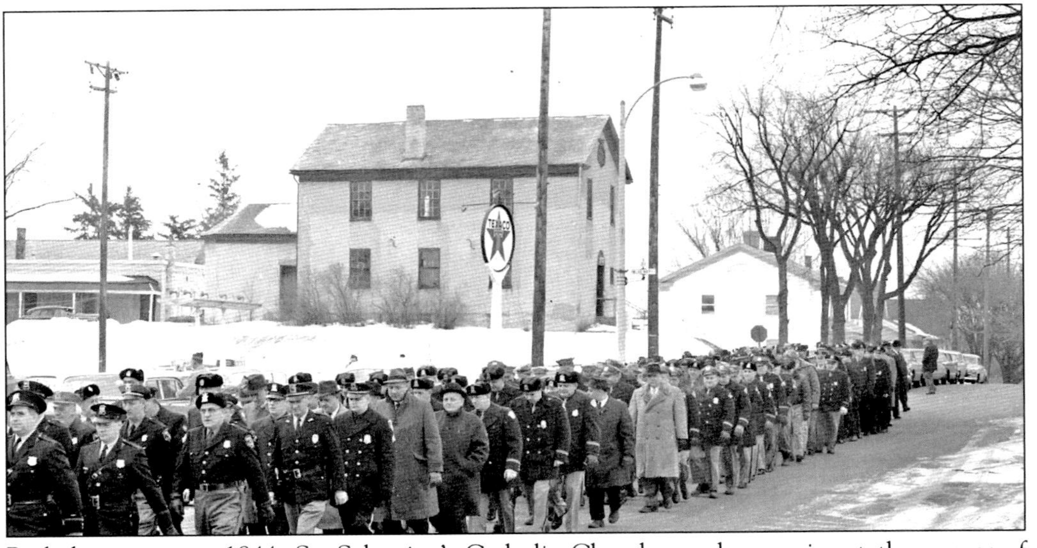

Built beginning in 1844, St. Sebastian's Catholic Church stood on a rise at the corner of Liberty (now State) and McHenry Streets. It served as the parish school after the Church of the Immaculate Conception was dedicated in 1859. In 1895, the St. Eustachius Society, a benevolent group that aided members and their families at the time of sickness and death, bought the property. Before the building was razed in 1965 to make way for a parking lot, the Veterans of Foreign Wars used it as their clubhouse.

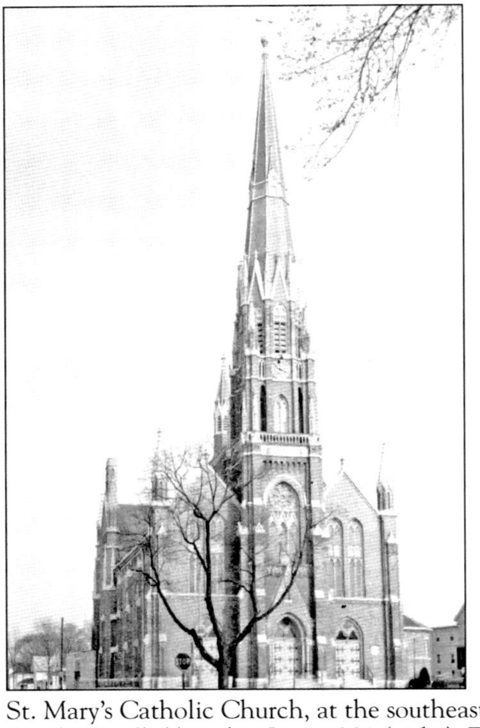

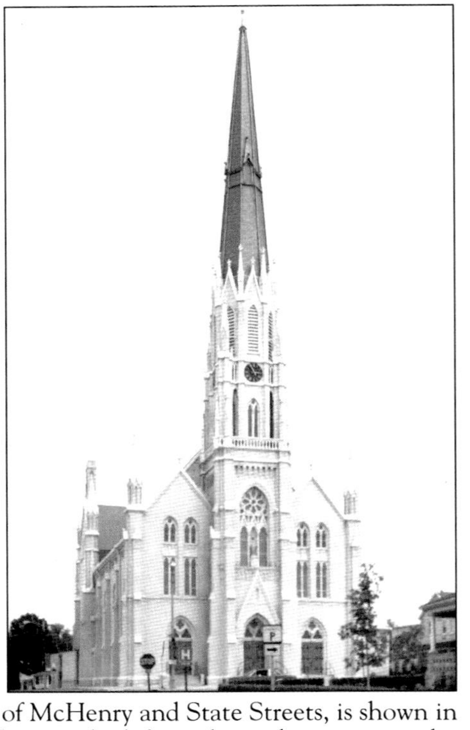

St. Mary's Catholic Church, at the southeast corner of McHenry and State Streets, is shown in April 1976 (left) and in June 1981 (right). The building on the left was burned in a spectacular fire in July 1977. The building on the right is the church after it had been rebuilt.

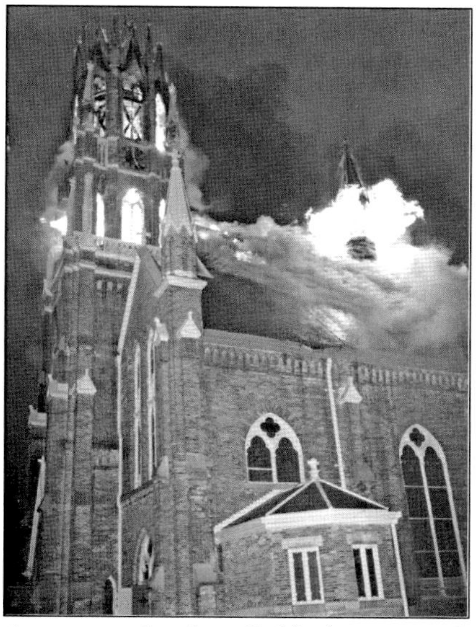

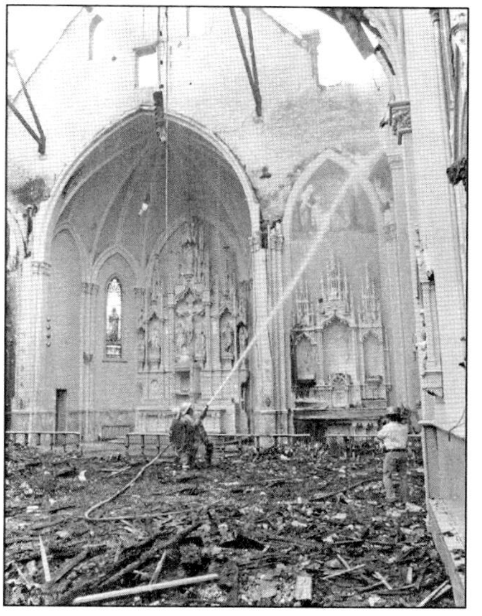

A spectacular fire (left) that started in the steeple of St. Mary's Catholic Church on July 24, 1977, destroyed the roof and gutted the church (right). But parishioners and others in the community came together with moral and financial support to rebuild one of the city's important landmarks. The new church was dedicated on December 7, 1979.

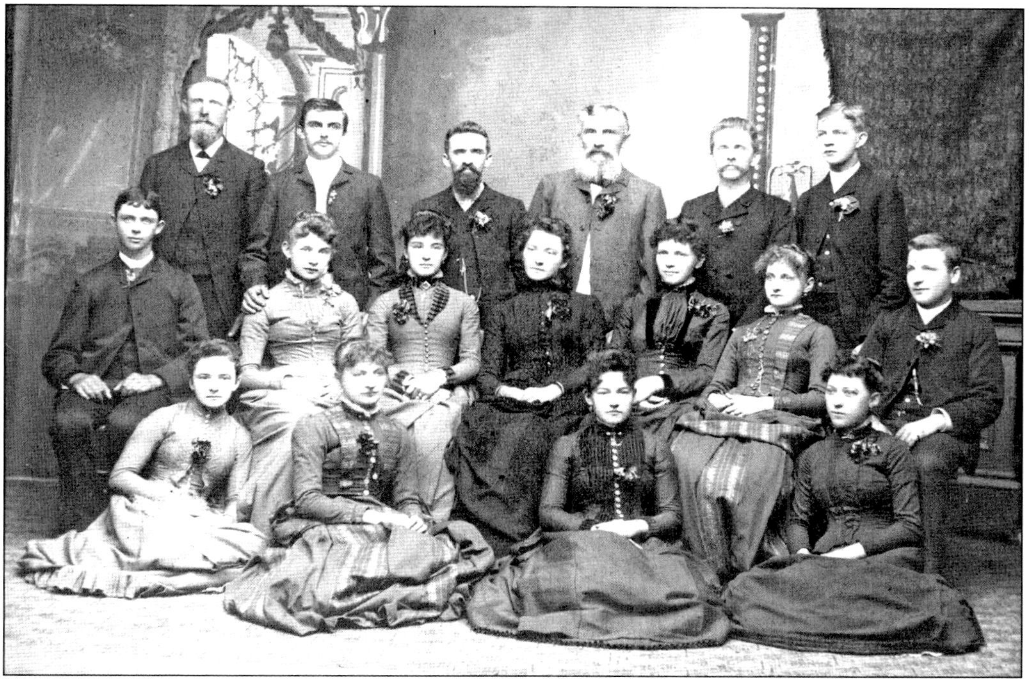

St. Mary's choir in 1889 included: (front, left to right) Mary Finke Gill, Emma Wagner Trier, Mary Brehm Mathews, and Eda Klingele Haitz; (middle) Willie Prasch, Ella Reuschlein Reinardy, Annie Brehm Zwiebel, Barbara Prasch Finke, Carrie Rittman Woeste, Theresa Wagner, and Sim Reinardy; (back) Sylvester Prailes, Mr. Stuebig, Martin Prasch, Francis Reuschlein, Frank Prasch, and Joe Reuschlein.

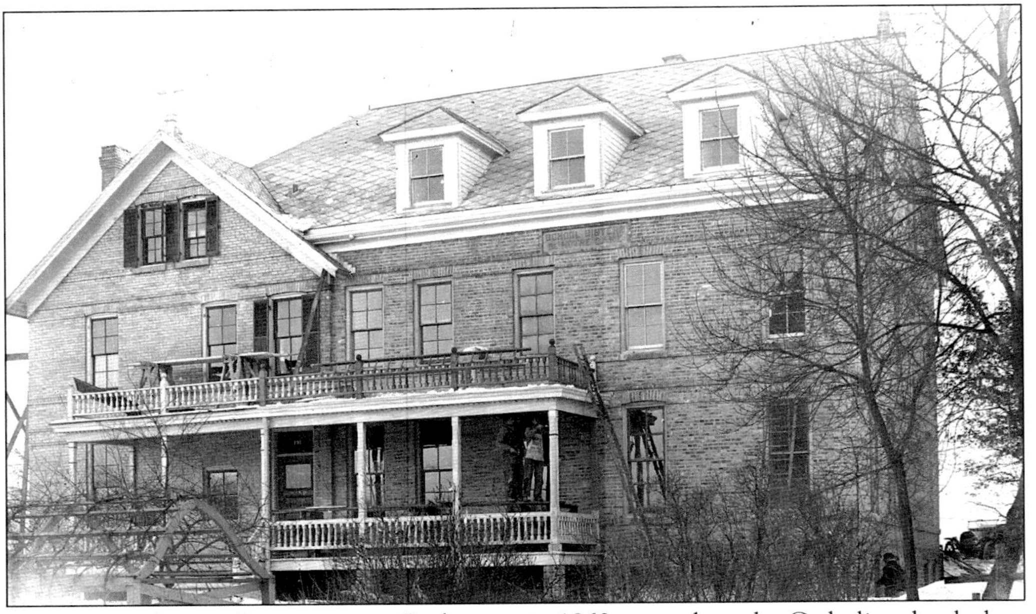

The Sisters of Notre Dame came to Burlington in 1860 to teach at the Catholic school, then called St. Joseph's. They lived for a few months on the first floor of the school building (now known as the Yanny building) at Jefferson and McHenry Streets, before moving to the old parsonage. In 1890, a new residence was built just east of the old one. In 1914, about the time of this picture, the frame portion of the residence was torn down and a brick addition was built.

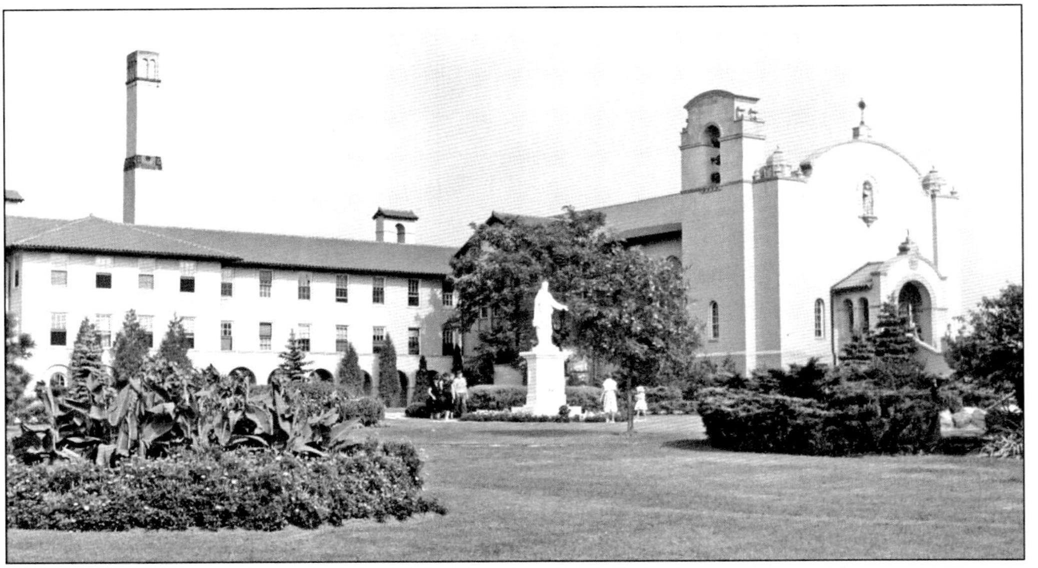

The Franciscan Fathers bought the Theresa Baumeister and Anton Kipp farms on County Trunk W near Highway 36 in 1929 and built a monastery and school, which were dedicated in 1931. Other facilities added over the years include a grotto area of nine acres added in 1935; a chapel replicating the Portiuncula at Assisi, Italy, constructed in 1940; an outdoor pavilion built in 1958; a retirement home for Franciscan friars built in 1992; and an assisted living facility, opened in 1999.

This frame church, shown c. 1900, was built in 1852 by Presbyterians on the southeast side of Geneva Street (now Milwaukee Avenue) near the Lewis Street intersection. In 1858, the Plymouth Congregational Church, made up largely of the Presbyterians, was organized and, in 1859, it acquired the building and property. This building was torn down in 1902 and replaced by a brick church building. During the construction, the congregation met in the former high school building, later called Lincoln School.

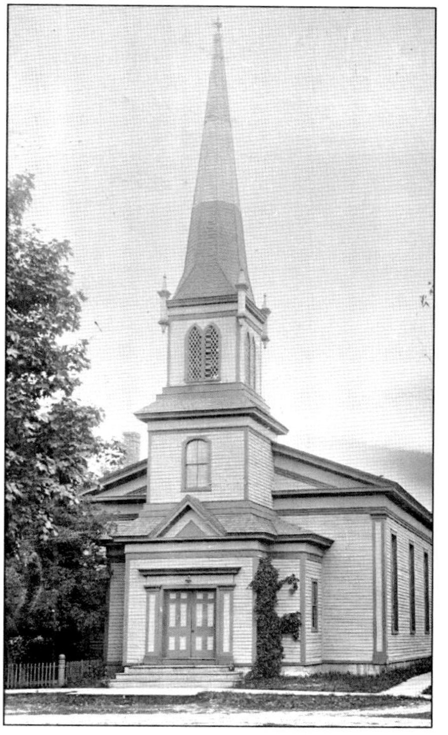

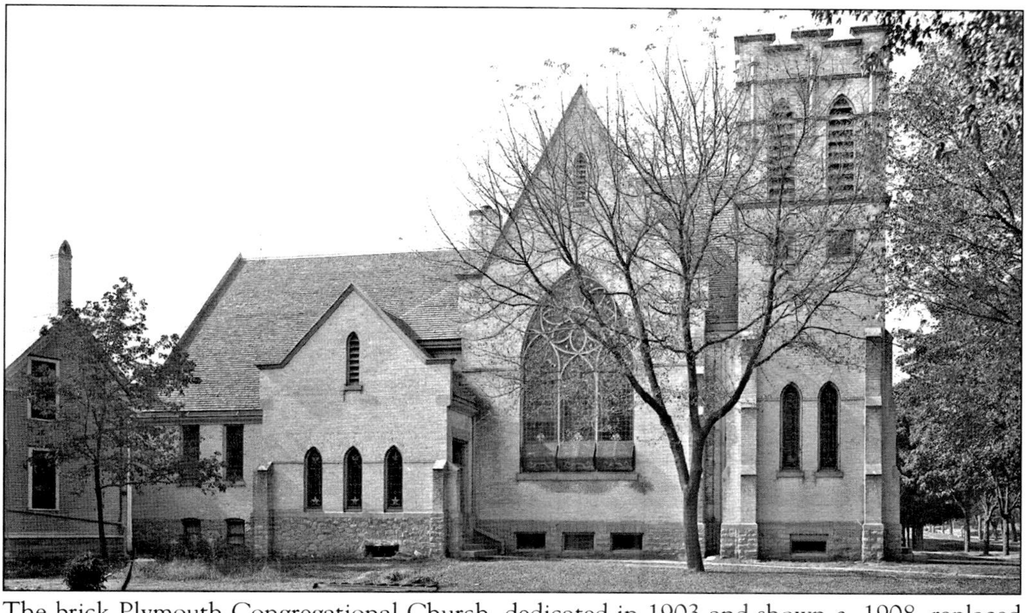

The brick Plymouth Congregational Church, dedicated in 1903 and shown c. 1908, replaced the earlier frame church. Eight stained glass windows, which had been in the frame building since 1891, were installed in the new building with some pieces added to make them fit. In 1951, an educational wing and chapel were added to the building. and in 1972, a narthex was built. The Plymouth Children's Center, a child care center and nursery school, also operates in church facilities.

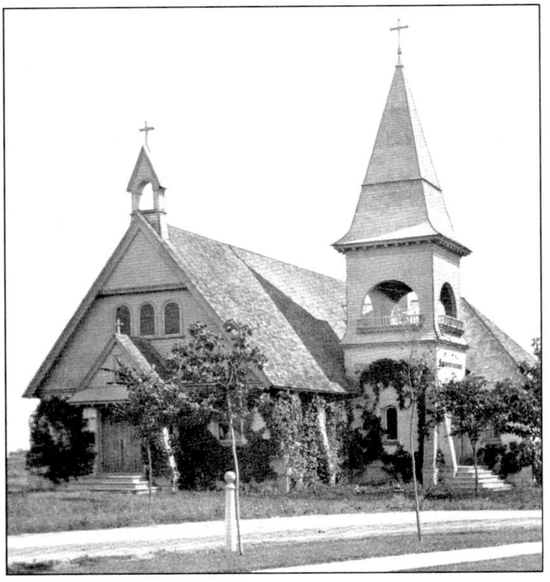

St. John the Divine Episcopal Church at Perkins Boulevard and Edward Street was dedicated in 1894, shortly before this picture. The stone for the basement came from the quarry at Voree, just west of Burlington. The brick was donated by Edward Brook of the Burlington Brick & Tile Co., located near Echo Lake. Before dedicating this building, church members met in a second-floor hall on the corner of Chestnut Street and Milwaukee Avenue and at the Cross Lutheran building, now the Historical Society Museum.

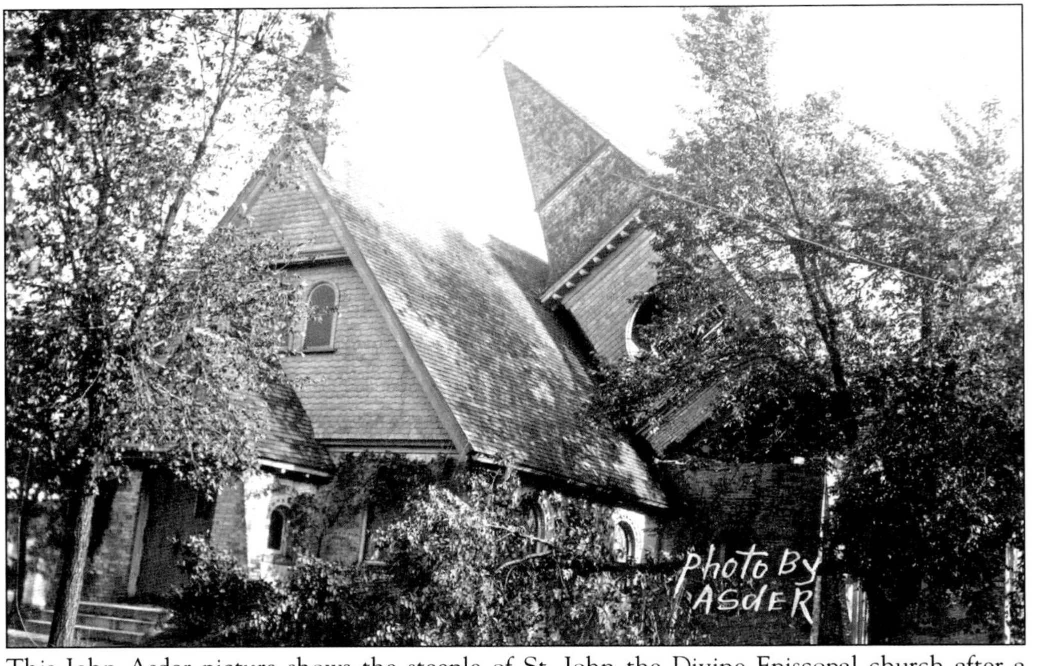

This John Asder picture shows the steeple of St. John the Divine Episcopal church after a terrific five-minute wind, rain, and hail storm on September 9, 1925. The storm caused the death of one man and serious injuries to another; blew down smokestacks at the Burlington Brass Works and at Klein's bottling plant and a number of chimneys on private homes; tore down trees and broke service poles, causing electric and telephone wires to go down; wrecked a number of buildings; broke many windows; and killed some farm animals. A falling chimney at the Citizen's Gas Co. punctured the gas reservoir and broke several valves and pipes causing gas service to be stopped for two weeks.

The Methodists bought a lot on the corner of State Street and Perkins Boulevard in 1903 and laid the cornerstone of this church in 1904. The basement was built of Voree quarry stone from the White River near what is now Highway 11 West. The superstructure was built of Burlington bricks manufactured by the Burlington Brick & Tile Co. on the northeast side of Echo Lake. The building, seen looking west across Perkins Boulevard, was dedicated in April 1905.

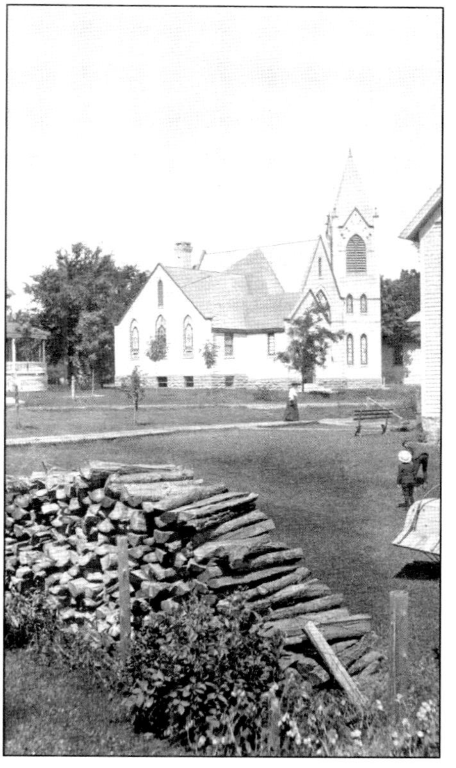

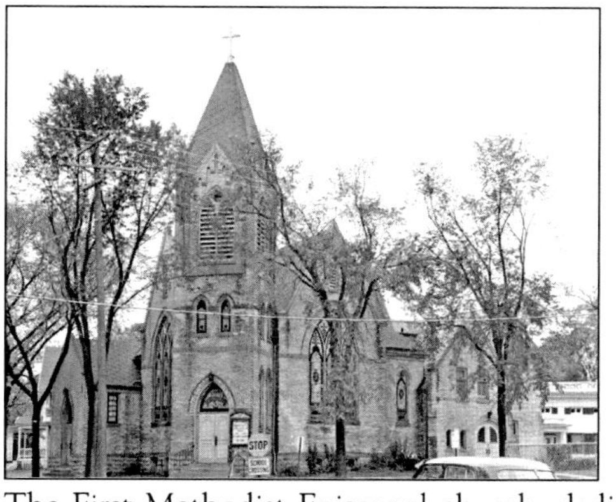

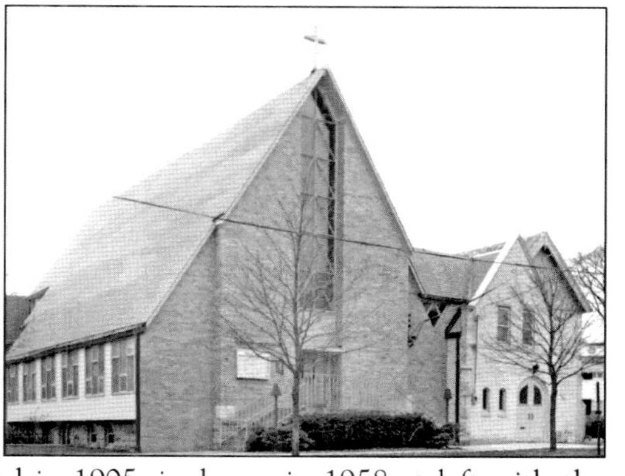

The First Methodist Episcopal church, dedicated in 1905, is shown in 1958 at left with the 1928 Fellowship Hall addition. Later in 1958, the original church building was demolished and replaced by the building at right c. 1976. The congregation broke ground in 2005 for a new building The church grew out of the Bible Christian Church—which was organized in 1862, became Methodist in 1884, and was discontinued in 1888—whose building was on Burlington Road (now Highway 142). After reorganizing, the members met until 1905 at the German Methodist Church that once stood at Washington Street and North Perkins Boulevard.

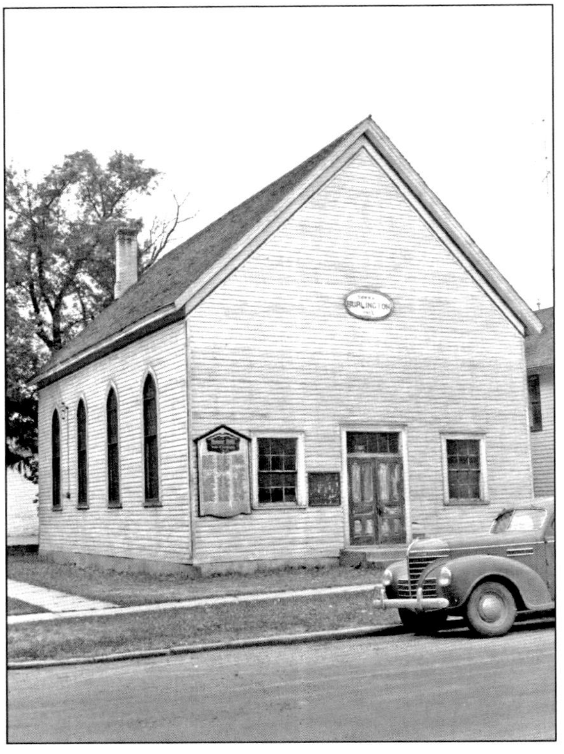

This building, shown shortly before being torn down in 1954 to make way for a telephone company building, was built as the German Methodist church in 1874 on the southwest corner of Washington Street and what is now North Perkins Boulevard. The First Methodist Episcopal church bought the property in 1922 and resold it in 1924 to the Town of Burlington, which used the building as the Town Hall until 1954. Burlington's little theatre group, the Haylofters, also used the building from 1938 until 1947.

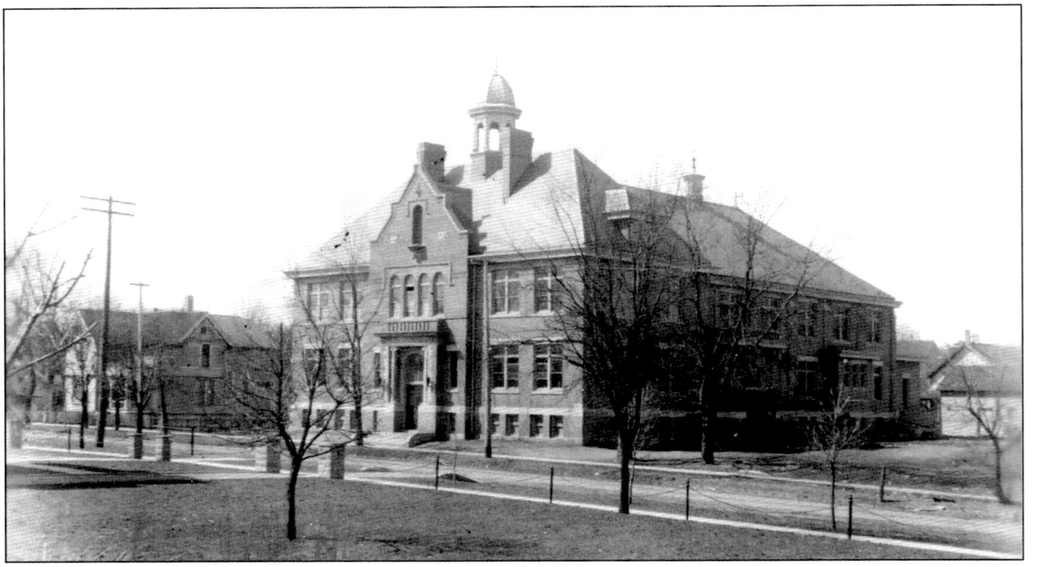

St. Charles Borromeo Catholic Church, on Conkey Street between Lewis and Chestnut Streets, was dedicated in November 1910. Located on the former Voorhees & Fiske planing mill property, the church building included four school rooms on the street side. The school opened in September 1910 with 112 scholars taught by three Dominican Sisters from Racine. The Gustave C. Rasch house, at left, was moved in 1956 to Edward Street to make way for a school playground.

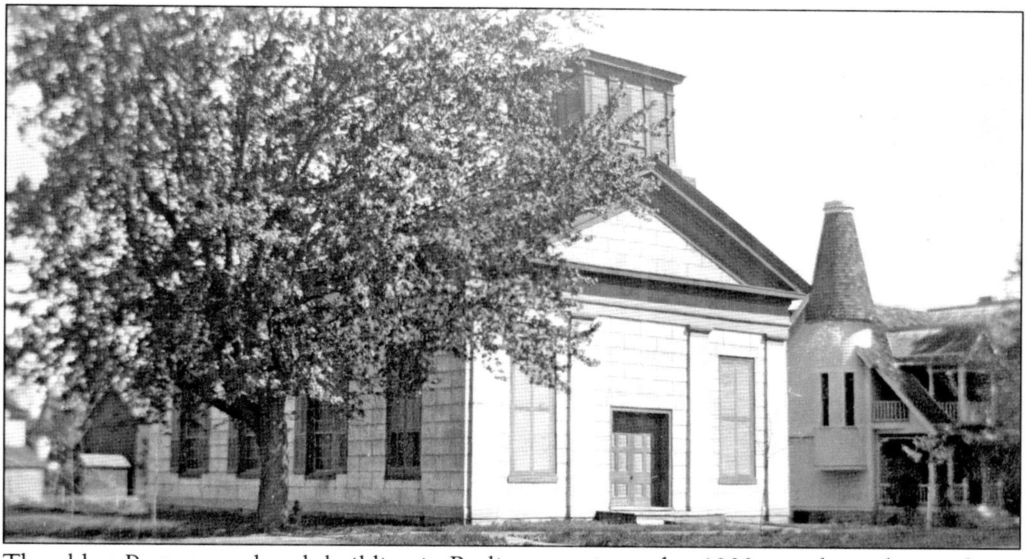

The oldest Protestant church building in Burlington, pictured c. 1900, stands on the northeast corner of Jefferson and North Kane Streets. It was built as the Union Free church in 1852 by a small group of Baptists, Unitarians, and German Methodists. The Baptists became the property owners in 1863. In 1922, the Baptist society of Burlington was formally dissolved and declared extinct by the circuit court. No services had been held since 1917. The Holy Cross Lutheran congregation bought the building in 1923 and used it first as its social hall and Sunday school and then as a church.

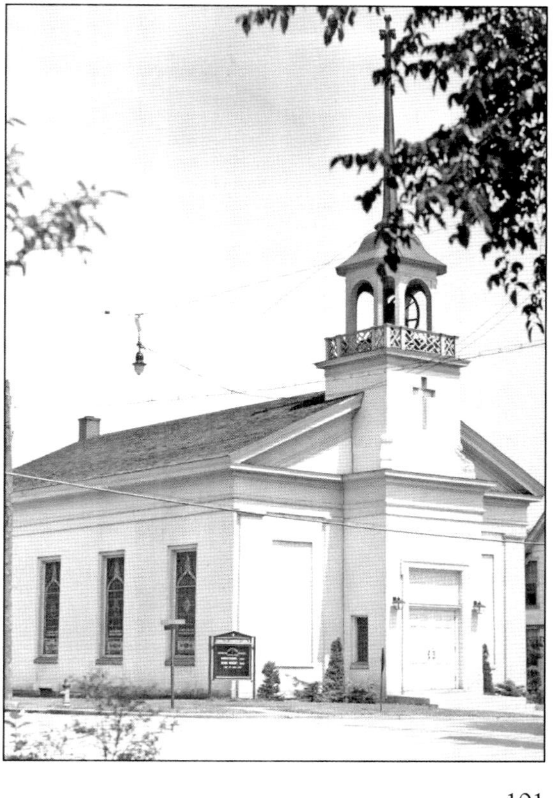

The Holy Cross Lutheran congregation, which bought the former Baptist church in 1923 for use as a social hall and Sunday school, remodeled the building (pictured in the 1950s) and used it as a church from 1940 until 1963. In 1963, the congregation moved to a new building on Chapel Terrace near Highway 11 East. The bell that had rung over the congregation's previous two church buildings now rings in the current church's tower. The Lutherans sold this building to a Baptist group in 1963, and it was later bought by its current occupant, the Church of the Nazarene.

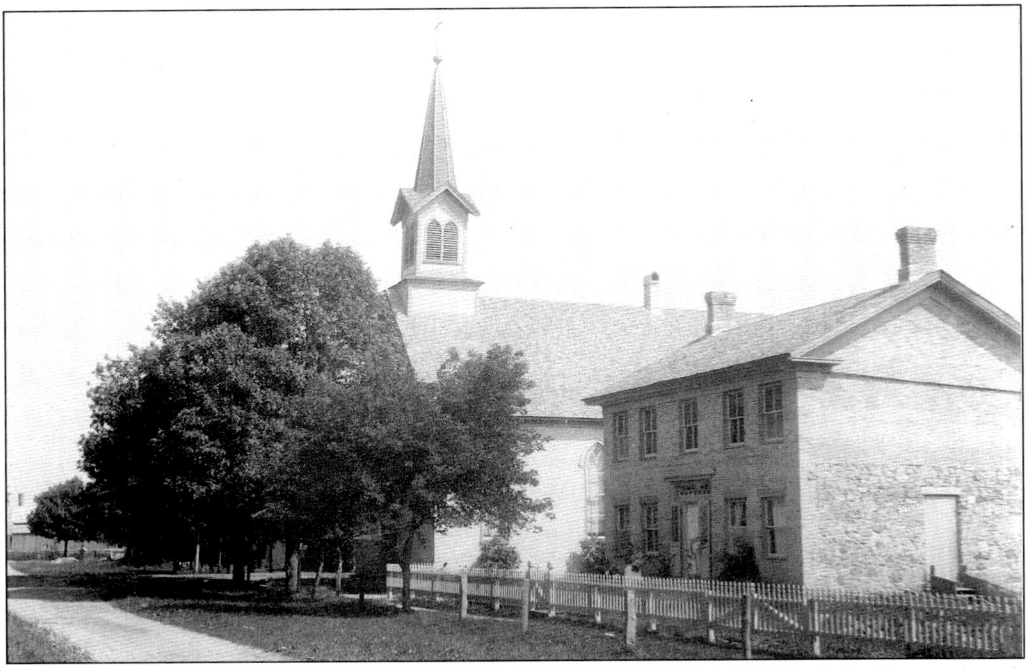

In 1883, the German Evangelical Lutheran Society withdrew from St. John's Lutheran church and built the Holy Cross Lutheran church, pictured in 1900, at Jefferson and West (now Perkins Boulevard) Streets. The stone parsonage at the right was replaced in 1918. In 1940, the growing congregation, which had bought the former Baptist church at Jefferson and Dyer (now Kane) Streets in 1923, moved its services there and used this building as its social hall and Sunday school. After the church moved again in 1963, Mrs. Antoinette Meinhardt Fulton, first president of the Burlington Historical Society, bought the church building and donated it to the Society for use as a museum.

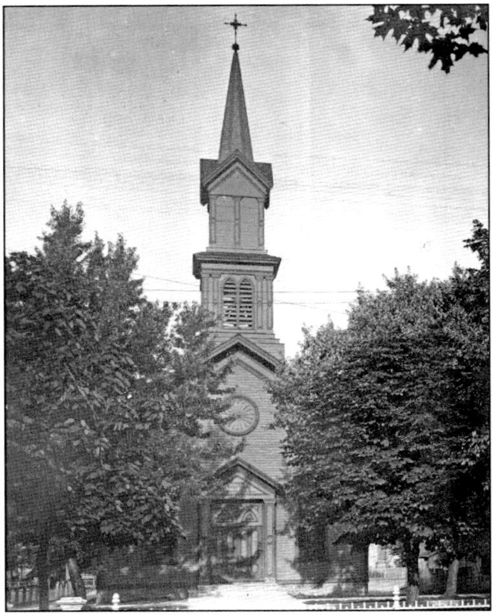

The St. John's Lutheran Church, pictured here in the early 1900s, replaced an earlier church building on the same site at the corner of Pine and Madison Streets. The church, which was organized in August 1858, also put up a parsonage in 1887 and a new school building in 1895 that replaced an earlier one. The school building was enlarged in 1908 and a second story was added. That same year, a new hall was dedicated.

The exterior of St. John's Lutheran Church at Pine and Madison Streets was remodeled in 1940. The congregation remained in this building, pictured in 1949, until 1980, when a new church was completed on Westridge Avenue. The congregation had opened a school at that location in 1962 and built a parsonage there in 1974. This church building, which housed a child care center starting in 1998, was sold in 2003, and the building was razed to make way for a parking lot in 2004.

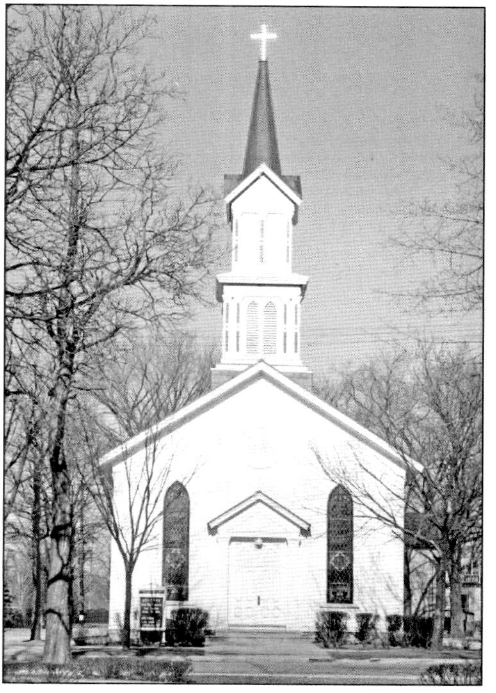

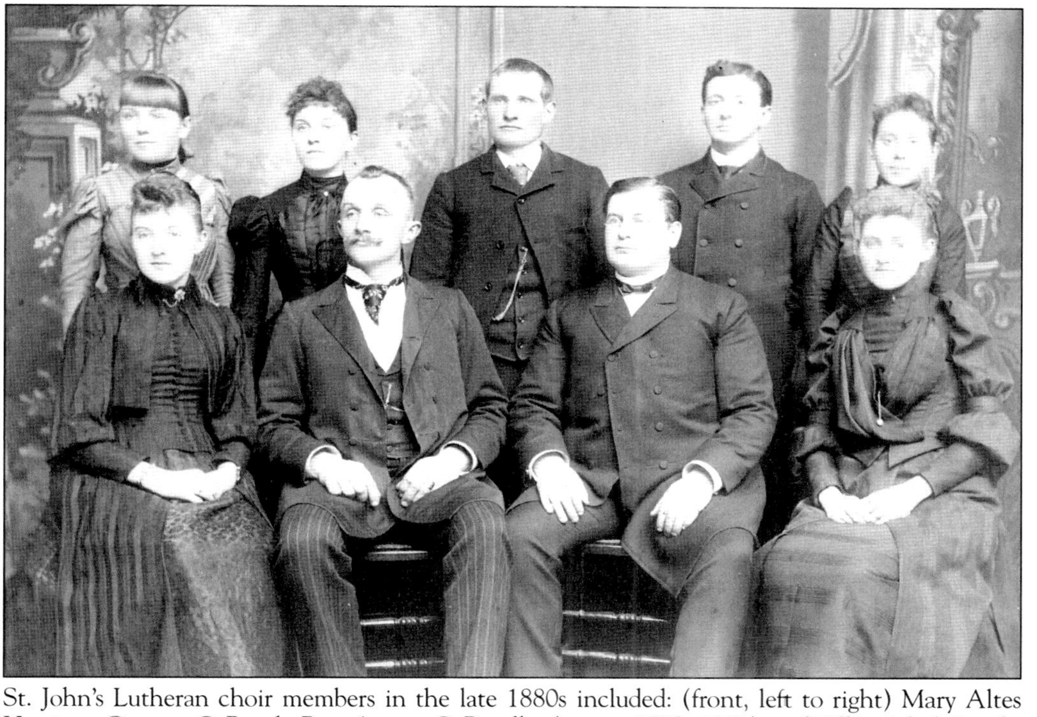

St. John's Lutheran choir members in the late 1880s included: (front, left to right) Mary Altes Hastings, Gustave C. Rasch, Rev. August C. Bendler (pastor, 1883–1890), and Tillie Geheb Rasch; and (back) Ida Kees Mole, Minnie Kees, William Gerloff, unidentified, and Louisa Wald.

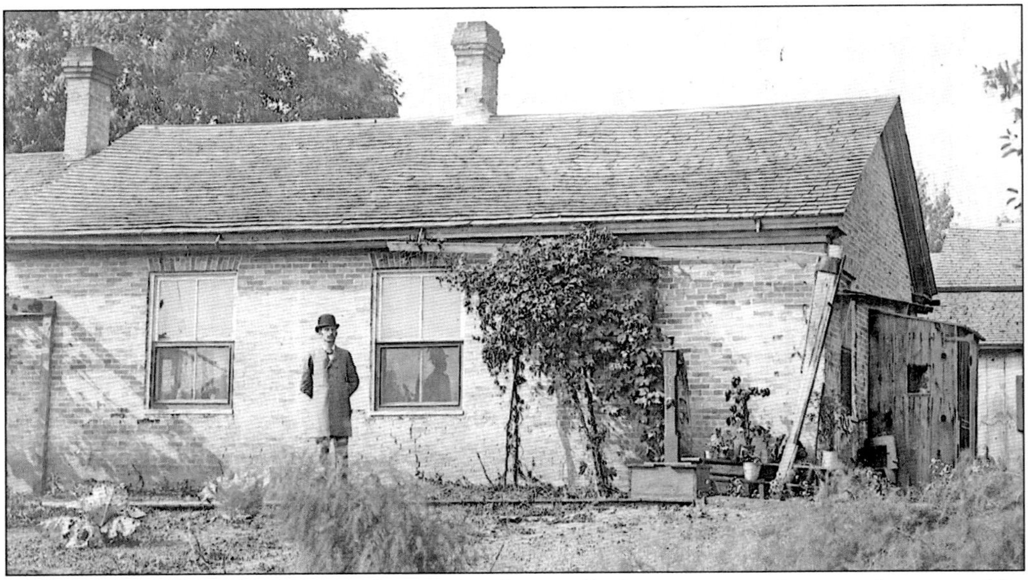

This brick building, built in 1840, was the first in Burlington erected expressly as a public school house. Sitting near the corner of Madison and Dodge Streets, it was also used by some Protestant denominations and other community groups as a meeting place. This *c.* 1890 picture by C. E. Clench shows Rev. L. A. Pettibone of Plymouth Congregational Church visiting the site. The building, now called Whitman School, was moved by the Burlington Historical Society in 1986 to Schmaling Park on Beloit Street.

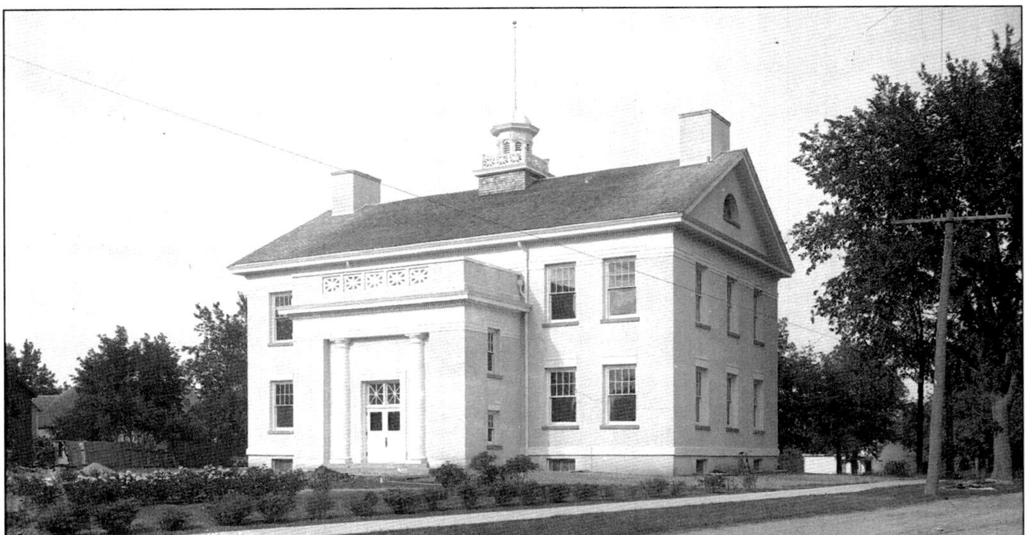

Used primarily as a manufacturing facility after it ceased being used as a school in 1896, the former Union School building at State and Dyer (now North Kane) Streets, originally built in 1859, was remodeled and reopened in 1912 as Lincoln School. Entrance wings were added on both the west and east sides, the interior plan was changed, and the exterior was stuccoed. Kindergarten and early primary classes were held here until 1981. School district offices now occupy the building.

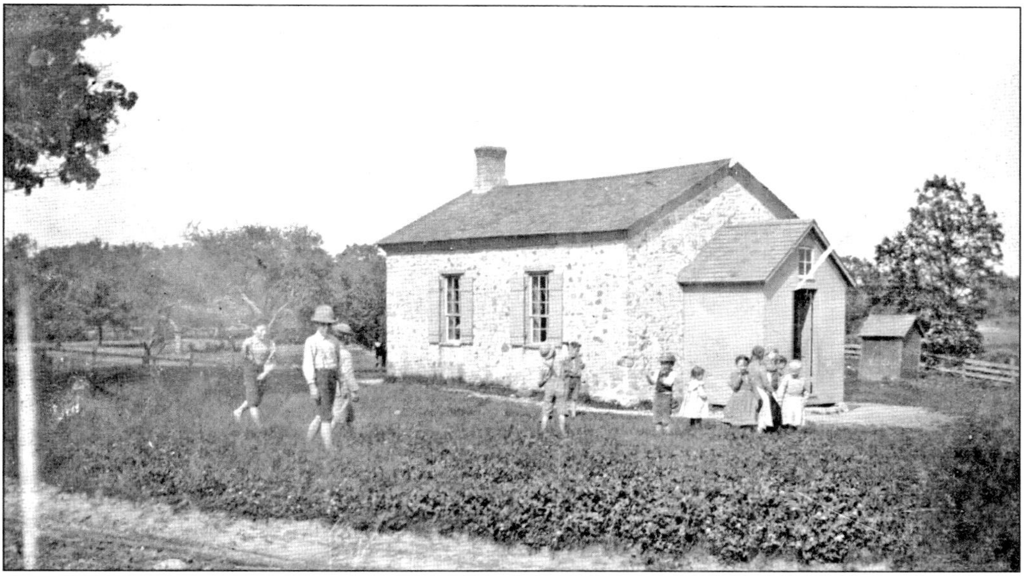

At a meeting at Anthony Bohner's home in December 1847, the residents of Town of Burlington School District No. 7 decided to build a frame school on land that Christopher Winkler donated on the southeast corner of his farm on McHenry Road (now County Trunk P). Before construction started, however, it was decided to build the stone school house, pictured here *c.* 1900. Following orders from the county superintendent of schools, the district built a new brick school in 1908.

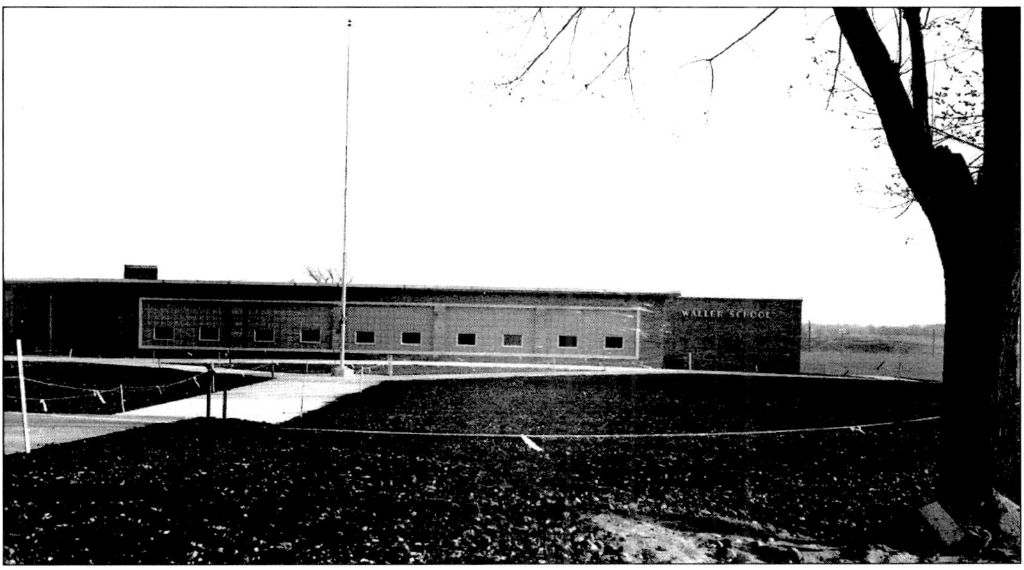

In 1953, the Waller property at Gardner Avenue and Randolph Street was chosen as the site for a new grade school, which opened as Waller School in November 1955 with nine classrooms in use. The school, to which additions were built in 1960 and 1963, was named for George Waller, an attorney and long-time school board member, who with his mother, Harriet, and sister, Annie, owned the property. Harriett Waller began the Christmas Seal program in Burlington and Annie carried it on for many years.

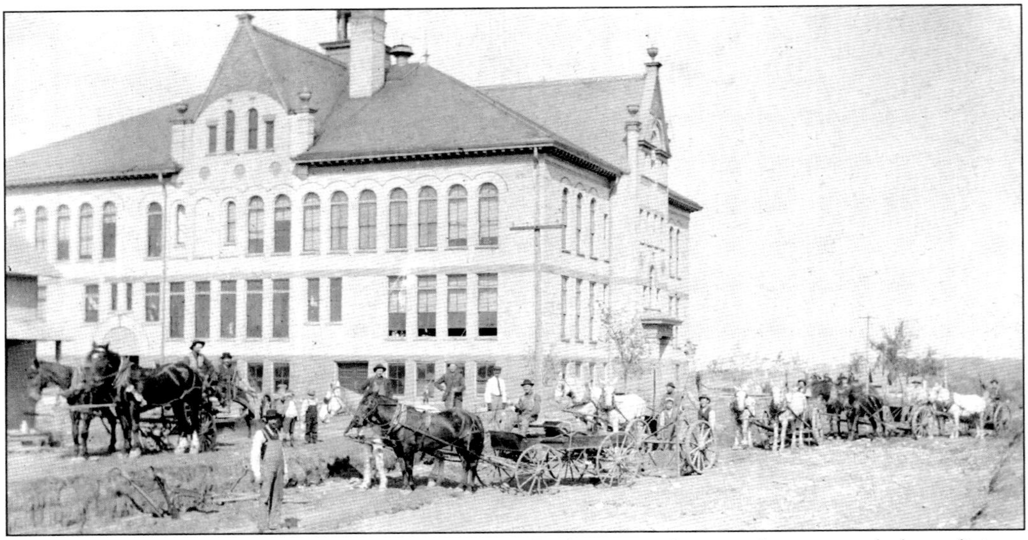

The Conkey Street School was built in 1896–1897 after several years of overcrowded conditions at the school house at State and Kane Streets. Burlington native and former school principal Edwin R. Smith, out of whose canteen President Abraham Lincoln had taken a drink during the Civil War, spoke at the dedication. The school, named Cooper School in 1940 for former Burlington resident Congressman Henry Allen Cooper, housed both grade and high school students until 1925, when a new high school was built.

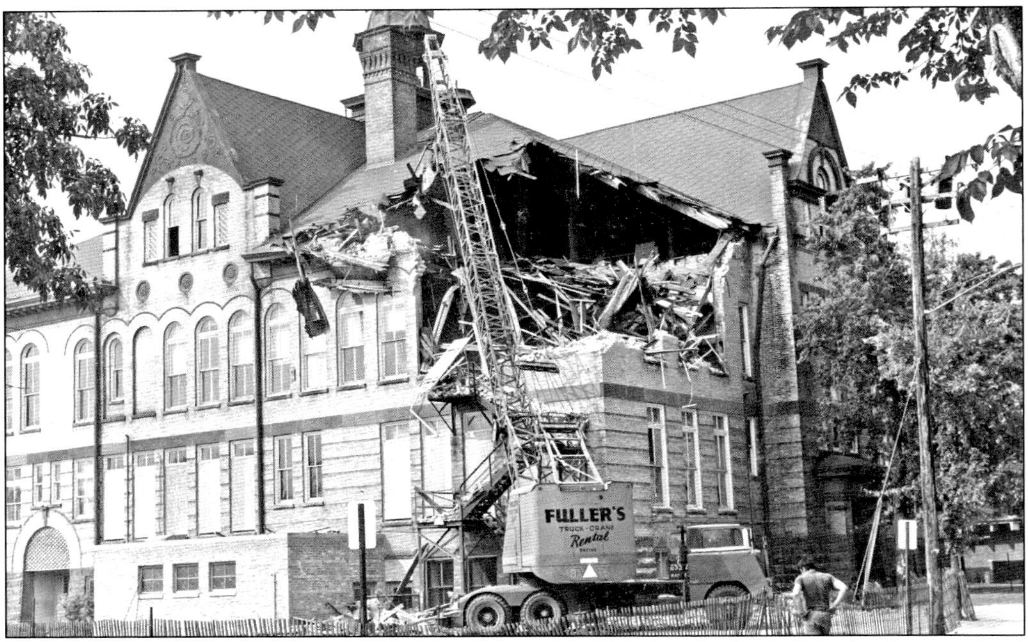

After a new school building was erected on the Cooper School grounds in 1968, the former school building, dedicated in 1897, was demolished, as this August 1970 picture indicates. The site is now a school parking area. At various times during its existence, the school provided a room for the Burlington Historical Society to display some of the community's artifacts. In 2004, a memorial for Revolutionary War soldier Aaron Smith, who was buried near the old school site, was dedicated.

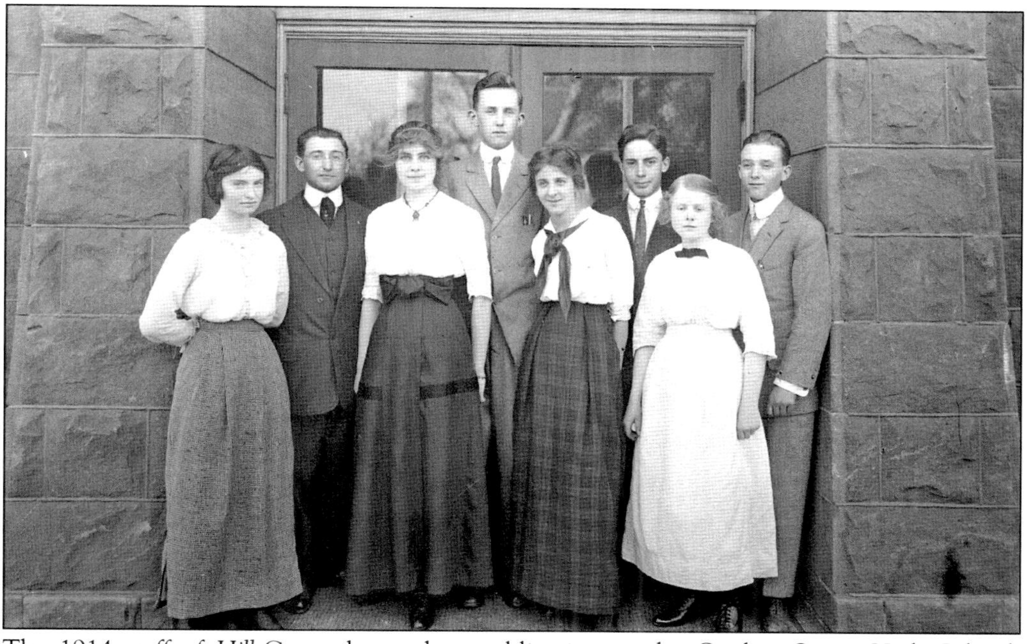

The 1914 staff of *Hill-Crest*, the student publication at the Conkey Street High School, included (left to right) Marguerite Pendergast, Francis Heiligen Thal, Erna Miller, Ray Pihringer, Charlotte Youngs, Bardo S. Verhalen, Selma Gehrand, and Alfred Hockings.

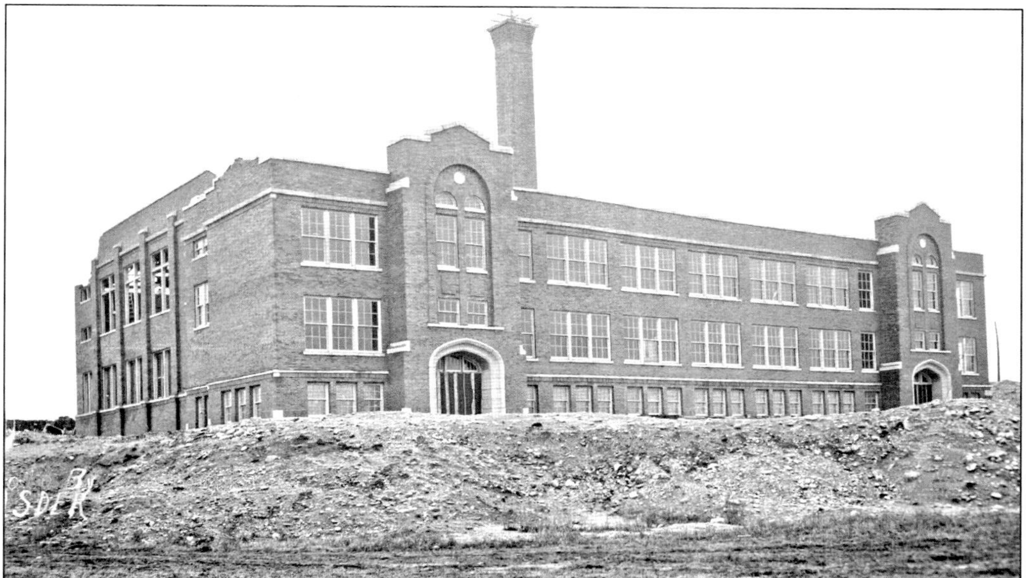

Although initial steps were taken in 1921 to build a new high school, it was not until September 1925 that this building was opened on Robert Street as Burlington High School. The adjacent athletic field, completed in 1929, was later named for Harry W. "Dinty" Moore, who started coaching the same year the school opened. After a new high school opened in 2000, this became Nettie Karcher Middle School, named for Racine County's first woman lawyer and local school board clerk for 32 years.

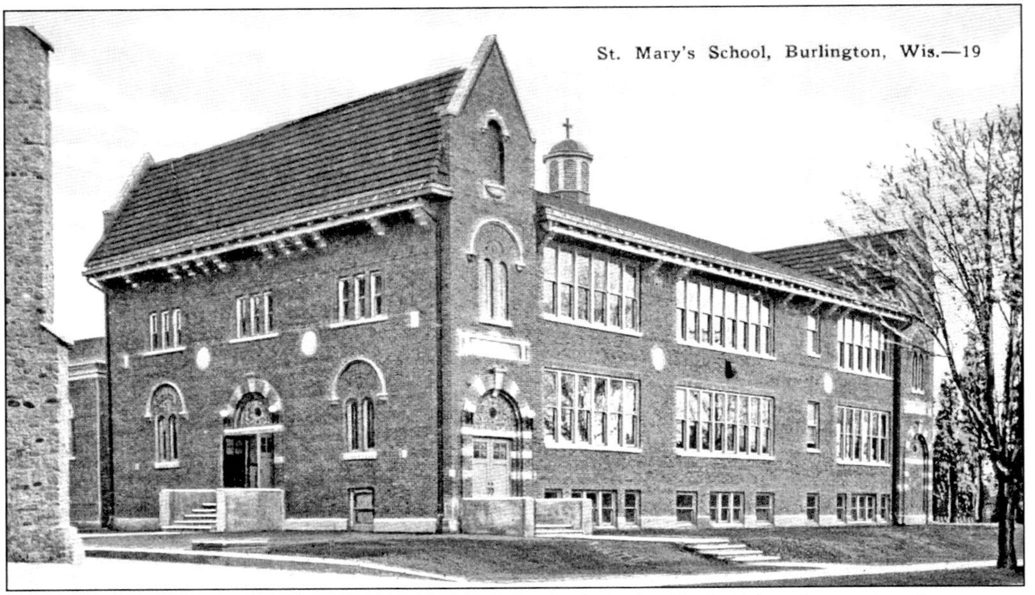

The dedication of this building in 1926 as St. Mary's Catholic High School completed a process that started in 1920, when pastor Rev. Joseph A. VanTreek proposed the project. The parish, which had earlier offered a commercial course with its first graduates in 1922, added a high school course in 1923. In 1974, the school board expanded to include representatives from other parishes. With 13 member parishes, the name was changed in 1984 to St. Mary's Catholic Central and shortened in 1989 to Catholic Central.

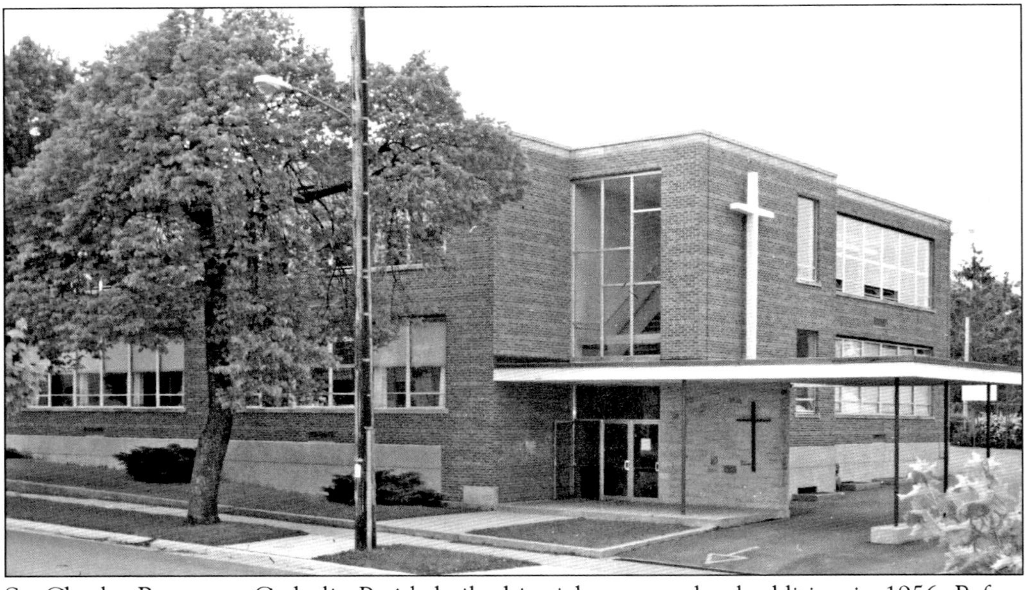

St. Charles Borromeo Catholic Parish built this eight-room school addition in 1956. Before the addition, the parish school accommodated from 160 to about 185 students a year. In 1961, about 350 students attended. In its earlier days, St. Charles was one of the few grade schools to have an active alumni association. The association, organized in 1917, held an annual banquet into the 1950s. St. Charles added a school and parish activity center to its facilities in 2003.

Six

Landmarks and Municipal Facilities

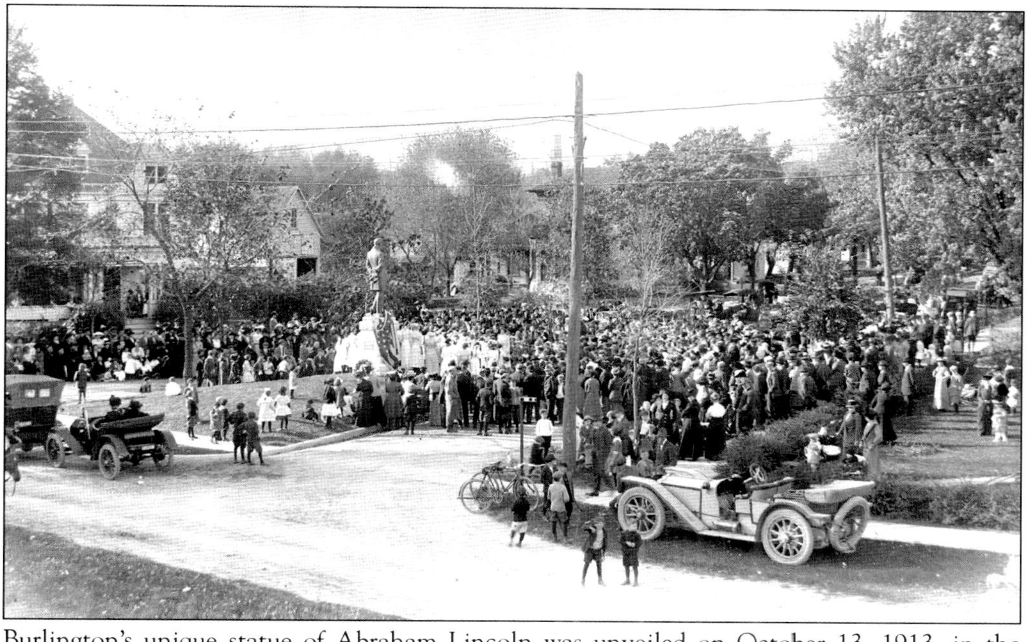

Burlington's unique statue of Abraham Lincoln was unveiled on October 13, 1913, in the presence of a large crowd. The idea for the statue had been suggested in 1911, when the school on State Street, built in 1859 when Lincoln was first nominated for the presidency and remodeled on the centennial anniversary of Lincoln's birth in 1911, was named for the slain president. Albert Meinhardt, brother of Dr. Francis Meinhardt who donated the statue to Burlington but who died before the dedication, gave the presentation speech. The Meinhardt brothers' nephew, Albert Francis Rogers, performed the unveiling. Rev. C. H. Beale of Milwaukee delivered the address.

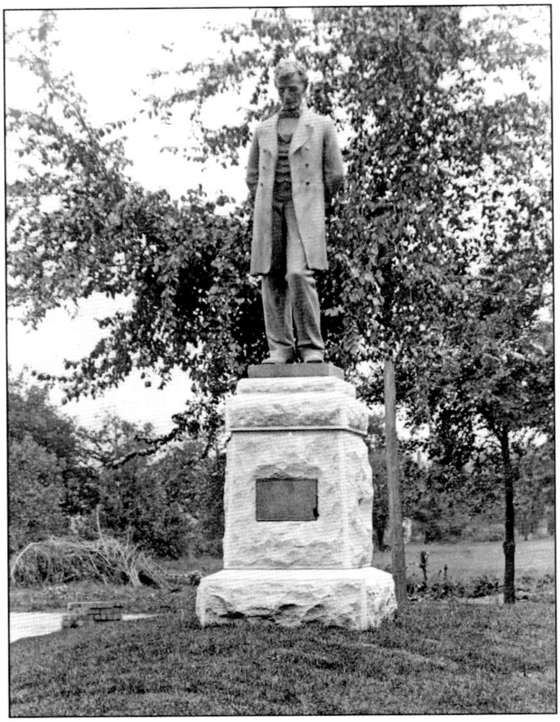

In a small triangle at the intersection of State and Kane Streets stands a one-of-a-kind statue of President Abraham Lincoln. It was a gift to Burlington from Dr. Francis W. Meinhardt, a Burlington dentist who died several months before the statue was dedicated in 1913. The statue depicts President Lincoln standing while giving his second inaugural address—"With malice toward none, with charity for all"—the notes for which are in his hands behind his back. The statue was sculpted by George D. Ganiere, a well-known Chicago artist.

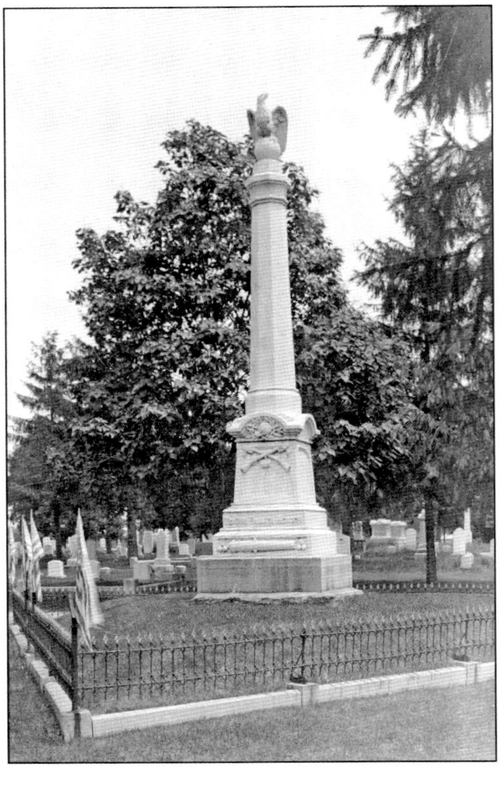

Believed to be the first Civil War Soldiers Monument to be erected in southeastern Wisconsin, this obelisk, created in 1880, still stands in Burlington Cemetery. The monument was suggested by Burlington's Henry Allen Cooper, who later served as Wisconsin First District Congressman for 31 years. Inscribed on the monument, which was unveiled by William Laske and Ernest G. Timme, both crippled in the war, are the names of Burlington Civil War veterans who had been killed or had died as of the time the monument was erected. The 20-inch iron fence on Joliet limestone coping was put around the monument in 1886.

The stone water tower at the top of Lewis Street, built in the era of outdoor privies and chamber pots, was part of Burlington's first community water system completed in 1890. It served the Village, and then the City, of Burlington's needs for more than 60 years. The original cypress wood tank on the 70-foot stone base, shown in this *c.* 1910 picture, was 30 feet high and 20 feet in diameter and held 70,000 gallons of water.

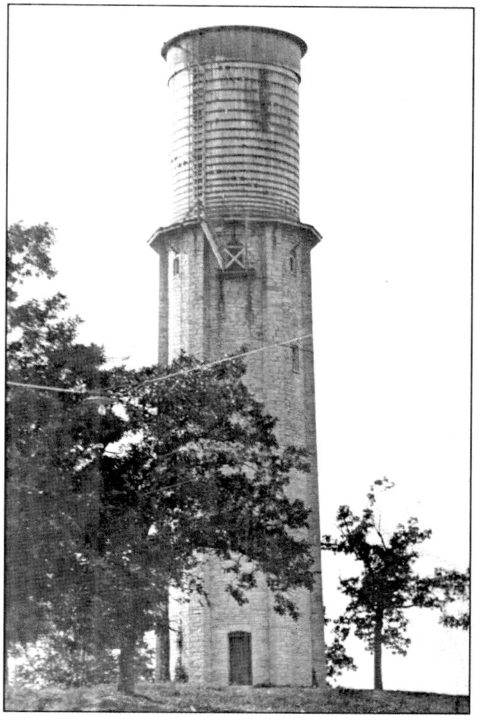

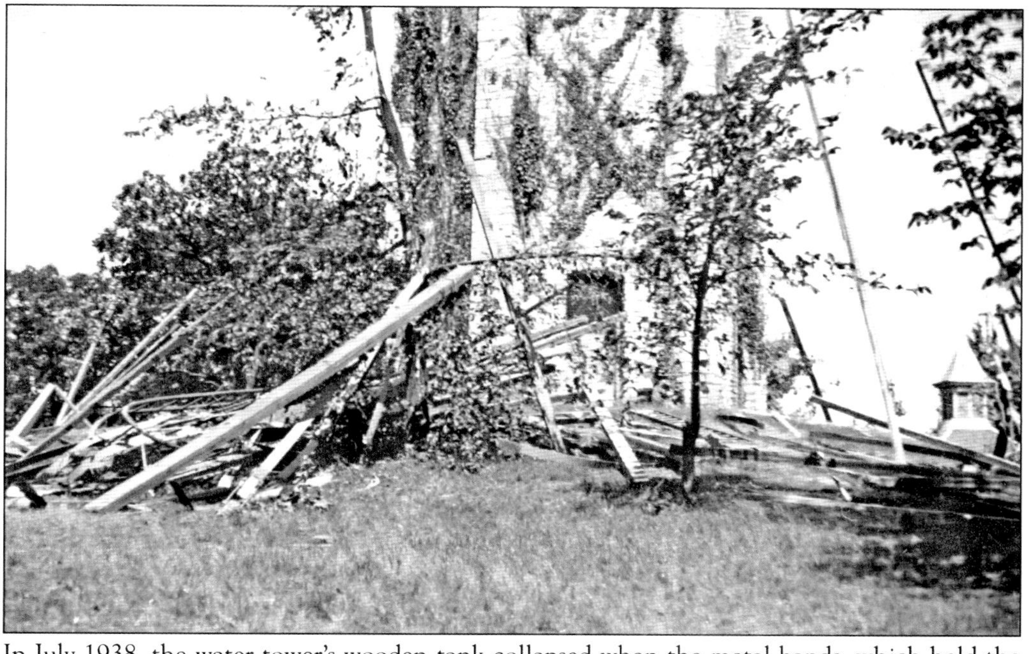

In July 1938, the water tower's wooden tank collapsed when the metal bands, which held the wooden staves together, broke. About 40,000 gallons were spilled, sending a wall of water about three feet high down James Street. The replacement tank, completed by mid-August 1938, served until the Origen Street tower was built in 1954. In 1981, a concrete liner was poured inside the old tank and a conical concrete roof was added. The tower area is now a city park.

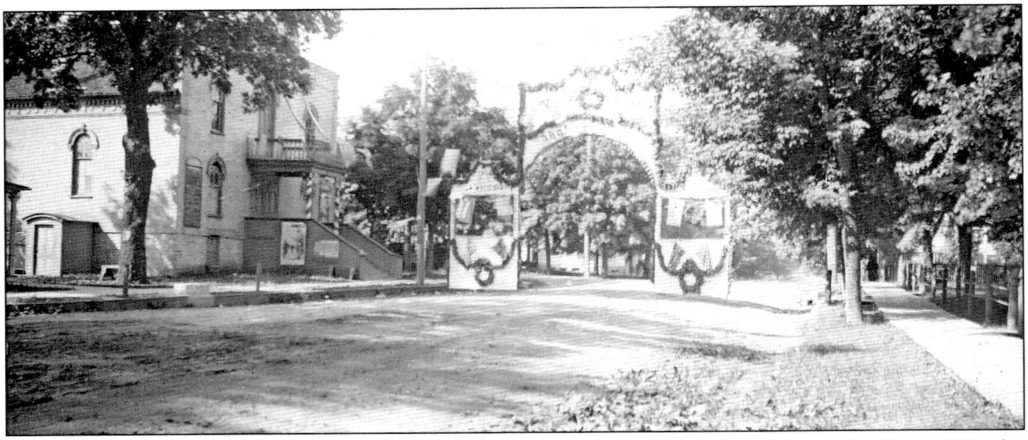

Teutonia Hall (left), at what is now Milwaukee Avenue and Kane Street, was built in 1871 by members of the Teutonia Society, a social club combining the Teutonia Society (a Catholic singing and social group), the German Dramatic Society (a theatrics group), and the Turner Society (a gymnastics and athletic group). The dedication banquet was scheduled for October 8, 1871, but hearing of the Chicago fire that night, society members packed the big roasts and everything that went with them and sent them to the sufferers. Perhaps ironically, this building was destroyed in a fire on January 23, 1930.

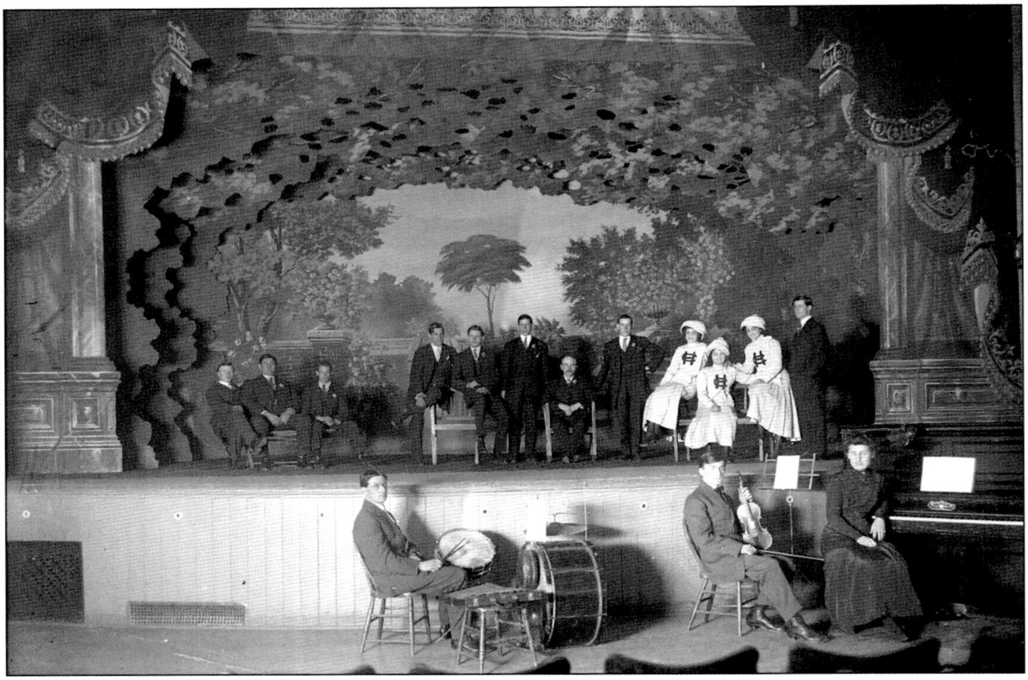

The Teutonia Hall stage was, at one time, the second largest in Wisconsin. Members of the house band, named LeGrande Trio, in this 1911 picture are Fred Boulden, drums, Theodore Korn, violin, and Laura Prasch, piano. Standing at right on stage with a vaudeville troupe is manager Howard Coburn. Teutonia Hall, later known as the Opera House and the Orpheum Theatre, was used for concerts, plays, dances, masquerade balls, banquets, school commencements, vaudeville shows, moving pictures, and other community activities.

The Old Settlers Monument, dedicated in 1926 on State Street opposite Lincoln School, lists the names of early Burlington settlers. The monument is topped by a Great Lakes sailing ship—the kind in which many settlers reached Wisconsin. It also marks a corner of the first frame house in Burlington, built by Dr. Edward G. and Ann Morse Dyer in 1840. The monument was donated by Mrs. Charles Dyer Norton following the expressed desire of her husband, a grandson of Dr. and Mrs. Dyer.

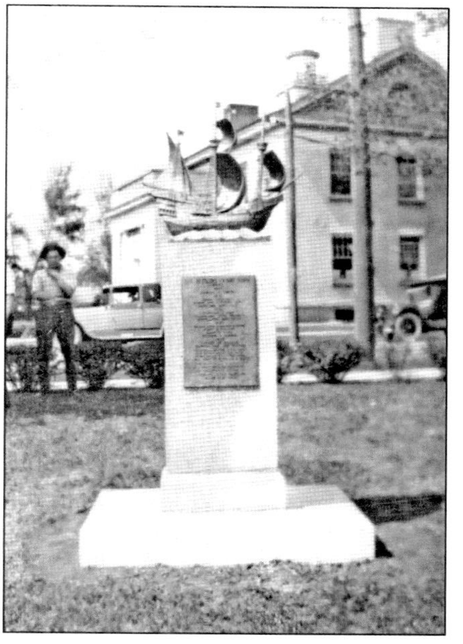

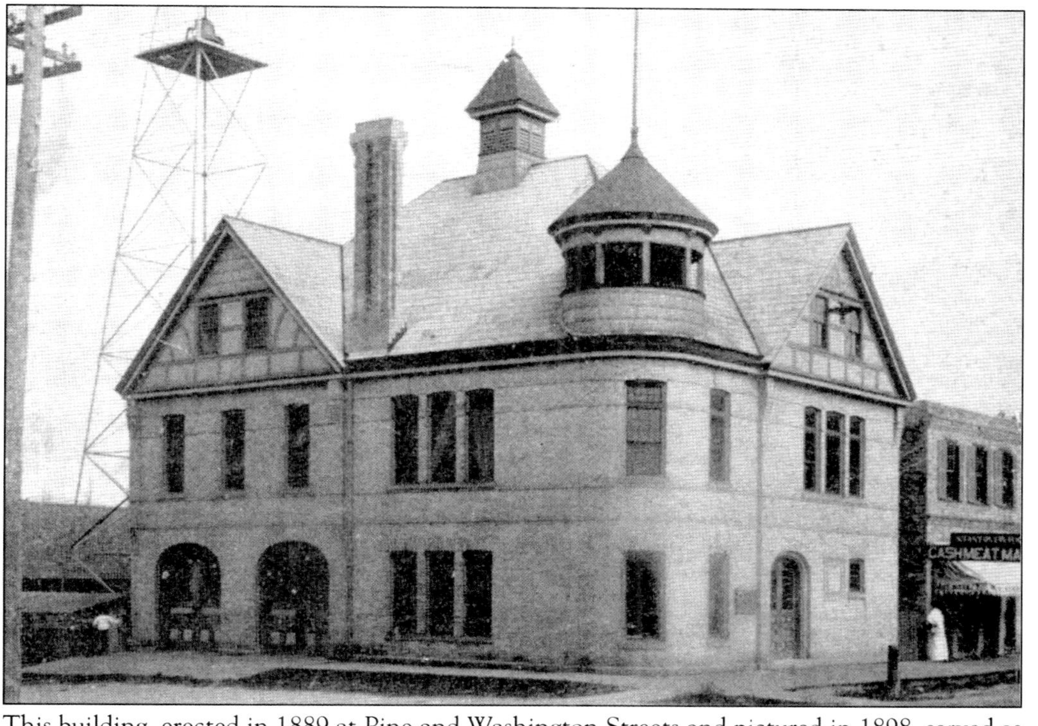

This building, erected in 1889 at Pine and Washington Streets and pictured in 1898, served as Village (and then City) and Town hall and fire station until 1924. The City then bought the Town's interest, and the Town offices moved to the corner of Washington Street and North Perkins Boulevard. After the City moved its offices in 1926, Joseph Bazal bought the building, removed the peaked roofs, and remodeled it into a creamery. He donated the fire bell and tower to Rochester.

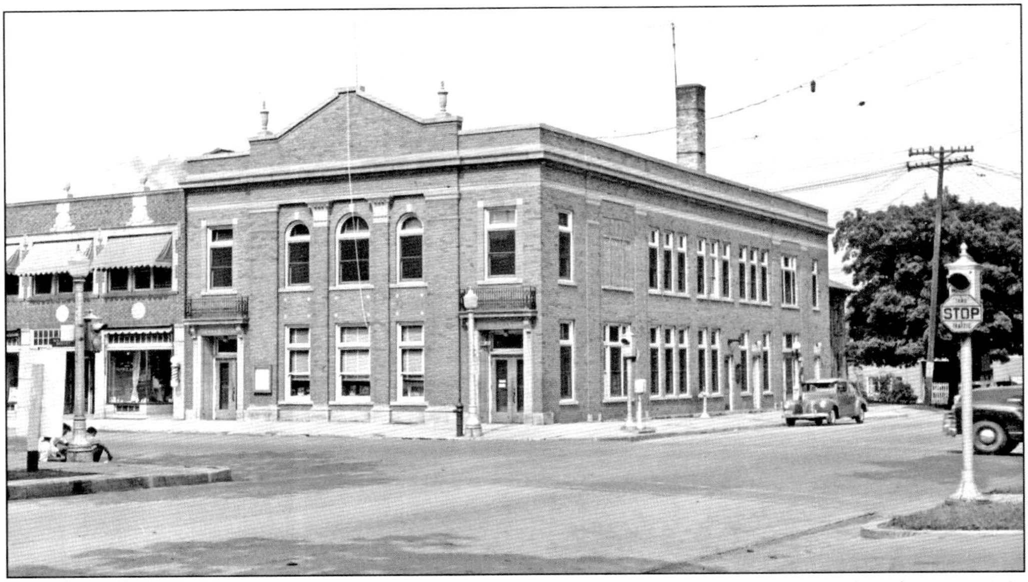

The current city hall at Pine and Jefferson Streets, pictured in 1949, was completed in 1926. It replaced a large red-brick house, built in 1875, which was moved to Madison Street and North Perkins Boulevard. When this building opened, the City occupied the second floor, with the library and the police department on the first floor, and the American Legion in the basement. The Legion moved to new quarters in 1963; the library, in 1964; and the police, in 1983.

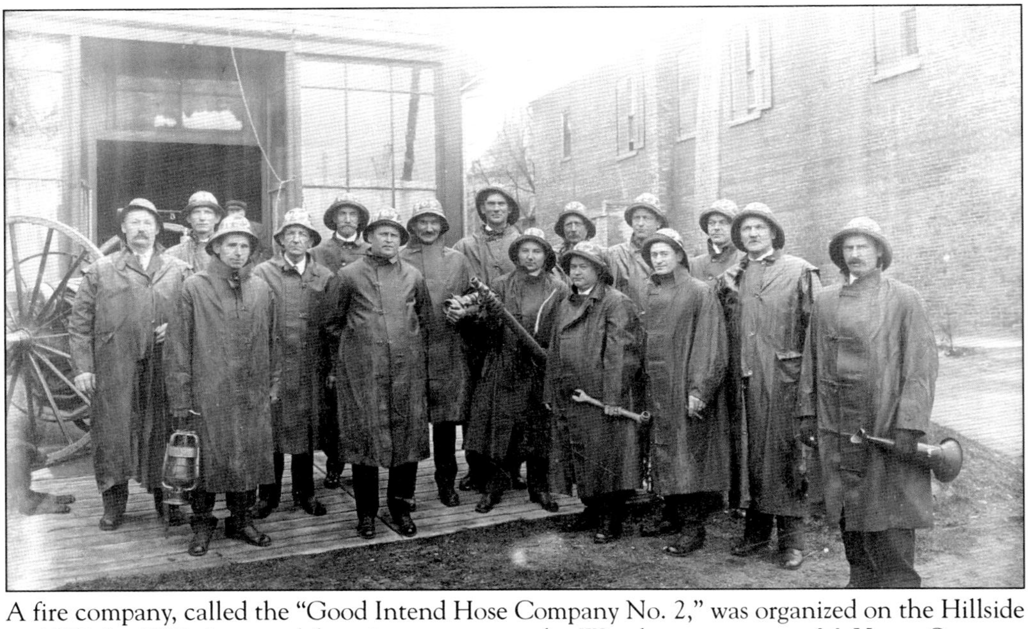

A fire company, called the "Good Intend Hose Company No. 2," was organized on the Hillside in 1890. In 1900, it moved from its quarters on the Wentker property on McHenry Street to Joseph A. Rueter's carpenter shop (left) on Jefferson Street across the alley from the Colburn tavern building, later known as the Log Cabin (right). Hose Company No. 2 met in the Rueter shop until 1939, when the company moved to the fire department building on Pine (now Commerce) Street.

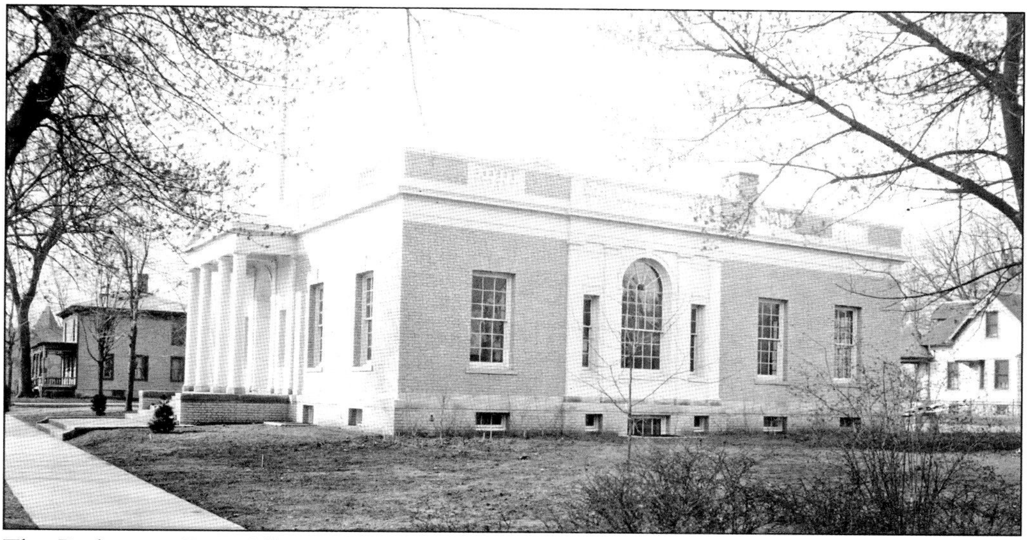

The Burlington Post Office occupied this building at Pine and Jefferson Streets from 1918, when this picture was taken, until 1961. Built by the government, the building replaced a 22-room residence and rooming house, which was demolished, and two 2-story houses and a barn, which were moved to other Burlington sites. The government deeded the building to the City in 1962 and the public library moved here in 1964. The house at the left was moved in 1930 to make way for a gasoline station. The house at the right was demolished in 1987 after an addition was built to the library and a parking lot was needed.

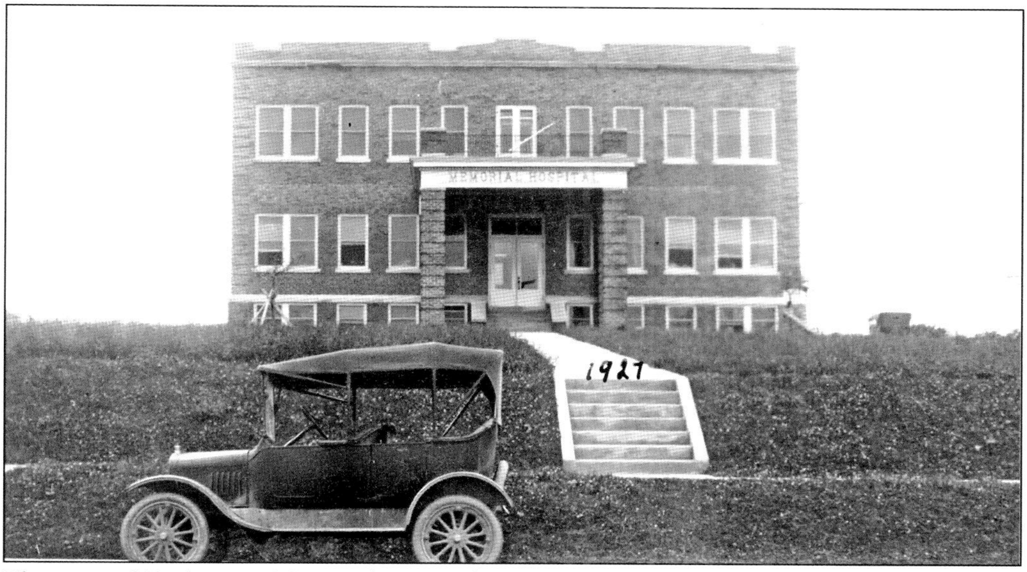

The original Burlington Memorial Hospital, now part of a large complex, opened in 1924 on Randolph Street on land donated by the Finke-Uhen Brewing Co. Building funds were raised in Burlington and nearby communities and included money remaining from residents' donations to the Racine County War Relief Fund during World War I. Donors also furnished some of the equipment. In the early years, an annual hospital donation day would be held to restock winter-keeping fruits and vegetables and canned goods.

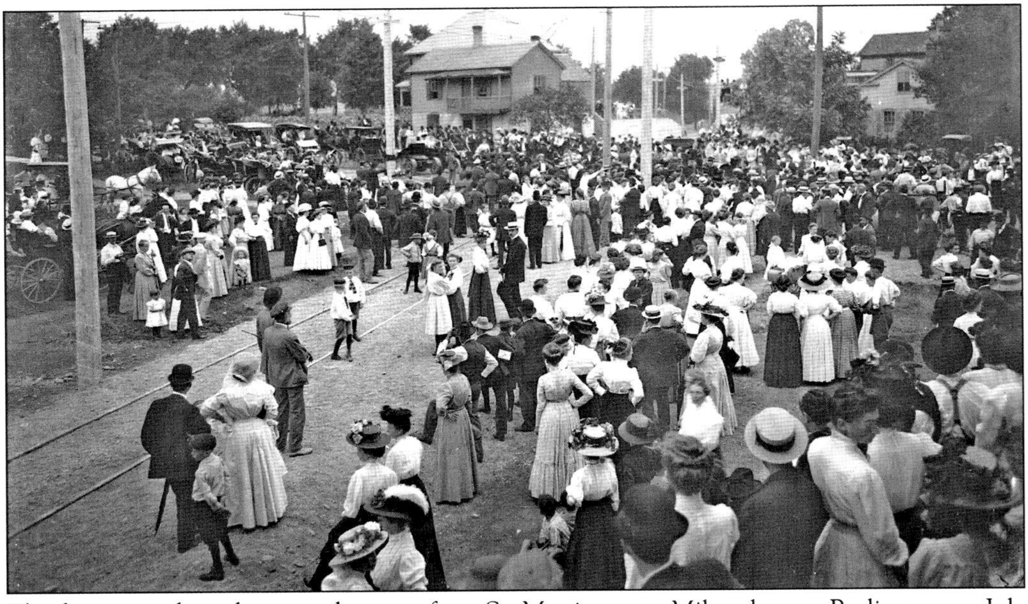

The first interurban electric railway car from St. Martins, near Milwaukee, to Burlington on July 1, 1909, was greeted by a great celebration—on the north side of the White River. At that time, the bridge over the White River and the track in the downtown area and up as far as St. Mary's Cemetery had not been completed. The line, with intermediate stops at Durham, Wind Lake, Norway, Waterford, Rochester, and Bellwood (near County Trunk W), operated until May 1938.

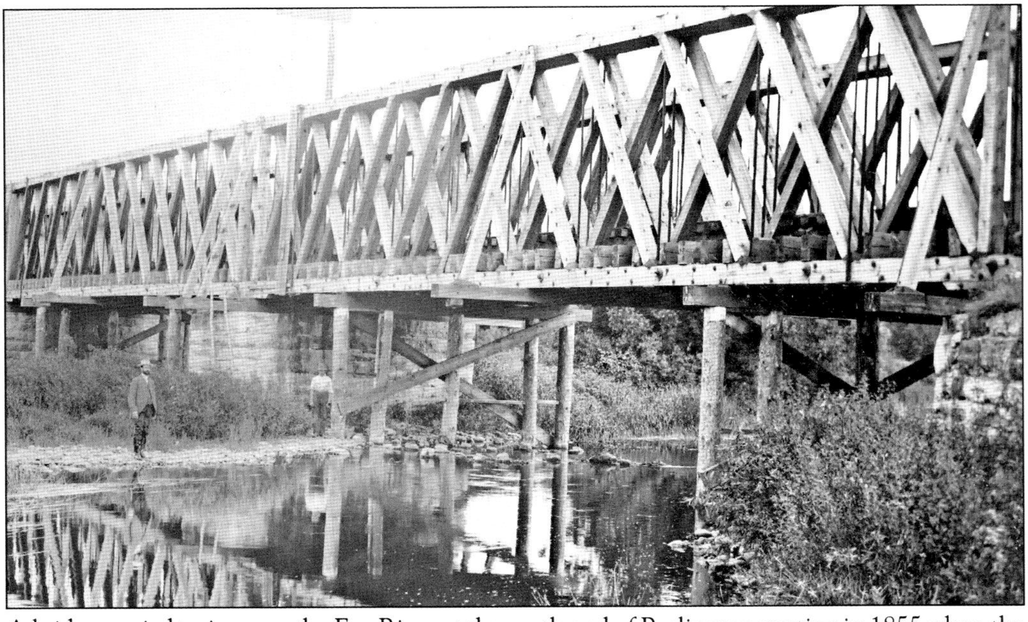

A bridge carried trains over the Fox River at the south end of Burlington starting in 1855 when the Racine and Mississippi Railroad first reached Burlington. That first bridge was replaced in 1875 by the Western Union Railroad, which acquired the Racine and Mississippi in 1866. The bridge here, pictured c. 1890, was built in 1881 by the Chicago, Milwaukee & St. Paul Railroad, after it had acquired the Western Union in 1879. An iron bridge replaced this wooden one in 1901.

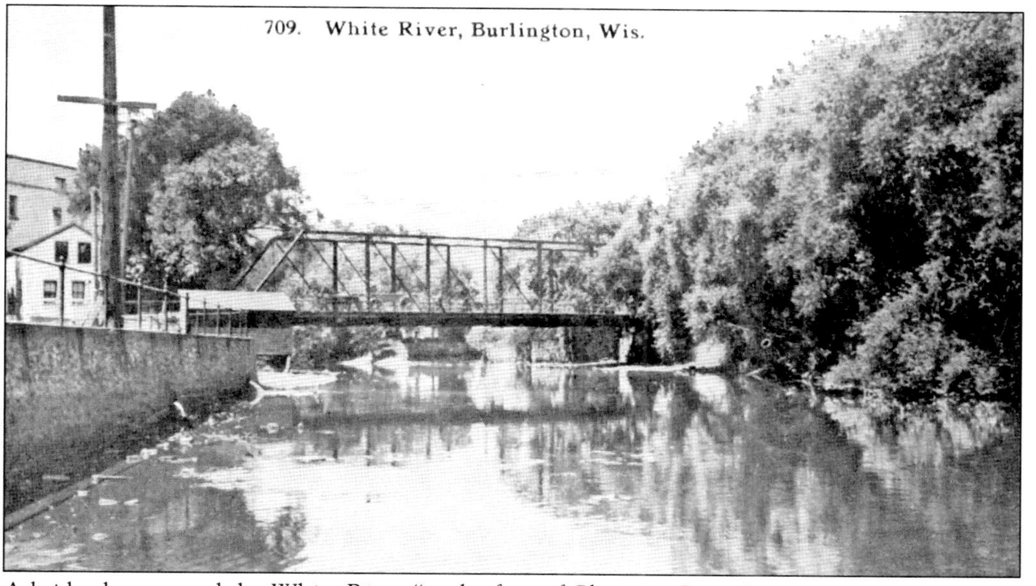

A bridge has crossed the White River "at the foot of Chestnut Street" since 1867, when a truss bridge was built. By 1877, that bridge had become unsafe and the bridge pictured here c. 1915 replaced it. As the 1877 bridge neared completion, a wind caused it to fall over into the river when it was not sufficiently braced before the high scaffold supporting both sides was removed. The mishap caused only a slight delay in completing the bridge.

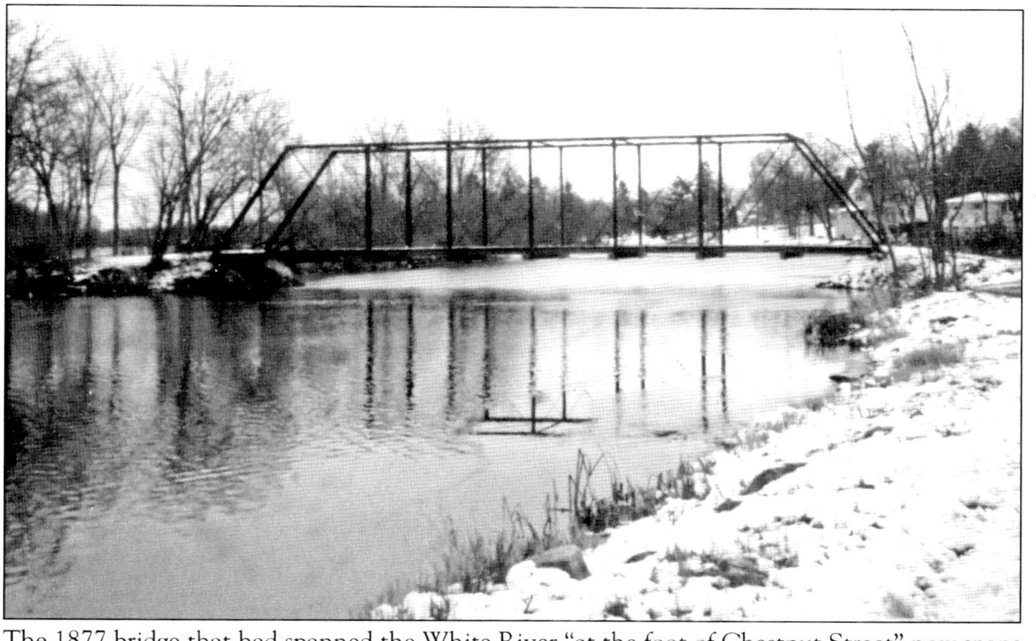

The 1877 bridge that had spanned the White River "at the foot of Chestnut Street" now spans Honey Creek at the Bieneman farm just north of Burlington on Bieneman Road. The bridge, now the oldest iron truss bridge existing in Wisconsin, was purchased by former farm owner John Frey and moved here in July 1922 after the City put in a concrete bridge to replace it. Work on the concrete bridge, started in September 1921, had been suspended for the winter.

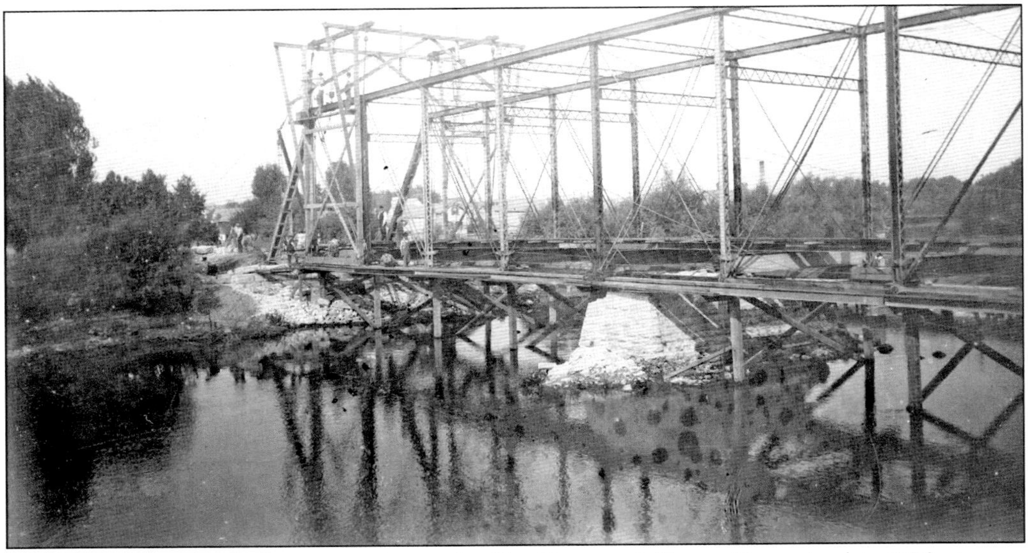

An iron bridge is being constructed over the Fox River at Jefferson Street in this 1893 picture, probably taken from the temporary bridge put up during construction. The 167-1/2 foot, 10-panel bridge was to have a 20-foot roadway and two 5-foot sidewalks, steel joists, and 3-inch oak planking laid diagonally. The bridge replaced an iron bridge put up in 1876 in place of a wooden bridge. The abutment pillow in the river, left over from the 1876 bridge, was removed after this bridge was completed.

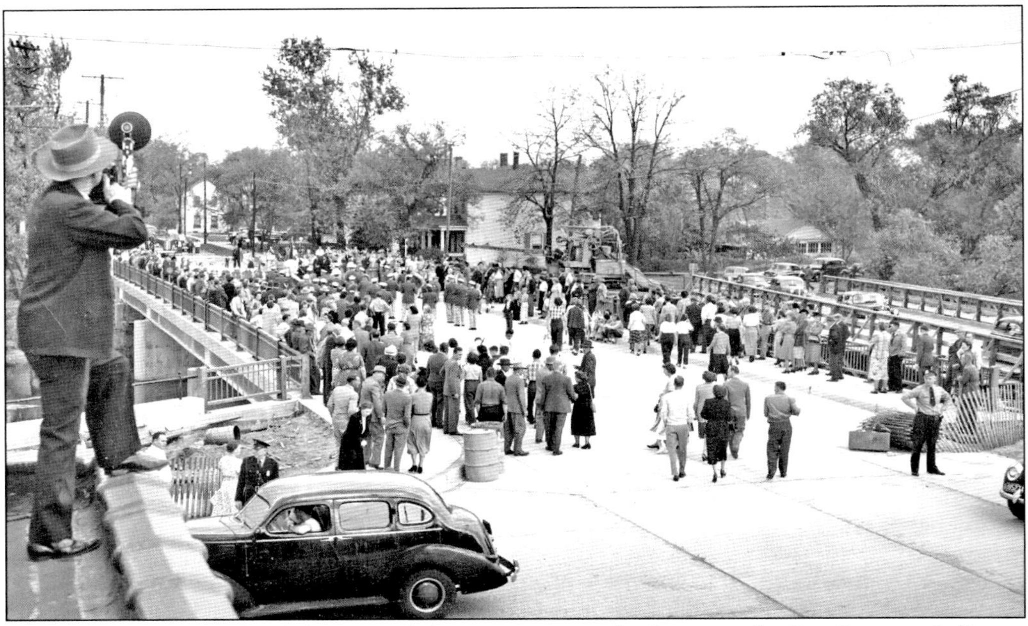

A crowd gathers for the dedication of the new concrete bridge over the Fox River at Jefferson Street in October 1949. This bridge replaced the 1893 iron bridge. The temporary wooden bridge used during construction is at right. Photographer Otis Hulett is at left on the roof of the former water works pump house at the corner of Jefferson Street and the former Mutter Avenue. Officers Roy McCourt (lower left behind car) and Elmer Rubach (lower right) help with traffic.

Seven

The Nearby Lakes

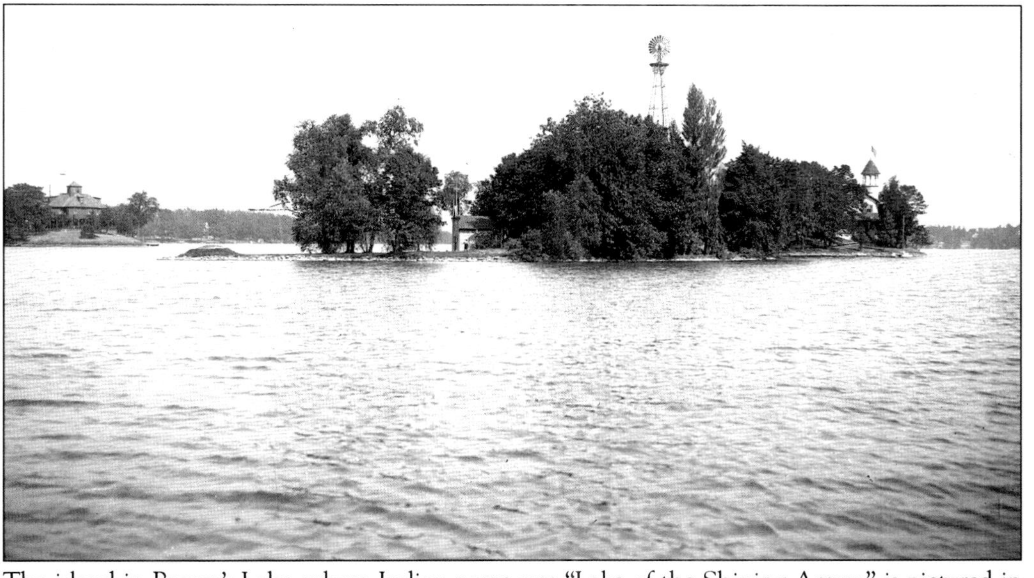

The island in Brown's Lake, whose Indian name was "Lake of the Shining Arrow," is pictured in 1908. At that time, the island, known by various names over the years, was called Bremner's Island. The island was first settled by Julius Lueck, who acquired it by "squatter's rights" and whose family lived there from the mid-1850s until 1863. About 1874, the island, becoming known about that time as Island Wild, became a summer retreat for members of Gideon's Band and their families. Gideon's Band was a social group of mainly Racine citizens and well-known western railroad men. In 1876, band member Fred Wild, general freight agent for the Racine & Southwestern Division of the Western Union Railroad, acquired the island from the federal government for $14 and conveyed it to Gideon's Band. The Band built a hotel in 1881. Hard times ensued, however, and the Band's mortgage was foreclosed in 1883. In 1885, the island was sold to the Iona Catholic Men's Club of Chicago, which renamed it St. Mary's Island. One of the Club members, David F. Bremner, president of Bremner Brothers Biscuit Co., bought the island in 1894.

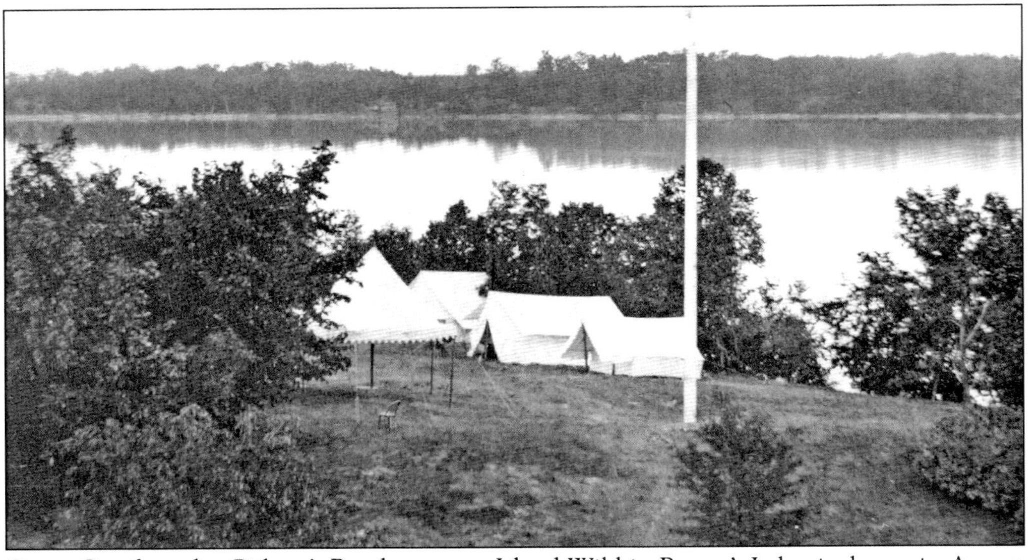

Camp Comfort, the Gideon's Band camp on Island Wild in Brown's Lake, is shown in August 1875. From 1874 until the early 1880s, Gideon's Band, a social group of mostly Racine and railroad men, annually camped on the island with their families. The Band, which acquired the island in 1876, built a clubhouse that year and added a hotel and other buildings in 1881. In 1882, a telephone line was completed between the island and the Burlington telephone "office" in Charles Wood's drug store.

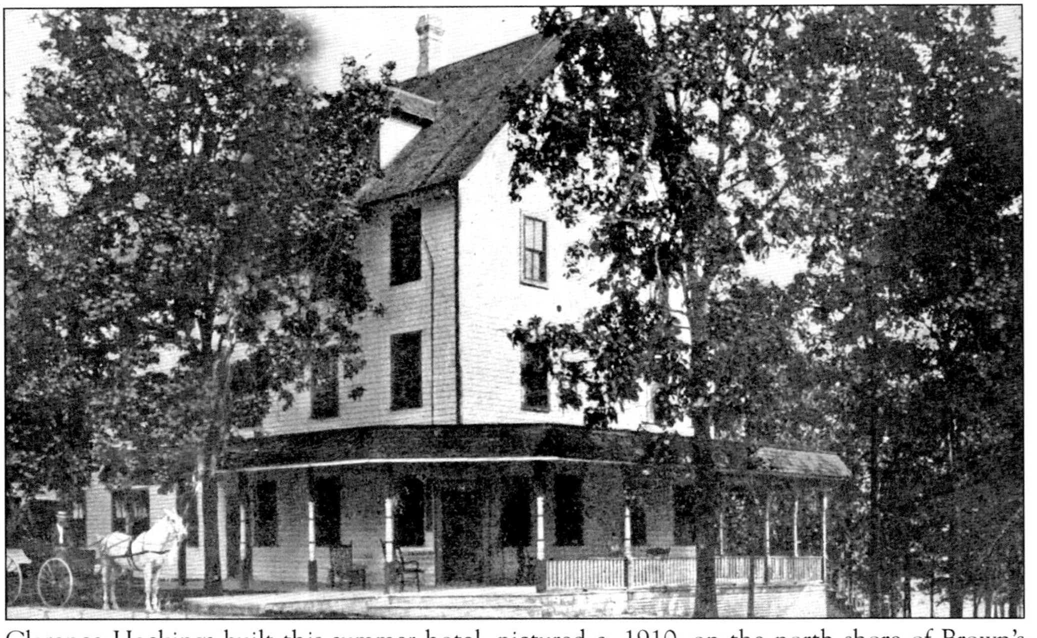

Clarence Hockings built this summer hotel, pictured c. 1910, on the north shore of Brown's Lake, opening it in 1893 as "The Columbian." In 1905, he added a two-story hotel building and changed the name of the resort to "The Antlers." Hockings also conducted a hatchery, raising chickens for serving to his guests and for sale. In 1920, the Royal Palm, a dance hall, was added, and in 1922, a nine-hole golf course. William Liggett bought the resort in 1940.

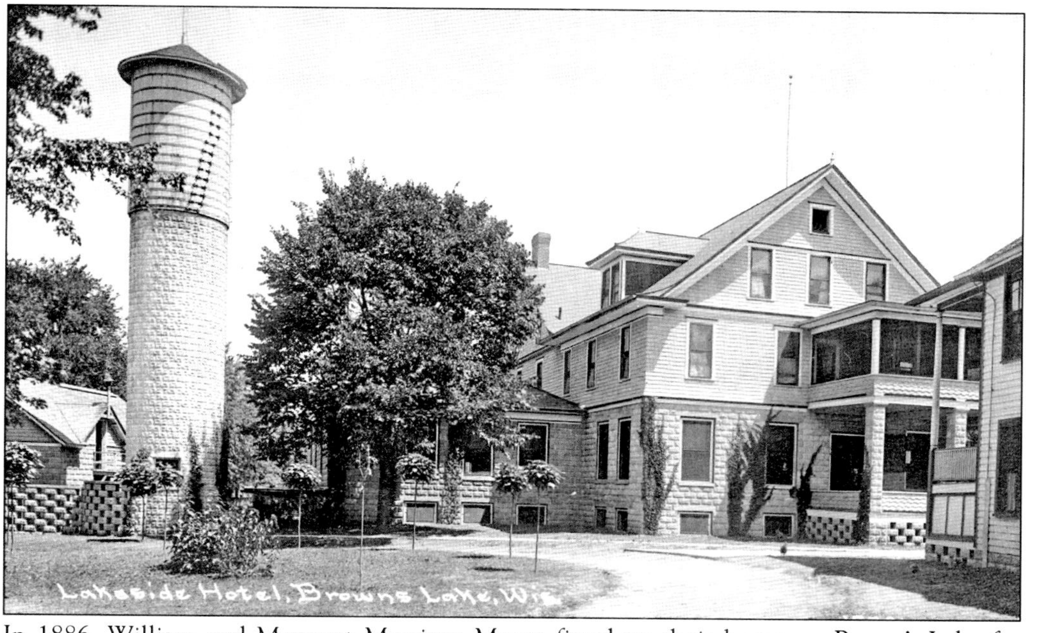

In 1886, William and Margaret Morrison Moore fitted up their home on Brown's Lake for summer boarders. Adding cottages and other facilities, Moore's Lakeside grew and, by 1898, was hosting up to 100 guests weekly. After three generations in the Moore family, the resort was acquired in 1947 by Harold Schlensky, who renamed it Brown's Lake Resort. In 1957 and 1958, the New York Yankees stayed at the resort during World Series play with the Milwaukee Braves. The resort was converted to condominiums in 1981.

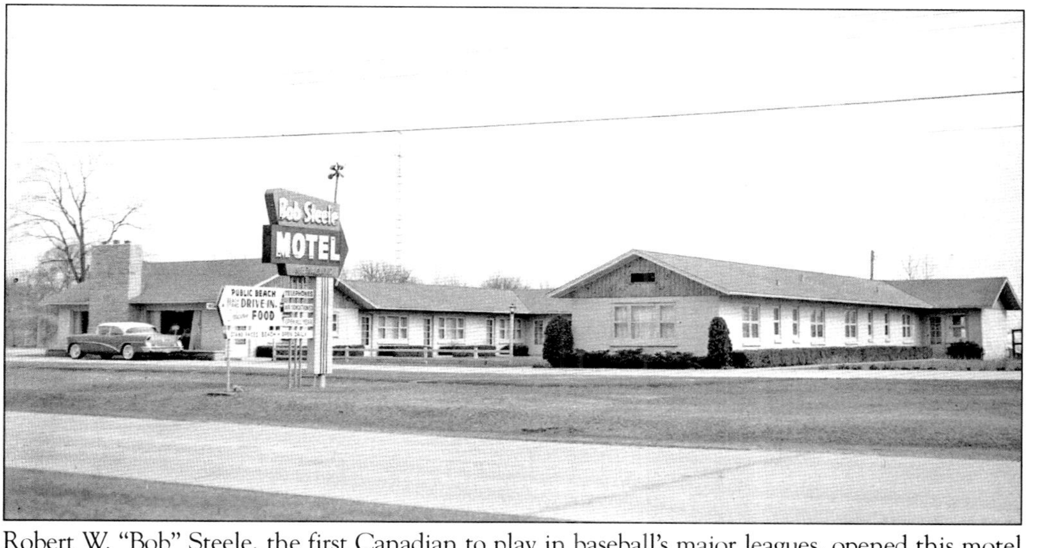

Robert W. "Bob" Steele, the first Canadian to play in baseball's major leagues, opened this motel across from Fischer Park at Brown's Lake in 1948. Steele spent 20 years in professional baseball, pitching in the National League from 1915 to 1922 for the Cardinals, Pirates, and Giants. He was the only man ever to pinch-hit for Honus Wagner and, while with the Giants, roomed with Jim Thorpe. In 1953, the American Institute of Television Manufacturers installed six television sets in Steele's motel as an experiment to find out if having TV in motels was practical.

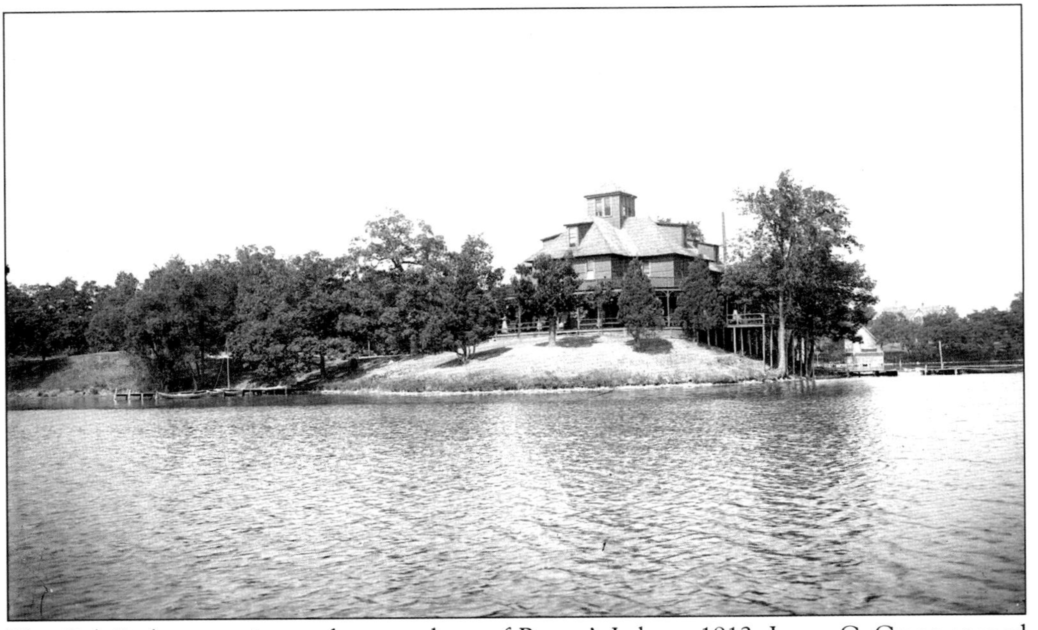

The Oak Park resort sits on the west shore of Brown's Lake *c.* 1912. James C. Grant opened the resort hotel in 1892 on the former Ostermann property. First called Brown's Lake Hotel and then Grant's Park, the resort was renamed by successive owners as Sherman's Park and Laurel Park, before becoming Oak Park in 1907. Mrs. Frances Kelnhofer became owner in 1913, operating the resort for 40 years. In 1952, Anthony and Pauline Cerami acquired the property and built Cerami's Island View Resort.

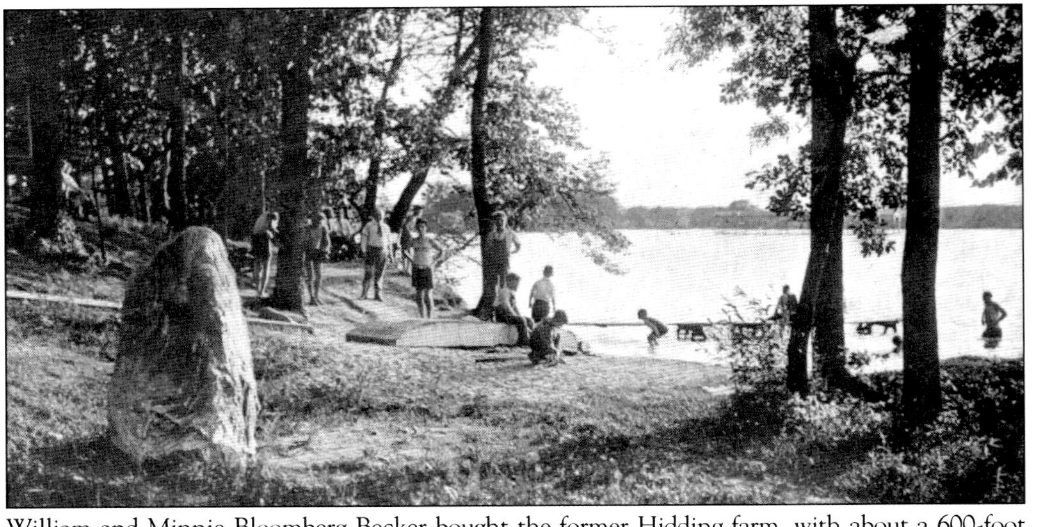

William and Minnie Bloomberg Becker bought the former Hidding farm, with about a 600-foot frontage on Brown's Lake, in 1911, moving there in 1912. In 1919, they added rooms for resort purposes and, in subsequent years, built additional facilities and enlarged others. In 1963, Becker's Farm Resort had about 100 rooms in hotel buildings and cabins. After retiring in 1967, the Beckers sold 62 acres to Racine County, which added the land to the adjacent Einar Fischer Park.

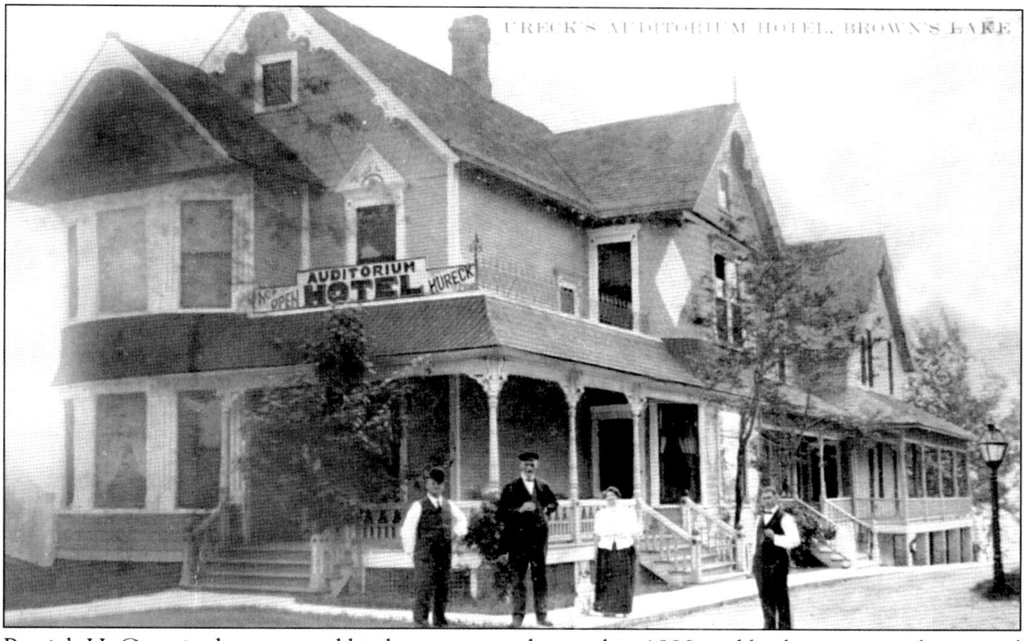

Patrick H. Cunningham moved his barns across the road in 1892 and built a new residence and summer hotel, called The Auditorium, on the west shore of Brown's Lake. In 1898, six-foot, nine-inch Harry Ureck (second from left) leased the hotel and, with his wife, Mabel, operated it for nearly 20 years. In 1926, the hotel became the club house for the golf course that was built across the road. In 1939, it was sold to Ben Hoffman, who changed it to the Colonial Club hotel and restaurant. Later called the Colonial Inn, the building burned in 1979.

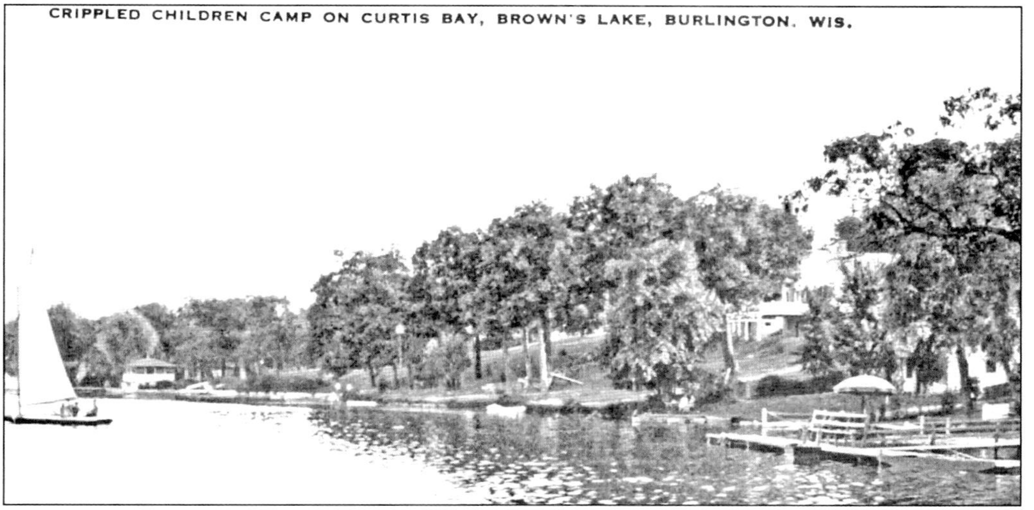

Emma Haskell, the first teacher of crippled children in Chicago, founded a summer camp in 1899. In 1909, about 40 children were brought to Mathias P. Petrie's Brown's Lake cottages for a five week outing. The next summer, about 50 children occupied the home and a cottage on the Curtis property, part of which the Crippled Children's Camp association eventually bought and operated until 1943. In 1944, an association of camp alumni bought the property and made it a private resort, called Brown's Lake Lodge. The Lodge operated until 1985.

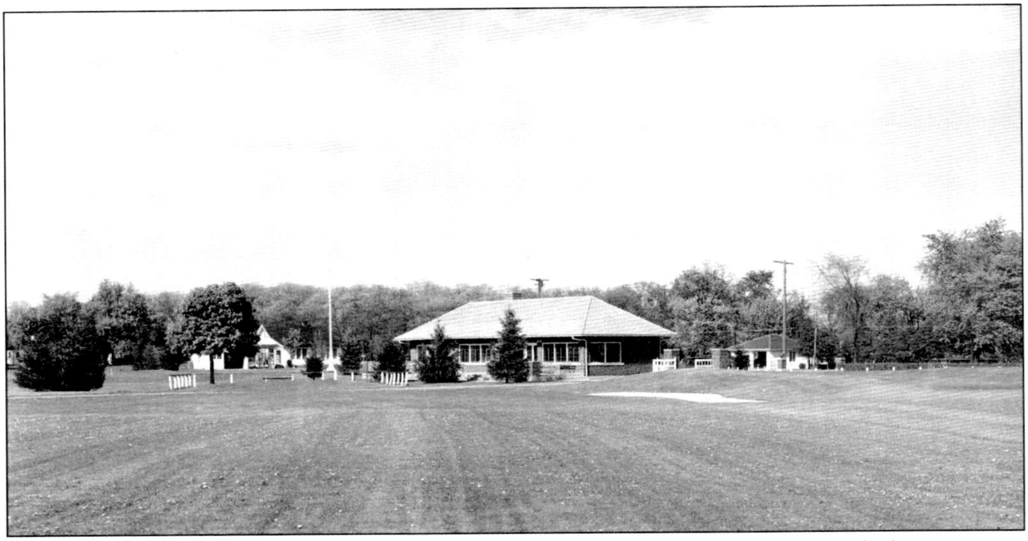

In 1925, the newly organized Brown's Lake Golf Association laid out an 18-hole course on portions of the former Cunningham brothers and Ayers farms, through which the Fox River flowed. For its clubhouse, the group bought the former Auditorium Hotel (later called the Colonial Club). A starting house (pictured in 1955 after remodeling) was built, a 150-foot suspension bridge was placed across the river, and about 400 Norway maple trees were set out. Racine County bought the course in 1979.

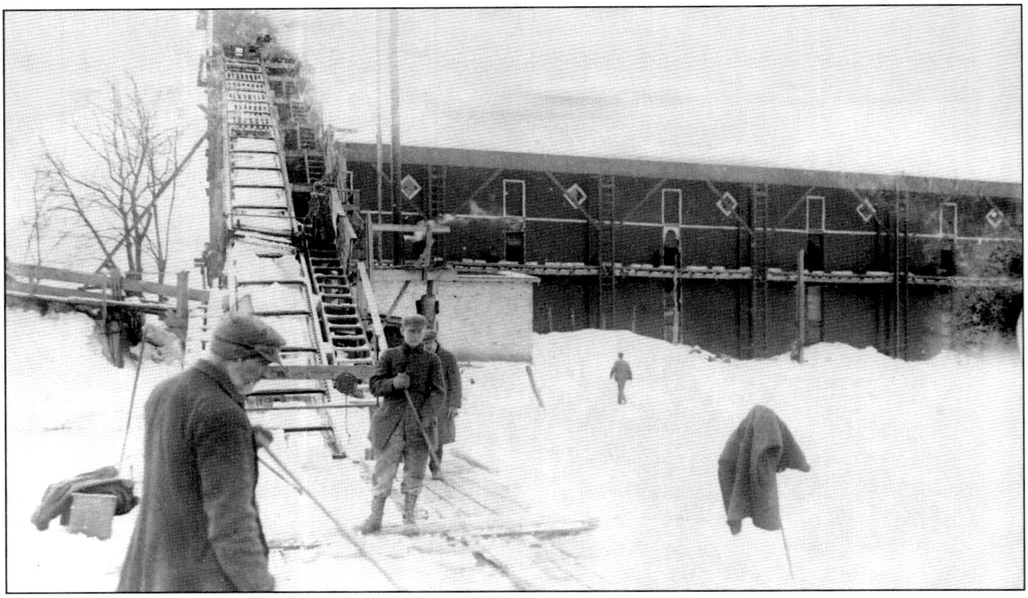

Ice harvesting, which had been done for local use since Burlington's earliest days, became a large-scale operation in the 1890s when Chicago ice companies bought farms at Norton's and Brown's Lakes, built large ice storage houses, and laid sidetracks to the Chicago, Milwaukee & St. Paul Railroad's main track. The companies, which employed hundreds of men each winter, as well as local farmers and their teams, started scaling back operations about 1920. The last of the ice houses at Brown's Lake was dismantled in 1936.

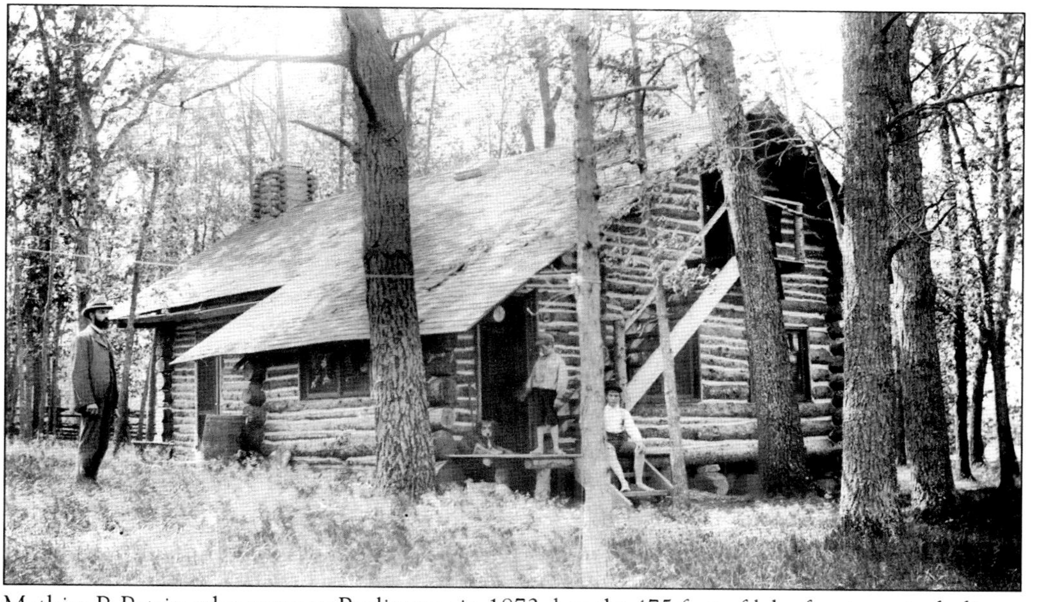

Mathias P. Petrie, who came to Burlington in 1873, bought 475 feet of lake frontage, including a former Indian camp site, on the south shore of Brown's Lake in 1888 and built a cottage. In 1896, he had this 18-by-36-foot, two-story log cabin, made entirely of tamarack logs, built. After Petrie's death in 1934, the property passed on to his son, Ervin. The cabin, which is still standing, was the site of several conventions of Indian relic collectors in the mid-20th century.

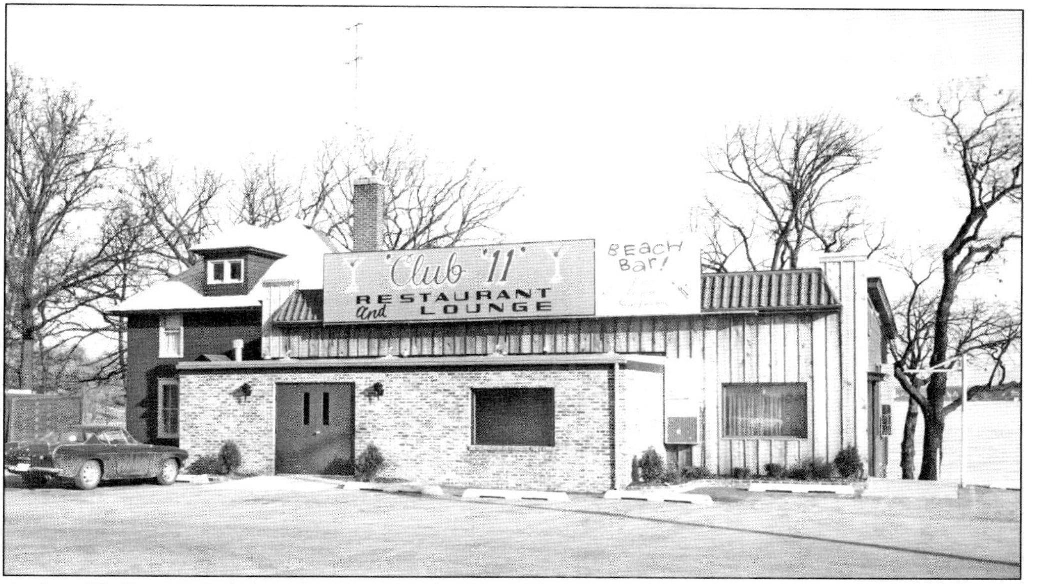

Arthur H. Kortendick bought property from Peter May on the south shore of Brown's Lake in 1938, built a new tavern and dance pavilion, and opened Club 11 in 1939. In 1960, Birge and Viola Kortendick Whitmore became the managers, and the Edgewater Room was opened on the lower level facing the lake. The business, pictured in 1975, was sold in 1971 and again in 1972, and the name was later changed to Brandy Bay. The Waterfront Restaurant has occupied the building in recent years.

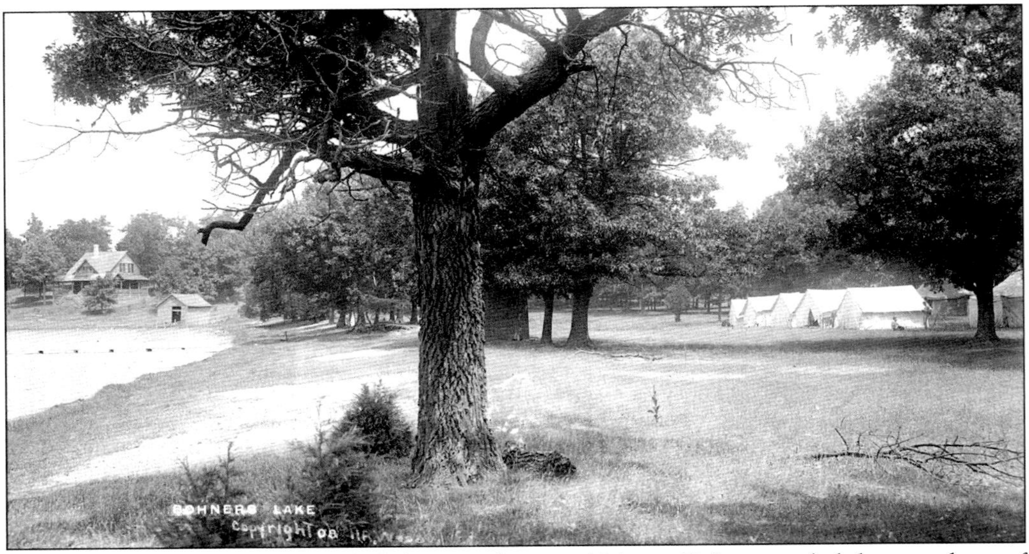

In 1843, Augustus Greulich settled the west shore and Martin Bohner settled the east shore of what became Bohner's Lake. Wilhelm Riel bought Greulich's land in 1848 and, in 1851, sold it to Augustus Jacobson. A portion of the land, subdivided in 1928, formed White Oak Park. William Grass bought Bohner's land in 1848. His son, Frank Grass, sold several lots starting in 1894; and William Robers bought the farm in 1910. Campers' tents were set up on the east shore in this 1908 Howard Wood picture.

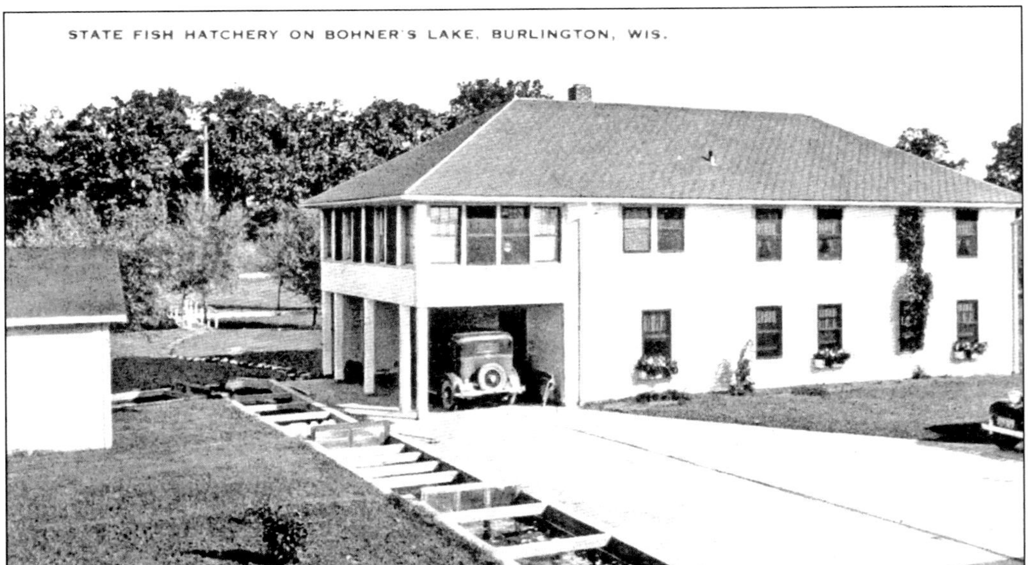

Although the Wisconsin Conservation Commission acquired land for a fish hatchery for Racine, Kenosha, and Walworth counties in the Spring Valley area west of Burlington in 1928, that location proved unsuitable. Instead, the hatchery, pictured *c.* 1935, was built on the former Jacobson farm at the outlet of Bohner's Lake in 1929. In 1941, Superintendent Fred Hewitt reported that over 102 million fish had been hatched during the past year. Over half were pike, followed by perch, black bass, bluegills, shiners, and bullheads.

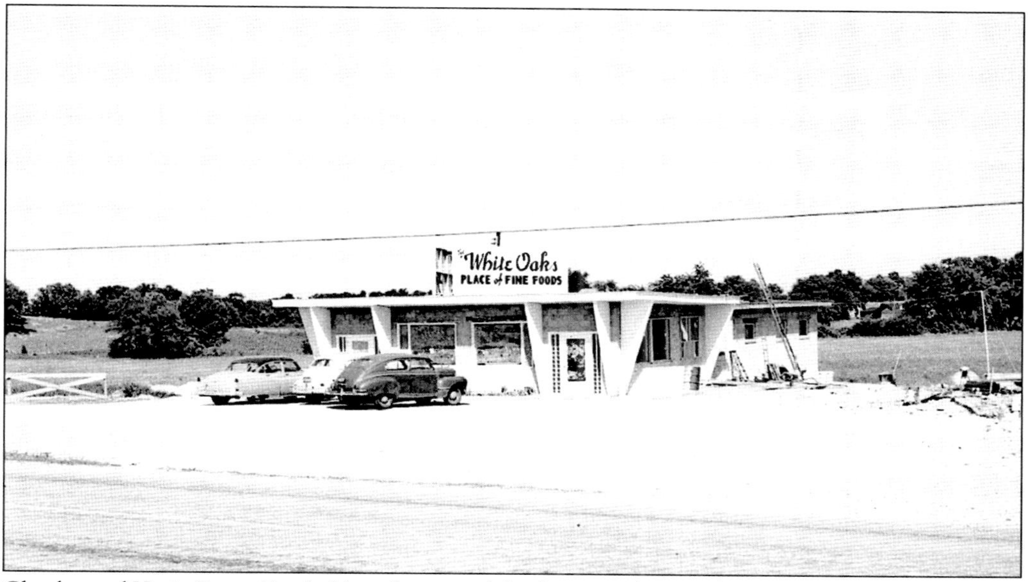

Charles and Katie Sgaga Dunkel bought part of the former White Oak golf course at Bohner's Lake and put up this building in 1952 to house "The White Oaks" restaurant, a drive-in "snack" stand, and a five-room apartment. At that time, the restaurant seated 65 to 70 people. The Dunkels built an addition to the restaurant in 1956. Richard Kiekenbush became owner in 1979 and operated the restaurant until 2000, putting up a new building after a disastrous 1985 fire.

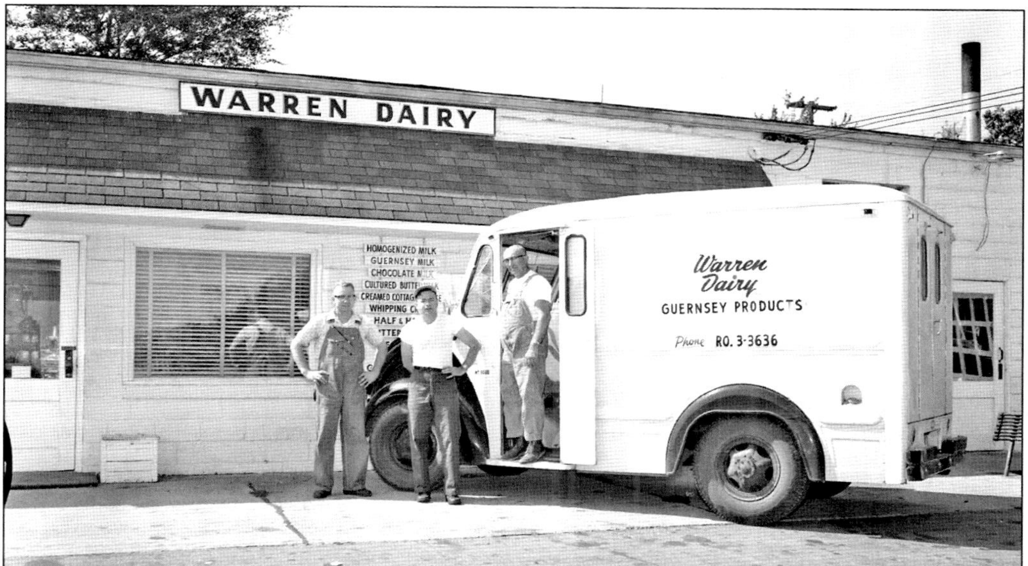

Bohner's Lake area farmers Art Winkler and James Warren combined their milk routes in 1931, starting Winkler & Warren Dairy. In 1932, they completed a new milk plant on the Winkler farm, and in 1939, started delivering milk in "Cream Top" bottles. In 1946, they completed a new dairy building on County Trunk P. In 1950, Warren's son, David, bought the Winkler interest, changing the name to Warren Dairy. David is at left in this 1961 picture with Gene Fuller and Al Forbes.

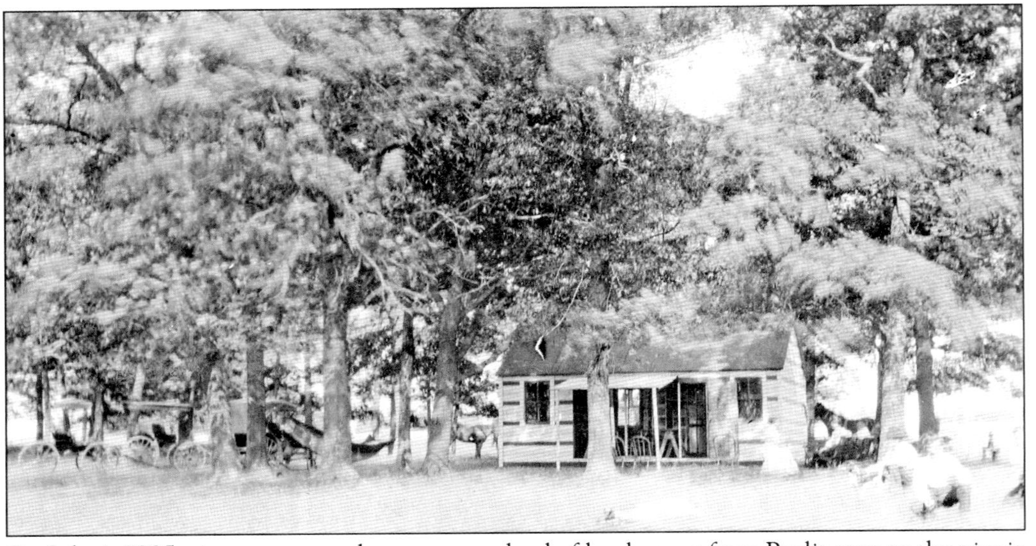

On July 4, 1905, six young men drove a wagonload of lumber out from Burlington to the picnic grove on the Frank Grass farm at Bohner's Lake. By evening they had erected the first cottage on the east side of the lake. The next week, they returned and painted it red, white, and blue. A friend commented on the lonesome spot, so they christened the place "Camp Lonesome." The area in which the camp was located was later known as Summerhaven.

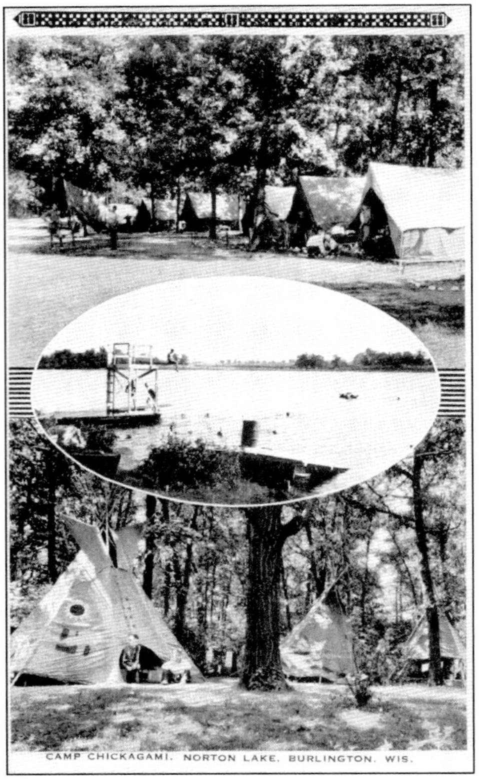

Although a spring-fed, crystal clear lake just east of Burlington is officially called Rockland Lake, it has been popularly known as Norton's Lake because Nelson R. and Clark Norton were early farm owners there. In 1882, a Chicago ice company built ice houses, laid a sidetrack, and began annual ice harvests that continued into the 1920s. The Racine Boy Scouts operated Camp Chickagami at the lake starting about 1921 until 1935, and the Boys Brotherhood Republic had Camp Freedom there in the 1930s. The Red Cross held swimming and water safety lessons at the lake for several years starting in 1939. In 1940, Mr. and Mrs. Hadden MacLean acquired about 240 acres of former ice company land, built a lodge and several cabins, and presented the camp to the Chicago YMCA in memory of their son, John. Camp MacLean, which is still operating, accommodated 460 boys the first summer. By 1976, annual usage was over 8,000 persons. In 1994, the Burlington school district bought the Koenen farm adjoining the lake and, in 2000, opened the new Burlington High School. A technical college branch is also on the district's property.